T0287777

# First Ladies

**by Marcus A. Stadelmann, PhD**
Professor of Political Science at the University of Texas at Tyler

for
dummies®
A Wiley Brand

## First Ladies For Dummies®

Published by: **John Wiley & Sons, Inc.,** 111 River Street, Hoboken, NJ 07030-5774, www.wiley.com

Copyright © 2022 by John Wiley & Sons, Inc., Hoboken, New Jersey

Media and software compilation copyright © 2022 by John Wiley & Sons, Inc. All rights reserved.

Published simultaneously in Canada

For general information on our other products and services, please contact our Customer Care Department within the U.S. at 877-762-2974, outside the U.S. at 317-572-3993, or fax 317-572-4002. For technical support, please visit www.wiley.com/techsupport.

Wiley publishes in a variety of print and electronic formats and by print-on-demand. Some material included with standard print versions of this book may not be included in e-books or in print-on-demand. If this book refers to media such as a CD or DVD that is not included in the version you purchased, you may download this material at http://booksupport.wiley.com. For more information about Wiley products, visit www.wiley.com.

Library of Congress Control Number: 2021948505

ISBN 978-1-119-82219-6 (pbk); ISBN 978-1-119-82220-2 (ebk); ISBN 978-1-119-82221-9 (ebk)

SKY10030907_102521

# Contents at a Glance

# Table of Contents

# Introduction

O ver the last 232 years, the United States has had 47 First Ladies. While presidents have dominated U.S. politics and history, most of our First Ladies are relatively unknown. The U.S. public might know about the most recent First Ladies, such as Michelle Obama, Melania Trump, or Dr. Jill Biden, and/or the most famous ones, such as Eleanor Roosevelt. However, most people are unfamiliar with many of the U.S. First Ladies.

While almost every American can name the current president, significantly fewer can name the current First Lady. Public school curricula and college courses focus on the U.S. presidents and not First Ladies. Academic books and autobiographies on American presidents and their administrations are readily available and fill many shelves in bookstores. Not so for First Ladies. The first memoirs of a First Lady didn't hit the bookshelves until the 20th century.

However, things have been changing. First Ladies are usually more popular than presidents and receive more media attention. Now, First Lady memoirs sell better than presidential memoirs. The media, beginning in the 1960s, started to spend more time disseminating information on the virtues and shortcomings of First Ladies. Then, in the 1980s, academics even started to rank First Ladies, and for the first time, their importance in American politics became well known. Select universities even offer college courses on First Ladies, and TV specials on First Ladies have begun to appear.

This book covers all 47 First Ladies — from the beginning of the republic in 1789 to the present time — in one place and makes it so you don't have to read 47 separate books just to read about the U.S. First Ladies. It shows how, over time, First Ladies have changed and the institution of the First Lady has also undergone changes. This work shows the slow transformation of the office of the First Lady to a powerful institution within the White House. Some First Ladies, such as Rosalynn Carter, played such a large role in their husband's administration that they were referred to as co-presidents.

Clearly, the time has come to study First Ladies. I am excited to share with you the histories and stories of these unique women.

# About This Book

This book is neither a textbook nor an autobiography; it combines the best elements of both. It won't bore you with little tedious facts or a lot of narrative. It doesn't shower you with a mass of statistics that prove to you what you already know. The information on the First Ladies gets to the point, highlighting only the major events in a First Lady's life.

The book covers all 47 U.S. First Ladies in chronological order. Some First Ladies have an entire chapter to themselves; others are grouped together. I detail some basic personal information for each First Lady, and I also cover some major events that took place during her tenure.

I designed this book to give a solid foundation on the First Ladies, whether you're studying political science, writing a paper, or reading for pleasure. I tried to make the book entertaining by including little-known tidbits. So whether you're a history buff, a student, or just someone interested in America's First Ladies, this book is for you. My hope is that this book will prove one point: The history of our First Ladies is fascinating and fun.

# Conventions Used in This Book

To avoid repeating certain procedures, facts, and ideas, this book uses certain conventions. For example, I use the common abbreviations *WWI* and *WWII* to refer to World War I and World War II, respectively. I also use familiar First Lady nicknames, such as Lady Bird Johnson rather than Claudia Johnson and Pat Nixon instead of Patricia Nixon. I always list the given name first and then explain her nickname, which I then use for the rest of the chapter.

I use the term White House for the executive mansion for most of this book. The only exceptions are the early years of the republic, from 1789 until 1800, when the executive mansions were located in New York City and Philadelphia, respectively. After 1800, when President Adams moved into the executive mansion, located in the new capital of Washington, D.C., I use the term White House instead.

I also provide information in a consistent format. For each First Lady, I include a part on her early years — when and where she was born, what schools she attended (if she attended school at all!), and how she met the future president. The next section then covers how she became First Lady and what her role as First Lady looked like. The final section focuses on what happened during her retirement from public office.

# Icons Used in This Book

As you read and enjoy this book, you'll discover four icons that alert you to specific aspects of America's 47 First Ladies.

This icon presents little-known information, or trivia, on the 47 First Ladies. Many of the First Ladies coined terms or set precedents for the office of the First Lady and the country.

This icon alerts you to famous statements or quotes made by or about the First Ladies. Some quotes you may be familiar with, and others you may not know. Some may shock you, and others may amuse you.

This icon points out important information you should be aware of as you read the section, the chapter, or the book. This icon covers only the most important events, people, and issues.

Historical information and other relevant material or events have this icon beside them. This information is included for the history buff, so feel free to ignore these paragraphs if you're not interested.

# Beyond the Book

In addition to what you're reading right now, this book comes with a free access-anywhere Cheat Sheet that includes key dates in the history of U.S. First Ladies. To get this Cheat Sheet, simply go to www.dummies.com and type "First Ladies For Dummies Cheat Sheet" in the Search box.

# Where to Go from Here

Feel free to start with any chapter and any First Lady who interests you. Keep in mind that all the chapters are nonlinear, so you can start with any topic in any chapter.

# 1
# Understanding First Ladies

Discover the roles First Ladies have been playing in the U.S. political structure and see how these roles have changed over time.

Examine the way First Ladies and their terms in the White House are evaluated and ranked. Uncover academic rankings of U.S. First Ladies and look at the upward and downward movement of some First Ladies through the years.

IN THIS CHAPTER

» Setting the foundation

» Being graceful hostesses

» Refusing the job

» Starting to matter

» Becoming copresidents

Chapter **1**

# The Changing Role of First Ladies in the United States

The story of the First Ladies of the United States is one of drama, personal struggle, and both great successes and failures. It's a story of ambition, joy, disappointment, and most often a total loss of privacy. In the early years of the republic, becoming First Lady imposed considerable dangers, both social and economic, on First Ladies and their families. The White House was open to just about everyone, and it had no security yet.

Today, First Ladies have professional roles and often aid in policy development. They work together with Congress and have become active policy makers. However, every First Lady decides how active they'll be. Hillary Clinton was one of the most active First Ladies in recent history, while Melania Trump was less active and played the role of a more traditional First Lady (see Chapter 20 for more). A First Lady's temperament, family situation, character, and even relationship with the president determines all of that. First Ladies with big political ambitions can use their office as a stepping stone to future offices. Eleanor Roosevelt did so with working for the United Nations after leaving her role as First Lady in 1945 (see Chapter 14), and Hillary Clinton ran and won a U.S. Senate seat after serving two terms as First Lady (see Chapter 18).

The role of First Lady has seen significant changes over the years. Women have made progress in society and are found at the highest levels of government, including now the vice presidency. Women today serve in Congress, even becoming the Speaker of the House of Representatives; they are members of the Supreme Court; and they govern states. It's only a question of time before a woman will become president and the U.S. will have its first "First Gentleman."

# First Ladies in U.S. History

Why become a First Lady? Most of the time, First Ladies had no choice. They were married to someone who just became president. In some instances, they had actually pushed their husbands into politics. Great examples include Sarah Polk and Helen Taft (see Chapters 7 and 12). They loved the game of politics and enjoyed the prestige of being First Lady. In fact, Julia Grant was so upset that her husband refused to run for a third term that she was in tears when she had to leave the White House (Chapter 10). More recently, First Ladies wanted to impact social and economic reforms and change the country and its people. Eleanor Roosevelt, Rosalynn Carter, Barbara Bush, and Hillary Clinton are examples of socially conscious First Ladies who wanted to bring about change (see Chapters 14, 17, and 18 for more on their stories).

## Defining a First Lady

Most of the 47 First Ladies in this book are famous because of the men they married. However, most First Ladies also impacted their husband's lives and directly and indirectly made significant contributions to U.S. history. From Martha Washington (Chapter 3) traveling with the Continental Army and improving soldiers' morale to Mary Todd Lincoln (Chapter 9) encouraging her husband to run for political office, in turn saving the Union, to Helen Taft (Chapter 12) pushing her husband to become president, American history wouldn't have been the same without the country's First Ladies.

Until recently, it was believed that First Ladies mattered and held their jobs only because their husbands had become president. That is true by definition but doesn't explain the whole story. Many claim that First Ladies owe their space in history to the men they married and that they didn't contribute much to the history and evolution of the United States. For them, First Ladies were basically footnotes in history. This is clearly wrong.

# FINANCIAL RAMIFICATIONS OF BEING FIRST LADY

Early on, the positions of President and First Lady imposed financial hardships. Presidents and First Ladies had to use their own resources to furnish the White House and to host dinners and parties. The amount of money Congress appropriated for these functions wasn't enough, and to top it off, the job of president wasn't compensated well, and the First Lady received no compensation at all. And, of course, after retirement, neither the president nor First Lady received a pension. This would not change until pensions for ex-presidents were approved in the 1950s, and presidents started receiving a comfortable salary beginning in 1969, when President Nixon received salary of $200,000.

Therefore, the job of First Lady involved personal sacrifices, and often a price, usually economic or even health-wise, had to be paid. Unlike today, when presidents and their wives make millions after they retire, usually by writing their memoirs and/or giving speeches, back then, being president could bankrupt a family. Early presidents and First Ladies left the White House often poorer than when they entered it. Dolley Madison, for example, was broke at the end of her life, and people left money in her house whenever she invited them over.

Not surprisingly, many First Ladies were quite upset when they found out their husbands had won the presidential elections and didn't celebrate but withdrew from the functions expected of a First Lady. Instead, they had their daughters or nieces take their place. Other First Ladies, like Sarah Polk, became penny pinchers and tried to run the White House the cheapest way possible.

Studies show that many First Ladies mattered more than people thought. They helped out with finances, managing family farms, teaching school, or working after getting married so that their husband could enter politics. In addition, most First Ladies came from social and economic backgrounds superior to the men they married. Without their contributions, their husbands couldn't have become presidents. Many First Ladies were even familiar with politics and had early exposure to politics through a father, a grandfather, or an uncle. Helen Taft, for example, decided to pursue a career in politics through her husband. Her father and grandfather had served in Congress, and she enjoyed the campaign for political office. This allowed her to give advice and help advance her husband's political career. Without her, there would have been no President Taft. (See Chapter 12 for her full story.)

It took quite some time to discover how important First Ladies actually were in the history of the U.S. The reason is that most early First Ladies, such as Martha Washington, didn't leave a lot of information for historians to study. Many burned all their correspondence with their husbands and friends that contained much information. The few who didn't, like Abigail Adams, left historians with a plethora of information and provided a picture of the time they lived in and information on their job as First Lady and how they contributed to their husband's career and successes.

This started to change, however, after the Civil War. First Ladies started leaving more information to be studied. In fact, Julia Grant, Helen Taft, and Edith Wilson all wrote their memoirs, giving us a lot of information on the role of First Lady and the gradual changes the office undertook.

Most First Ladies accomplished great things, often before becoming First Lady. Here are some examples:

» Elizabeth Monroe single-handedly saved the wife of the American war hero the Marquis de Lafayette in Paris during the French Revolution. See Chapter 5.

» Louisa Adams traveled by herself with a young child during the wintertime from Russia to France during the Napoleonic wars. See Chapter 5.

» Lou Hoover, who was in China during the Boxer Rebellion, carried a gun and got involved in shoot-outs. See Chapter 13.

# Powers of the First Lady

The position of First Lady isn't mentioned in the Constitution. However, the position soon became attached to the presidency and received some informal powers.

REMEMBER

The position of First Lady has been defined by culture and not the Constitution. There's no job description and no laws regulating First Lady behavior. However, changing American culture has put both limitations and opportunities on the role of First Lady. Cleary, back in the 19th century, an active First Lady campaigning for her husband and trying to impact policy making publicly wouldn't have been tolerated. Today, the American public expects First Ladies to be educated, to campaign for their husbands, and to even run for office themselves.

For this reason, the position of First Lady has considerable power today, and the First Lady has become one of the most powerful persons in Washington, D.C. From Betty Ford (see Chapter 16) who encouraged her husband to pardon President Nixon to Hillary Clinton who was put in charge of reforming healthcare in the United States, First Ladies have shown that they matter and can impact policy making.

## Assuming head of state roles

The Constitution provides a president with two jobs. First, there's the head of state position; and second, there's the head of government position. The first is ceremonial and doesn't matter that much; therefore, presidents have given ceremonial powers to First Ladies. Martha Washington attended church on her husband's behalf (see Chapter 3); Nancy Reagan was the president's stand-in after the assassination attempt on her husband (see Chapter 17); and Lady Bird Johnson represented for her husband campaigning in the South (see Chapter 16).

## Having unseen powers

In the first years of the republic, First Ladies were mostly concerned with their hostess role and arranging social events. They further oversaw renovations of the White House. While many dismiss these functions as irrelevant, they had very political undertones. Every teatime, soiree, and formal dinner can be used politically, as Louisa Adams showed in 1825, when during a soiree the night before Congress picked her husband as the new president, she convinced several Congressmen to vote for her husband.

Dolley Madison organized weekly Wednesday evening get-togethers where she invited Congressmen from both parties and often took the place of her husband, who can't take sides on issues, discussing politics with her guests. Soon she became one of the most powerful political brokers in the capital.

## Getting into the limelight

Some First Ladies have made an imprint quietly, while others have gone public. Abigail Adams was able to discuss politics and convince her husband on issues in more than a thousand letters written to her husband. Others have used media, such as the radio or television, to make or even change policy. Both Betty Ford and Rosalynn Carter went public on issues such as the equal rights amendment, abortion, and mental health.

With the New Deal and WWII, more government power became centralized in the office of the president in the 1930s and 1940s. Not surprisingly, the media began to focus more on Washington, D.C., and the office of the president. Increased focus on the president also led to more attention being paid to the First Lady. The advance of television further increased this coverage. Suddenly, people could see the First Ladies in action and listen to them speak. By 1960, half of all Americans owned a television set, and this increased coverage of the First Ladies immensely.

## Becoming institutionalized

With Edith Roosevelt, at the turn of the 20th century, the office of the First Lady became more institutionalized (see Chapter 12). She hired highly paid and educated professional staffers, and suddenly staff weren't just helpers in the kitchen but full-time professional advisors. These advisors attended morning briefings with the First Lady and on occasion worked closely with the president's staff. Lady Bird Johnson then took it a step further and turned the East Wing of the White House into a business organization and ran it as such (check out Chapter 16). Rosalynn Carter completed the process of institutionalization by moving her office to the East Wing and creating a formal Office of the First Lady.

# The Evolution of the Position of First Lady

The office of First Lady, and likewise the women who fill that role, has gone through an evolution since its conception to present day. I discuss those changes in four phases in this section.

## Phase I (1789–1829)

Part 2 of the book covers the First Ladies of this phase. Martha Washington set the foundation for First Lady obligations. On occasion, she played the part of head of state, and she set the precedent of being a great hostess who wasn't involved in policy making.

Martha Washington's role as First Lady was undefined. She herself didn't know what to expect of the position. She was surprised when she received a 13-gun salute and shouts of "Long live Lady Washington!" when she arrived in the then-capital New York City. She decided to become the perfect hostess, because the democratic spirit of the time called for the president to open the doors of the executive mansion in New York City anytime. Soon this led to problems. Too many people took advantage of the open doors and just showed up. No work could get done, and no privacy existed. So it was decided to limit open houses and receptions.

Another hostess function was to deal with callers, usually the wives of Senators, House members, and foreign diplomats, who came to the door of the White House and left their cards. It was customary that a First Lady returned their visits. Often, First Ladies would have to make up to 60 visits a week. To make matters worse, the White House was open to everybody who wanted to show up on New Year's Day, with the exception of wartime or periods of mourning. Thousands would stop annually, and the practice wasn't stopped until the Hoover administration in 1933.

While Abigail Adams was an opinionated woman who influenced her husband in private, publicly she mostly fulfilled her hostess function. Dolley Madison was the first to help a widower, Thomas Jefferson, and then served eight years as First Lady. She dominated the White House for a long time. She was such a superior hostess that future First Ladies would ask her advice on becoming a hostess as late as 1845, but she also managed to mix the social part of being a hostess with the political part. Not only did she start the tradition of having an inaugural ball, but she also was truly nonpartisan at her receptions and everybody loved her for it. In addition, she called upon every wife of a Congressman and invited them to the White House, creating goodwill among the spouses of all Congressmen at the time.

The country's early First Ladies were sweet, quiet, and gracious hostesses in public and played a supportive role to their husband, which reflected the times they lived in. In private, they displayed courage, had exceptional training, spoke foreign languages, read French philosophers, and traveled abroad creating goodwill for the U.S. in Europe.

## Phase II (1829–1869)

Phase II is dominated by young substitutes — either daughters, daughters-in-law, or nieces — for First Ladies. There were few mature or strong First Ladies during this period; most were youthful surrogates who didn't impact policy making much. (Turn to Part 3 for a closer look at these ladies.)

Six out of nine first ladies during this time period pleaded ill health or grief as reasons for not being able to perform First Lady functions. They were Anna Harrison, Letitia Tyler, Margaret Taylor, Abigail Fillmore, Jane Pierce, and Eliza Johnson. Rachel Jackson had made arrangements for her niece to serve as First Lady in case she died, which she did. In some cases, there was no other way. Andrew Jackson's wife passed right after he got elected president in 1828 and was unable to serve as First Lady. The same situation occurred in Martin Van Buren's case. In both instances, younger nieces had to take over as First Lady.

Only two First Ladies were exceptions. Both Sarah Polk and Harriet Lane, the niece of President Buchanan who was a bachelor, were excited to become First Lady and were quite active. Not surprisingly, both are among my top ten most influential First Ladies (see Chapter 21).

## Phase III (1869–1933)

The role of First Lady changed again after 1869. Suddenly, there were no more youthful surrogates being used as First Ladies. The new First Ladies came from different backgrounds compared to the First Ladies in Phase I. The ladies discussed in Part 4 weren't married to founding fathers nor were they the wives of rich plantation owners. However, they were well educated, and many came from small-town America.

The press started talking about the First Ladies reflecting the ideal of the new woman. The new woman was educated, as universities had opened up enrollment to women. The new woman was also involved in political organizations. The Civil War had gotten many women involved in public organizations, and all female political and social clubs were founded.

Many political and social barriers were broken down during this period. Some political gains happened, too. Women got the right to vote at the local and state level, and the country saw its first female politicians elected at the local level. Some women were even appointed to state and local government positions. By 1900, women could vote in four states: Wyoming, Idaho, Colorado, and Utah. Even though women still had to attach themselves to their husband's career, many spoke out in public and created and joined national organizations. Not surprisingly, the suffrage movement gained steam, too, and by 1917, the first female member of Congress, Jeannette Rankin from Montana, was elected.

With the outbreak of WWI, the role of women and First Ladies changed yet again. After becoming a part of the war effort, women suddenly stayed a part of the workforce and in 1920 received the right to vote at the presidential level. Florence Harding was the first woman to cast a ballot for her husband in 1920. Right before, Edith Wilson basically became the president herself after Woodrow Wilson suffered a debilitating stroke. She became his guardian and gatekeeper and studied every paper and decided what would go to the president and what wouldn't. In other words, she became responsible for policy making, and letters sent to her addressed her as "Mrs. President."

## Phase IV (1933–Present)

In the 20th century, with wars and the second industrial revolution, the role of women dramatically changed in the U.S. This brought about a change in the role First Ladies performed and also changes in American culture. Here is where the modern era for First Ladies began. They became public figures pursuing their own causes, which made them not only more famous but also resulted in the media scrutinizing them even more. (Check out Part 5 for these First Ladies.)

Then, after 1960, First Ladies' roles changed rapidly one more time. For the first time, First Ladies started campaigning for their husbands, even on their own, which previously had been considered not proper. Today, First Ladies campaigning for their husbands hasn't just been accepted but is expected. In addition, First Ladies today are expected to pick a public cause to focus on, which in turn gets them involved in political issues. They truly have become a first partner to today's presidents. By now, First Ladies often outstrip their husbands in popularity, emotional access by the public, and even book sales.

In the beginning, First Ladies were mostly nonpartners in their husband's presidencies, and today they have become full partners. They are now equal in not just social or charitable matters but also in political matters. From Edith Wilson to Eleanor Roosevelt to Hilary Clinton, First Ladies have become trusted allies and advisors for their husbands and have asserted themselves independently.

Today, many First Ladies are highly educated, have professional portfolios, and have ambition to seek political office. Traditionally, a First Lady's background has impacted how influential and assertive she will be.

Educational achievement and professional experience are great predictors on how strong First Ladies will be. Based on this, it's possible to predict that future First Ladies will be more independent, more politically involved, and possibly more controversial in the public's eyes compared to the First Ladies of the past.

# Chapter **2**

# First Lady Rankings and Evaluations

This chapter looks at how experts rank U.S. First Ladies. The public is aware of some of the First Ladies, namely the wives of our most famous presidents. This knowledge comes mostly from schools and the emphasis that the media places on these important First Ladies. But when was the last time you read about or saw a show on Lucy Hayes or Grace Coolidge? On the other hand, you can choose among several movies or books about Eleanor Roosevelt or Jaqueline Kennedy.

Polls show that most U.S. citizens know about the First Ladies in office during their lifetime but don't know much about the First Ladies of the past. Most Americans are familiar with Michelle Obama, Nancy Reagan, and even Jaqueline Kennedy. But what about Helen Taft or Sarah Polk? Therefore, the public ranks current and famous First Ladies higher than lesser-known first ladies. Academics who study First Ladies, on the other hand, have a better historical perspective and do rank some of our founding First Ladies, such as Abigail Adams and Dolley Madison, very high.

Over time, the standing of a First Lady may change within the rankings of the U.S. public and academics, providing for renewed interest in her life and actions while serving as First Lady. Some First Ladies are highly regarded after they leave office, only to end up being considered disappointments in the long run. Other

First Ladies may be considered failures shortly after the end of their term and then become popular later. Nancy Reagan is a great example of this. When her husband left office in 1989, she was ranked very low, among the ten least influential First Ladies. This changed over time, as people took a look at what she had done and how influential she was with her husband, especially during his second term. By the time the newest rankings came out in 2014, she made it into the top 15 list of First Ladies.

This chapter looks at the one consistent academic survey of U.S. First Ladies, the Siena College Research Institute Survey on First Ladies, which is taken just about every decade.

# Evaluating the First Ladies

Unlike U.S. presidents, academics and the American public rarely evaluate First Ladies. It wasn't until the 1980s that the Siena College Research Institute in New York established an academic survey to rate and rank First Ladies. The survey continues but isn't taken often, usually only about once a decade. To this date, it has been conducted only five times since its inception in 1982. The most recent survey, discussed later in the chapter, was taken in 2014.

**REMEMBER**

Keep in mind that times change and First Lady rankings reflect this. Early in U.S. history, First Ladies were mainly hostesses in and caretakers of the White House. Some even refused to do that and had their daughters step into their place. Only a few First Ladies mattered when it came to impacting policy making. They were Sarah Polk, Dolley Madison, and, of course, Abigail Adams. Not surprisingly, many First Ladies of the 19th century don't rank very high in the survey. They just didn't do much besides being a great White House hostess, if that. Keep in mind that this isn't a negative thing; that is all that was expected of them, and if they had been more engaged, the American public may not have stood for it.

It wasn't until the 20th century that stronger First Ladies emerged. They suddenly took their place next to the president and influenced policy making. Some were even quite public about it. Eleanor Roosevelt was the first First Lady who was actually publicly involved in policy making and openly conversed with the America public about her political stands and preferences.

Media scrutiny of First Ladies is also a recent phenomenon. During most of the 19th and 20th centuries, the media didn't delve into the lives of First Ladies. Much of what we know, we get from letters written by First Ladies, their husbands, and their acquaintances, and even that isn't much because often First Ladies would burn their correspondence when leaving office. It was considered taboo to report on the private lives of First Ladies — the public didn't know much, if anything, about Eleanor Roosevelt's live-in girlfriend or Helen Taft smoking cigarettes and playing cards with the boys. A president's or First Lady's private indiscretions were kept secret. This code of silence held well into the 20th century.

The Watergate scandal in the 1970s changed things. Suddenly, the media believed that it had an obligation to be a watchdog over the presidents and First Ladies. This new role allowed the media not only to check presidents for public mistakes and policy failures but also to report on First Ladies and their activities. This role for the media won't change as long as juicy scandals continue to garner large audiences. Future First Ladies have to expect to have their lives scrutinized and any minor wrongdoing reported. Hillary Clinton found that out the hard way in 1993 with the Whitewater scandal, where the Clinton's were accused of financial wrongdoings (see Chapter 18) and again in 2015, after her term as First Lady had ended in 2001, when the media reported on her using her private server for classified emails. Today, scrutiny of First Ladies does not even end after their terms have ended. Melania Trump ran into a similar problem when her nude photoshoot of 2000 was revealed during the 2016 campaign.

# Ranking U.S. First Ladies

One of the best academic evaluations of U.S. First Ladies was released in 2014, in a joint effort by both the Siena College Research Institute and C-SPAN (National Cable Satellite Corporation), a network created to show public affairs programming. The survey was conducted in 2013, and its results were released in 2014. A total of 242 experts on First Ladies in the United States were asked to rank the First Ladies based on ten criteria (see the section "Discussing ten evaluation criteria"). Rankings of all the First Ladies are rare, they are-time consuming, expensive, and there isn't much demand for them.

*Note:* Because the study was done in 2013–2014, it obviously doesn't include either Melania Trump or Dr. Jill Biden, who became First Lady in 2017 and 2021, respectively. It further excludes Harriet Lane, who was President Buchanan's niece and became his First Lady because he was a lifelong bachelor. I and many other academics do count her as a First Lady, and in Chapter 21, she is among my choices for the ten most influential First Ladies. Finally, the study excludes the four First Ladies who died before their husbands became president and Anna Harrison who never had a chance to became First Lady after her husband died a month into office.

# The Siena Research Institute Survey

**REMEMBER**

The Siena Research Institute Survey was the first survey on First Ladies in the United States. It's conducted about every ten years, and it asks history and political science professors at American universities, as well as other experts on First Ladies, to rank the U.S. First Ladies on a scale of one to five based on ten separate categories (see the section "Discussing ten evaluation criteria"). Unlike surveys on American presidents, there were no other surveys to compare results to and thus the Siena College Research Institutes findings are the only comprehensive survey on U.S. First Ladies, establishing a benchmark for First Lady studies. Table 2-1 presents its rankings in order.

**TABLE 2-1**  ## First Lady Rankings

| Ranking | C-SPAN Academic Survey |
|---------|------------------------|
| 1 | Eleanor Roosevelt |
| 2 | Abigail Adams |
| 3 | Jaqueline Kennedy |
| 4 | Dolley Madison |
| 5 | Michelle Obama |
| 6 | Hillary Clinton |
| 7 | Lady Bird Johnson |
| 8 | Betty Ford |
| 9 | Martha Washington |
| 10 | Rosalynn Carter |
| 11 | Barbara Bush |
| 12 | Laura Bush |
| 13 | Edith Roosevelt |
| 14 | Edith Wilson |
| 15 | Nancy Reagan |
| 16 | Bess Truman |
| 17 | Lou Hoover |
| 18 | Louisa Adams |
| 19 | Ellen Wilson |

| Ranking | C-SPAN Academic Survey |
| --- | --- |
| 20 | Lucy Hayes |
| 21 | Grace Coolidge |
| 22 | Julia Grant |
| 23 | Sarah Polk |
| 24 | Mamie Eisenhower |
| 25 | Helen Taft |
| 26 | Francis Cleveland |
| 27 | Julia Tyler |
| 28 | Lucretia Garfield |
| 29 | Caroline Harrison |
| 30 | Elizabeth Monroe |
| 31 | Mary Lincoln |
| 32 | Abigail Fillmore |
| 33 | Pat Nixon |
| 34 | Ida McKinley |
| 35 | Margaret Taylor |
| 36 | Florence Harding |
| 37 | Letitia Tyler |
| 38 | Eliza Johnson |
| 39 | Jane Pierce |

*Source: Siena College Research Institute/C-Span study of the first ladies of the United States, 2014. Retrieved at: https://scri.siena.edu/first-ladies-study/*

If you compare the results from the first survey taken in 1982 to the last one, conducted in 2014, the top ten and bottom ten First Ladies have been fairly consistent. At the bottom are Jane Pierce, Eliza Johnson, Letitia Tyler, and Florence Harding. Even Mary Lincoln falls into the bottom ten category. Mary Lincoln and Jane Pierce are considered neurotic women whose behavior and attitude made their husband's life more difficult. Instead of being helpful during their husbands' presidencies, they did the exact opposite and undermined their husband's reputation and proved to be a handicap for effective policy making. Florence Harding is often blamed for being too ambitious and pushing her unqualified husband to become president. He turned out to be one of the worst presidents in American history. Letitia Tyler and Eliza Johnson, on the other hand, had no interest in being First Lady. Both claimed to be ill and made their daughters surrogate First Ladies for their husbands.

At the same time, Eleanor Roosevelt has held the top spot in all five surveys taken since 1982. She was an exceptionally active First Lady who became a co-president to her husband. She clearly changed the role of First Ladies in U.S. history, and for this she is still admired and rewarded with the number one spot in all surveys on First Ladies.

# Discussing ten evaluation criteria

The ten criteria included in the Siena Research Institute Survey were White House steward, value to president, own woman, public image, accomplishments, value to country, leadership, integrity, background, and courage. I define the ten criteria in this section in my own words and use them to rank the ten most influential First Ladies in Chapter 21.

## White House steward

This category refers to a First Lady being a gracious hostess in the White House, holding dinners, balls, and teas. In addition, it includes taking good care of the building itself, providing new furniture and necessary repairs and renovations. Dolley Madison excelled in this category as did Jackie Kennedy, who established the White House Historical Association 60 years ago, which continues to steward the White House.

## Value to president

*Value to president* refers to how helpful a First Lady was when it comes to the presidency. This can include having private policy discussions or a letter exchange on ideas, as was common. In addition, the criterion includes helping with correspondence and even going over campaign speeches as Eleanor Roosevelt used to do for her husband. Finally, it can include campaign activities that now every First Lady undertakes.

## Own woman

This criterion refers to a First Lady being willing to express her own ideas publicly and privately. More recent First Ladies have been willing to give press conferences, campaign by themselves for the president, start pet policy initiatives, and even contradict the presidents publicly on occasion. Betty Ford and Eleanor Roosevelt score high in this category.

## Public image

This criterion refers to whether a First Lady is well liked by the public. A well-liked First Lady can help the president overcome popularity problems. On the other hand, if a First Lady is disliked by the public, as Mary Todd Lincoln was, she can drag the president down with her. Some First Ladies were admired to a point where people would copy their looks and outfits and goods were named after them to take advantage of their popularity. From Dolley Madison snuff boxes to Frances Cleveland cigars, we've had it all in our history. Jacqueline Kennedy excelled with this category when she helped the country overcome the shock and grief at her husband's funeral after his assassination. She displayed an extraordinary brave behavior, which helped the nation heal.

## Accomplishments

This category ranks what First Ladies accomplished in their tenure. Did they start projects to help the American public, were they concerned about certain segments of the population, or did they just hide from the media and the public and not accomplish anything? Both Barbara Bush and Laura Bush excelled in this category with their literacy program as did Michelle Obama with her school lunch program.

## Value to country

This category ranks a First Lady on how they were able to improve American reputation globally and how or whether they were able to increase morale in the U.S. during times of crises. Eleanor Roosevelt again excelled in this category. She traveled to meet with troops in the Pacific and in Europe during WWII and later received a global reputation for being responsible for the Universal Declaration of Human Rights. Most recently, both Laura Bush and Michelle Obama scored high in this category for trying to improve the status of women in Third World countries.

## Leadership

Often First Ladies pick projects they intend to pursue while in office. They have to assume leadership roles for these projects to succeed. Lady Bird Johnson was concerned about the environment and the beautification of the country. She successfully assumed a leadership role and did succeed and continued her passion for her causes after she left office. Nancy Reagan assumed a visible role in the Just Say No program, targeting substance abuse, and the program survived her retiring in 1989. Most recent First Ladies rank high in leadership because today it's almost expected that a First Lady focuses on a program and puts their stamp on it. That wasn't expected before WWII, and, not surprisingly, most of the First Ladies of this period rank lower on the leadership scale.

## Integrity

Most First Ladies score high on integrity. However, there were a few who manipulated their husbands for their own good and pushed them into an office they didn't want or even pushed for policies that weren't good for the nation. Florence Harding, who constantly pushed her husband until he became president, comes to mind. As stated previously, her husband, Warren G. Harding, turned out be one of the worst president's in U.S. history.

## Background

This category looks at how much a First Lady accomplished before she became a First Lady. Hillary Clinton scores high here, being selected twice as one of the top 100 lawyers in the country. Another one is Lady Bird Johnson who built a media empire and became a millionaire before she became First Lady. More recent First Ladies score higher in this category because early on in U.S. history, it was uncommon for women to be educated, become business leaders, or participate in public policy making.

## Courage

There are many ways to define courage. Dolley Madison risked being captured by the British in the War of 1812 when she single-handedly saved many rare and historical items in the White House before the British burned it down. Betty Ford displayed courage when she came forward and publicly discussed her breast cancer and subsequent mastectomy. The point here is all these First Ladies displayed enormous courage in different areas and need to be given credit for it.

# 2
# Setting the Precedent

Discover how Martha Washington became the first First Lady of the United States. Look at her tenure as First Lady and see what precedents she set for First Ladies to follow.

Examine how Abigail Adams became one of the most influential First Ladies in U.S. history. And, find how Martha Jefferson died before her husband took office. Also, see how Dolley Madison not only became a national heroine but also was the best hostess the White House has ever seen.

Discover how Elizabeth Monroe and Louisa Adams became famous before becoming First Ladies and see how their turn in the White House was a letdown for both of them. And find out why Rachel Jackson hated Washington, D.C., and never wanted to be a First Lady.

Chapter **3**

# Becoming the First First Lady

Martha Washington was the first American First Lady, and she proved to be one of the best. With the exception of Abigail Adams (see Chapter 4), the early First Ladies adopted the contemporary 18th-century model of womeness. They were great hostesses and docile wives in public, but they weren't afraid to speak their mind in private. Even though Martha didn't discuss politics publicly, she was the most influential person with George Washington.

When it comes to formal and social traditions, Martha was the one who gave the position of First Lady many of its current traditions. She didn't enjoy being around rowdy crowds or hosting social events, but she adapted well to changing circumstances in her life.

This chapter looks at Martha Washington's childhood and how she met George. After playing an important part in the Revolutionary War, Martha becomes First Lady in 1789 and sets many of the traditions subsequent First Ladies would follow.

# Martha Dandridge Custis Washington (1731–1802)

Martha Dandridge (see Figure 3-1) was born on June 2, 1731, on a plantation near Williamsburg, Virginia. She was the oldest of eight children and didn't receive any formal schooling, as was common back then for young females. She enjoyed horseback riding and was taught how to manage a household to be able to become a proper wife.

**FIGURE 3-1:** Martha Dandridge as a young woman.

Source: Library of Congress, Prints & Photographs Division, Reproduction number LC-DIG-pga-04936 (digital file from original item)LC-USZC2-3273 (color film copy slide)

Martha married Daniel Park Custis, a wealthy plantation owner who was 20 years older, when she was 17. At this point, she moved into his mansion, which ironically he called the white house. During the next seven years, she was happily married and had four children. Only two of her children survived, the other two died before the age of six. Then Daniel died in 1757, and Martha was suddenly a widow.

TECHNICAL STUFF

Martha inherited a 17,500-acre plantation and nearly 300 enslaved people from her husband, making her, at the age of 26, one of the richest people in the American colonies.

# Joining Forces with George, the Love of Her Life

While staying with friends in 1758, Martha met George Washington, who was a military officer trying to settle back into civilian life. Over dinner, Martha, who was referred to as the prettiest and wealthiest widow in Virginia, hit it off with George, and they were married on January 6, 1759.

**REMEMBER**

The couple never had children, a fact George and Martha regretted. George, however, treated her two surviving children, John, referred to as Jack, and Martha called Patsy, from her previous marriage as his own. Both Jack and Patsy died before George became president. Patsy died of epilepsy and Jack died during the Revolutionary War. Martha and George raised their grandchildren as their own.

The next 15 years were happy ones for Martha. She and George enjoyed the quiet life on his estate Mount Vernon. For Martha, Mount Vernon became the training ground for the White House. She was expected by the Virginia social elites to host large parties and dinners. She didn't enjoy hosting but soon became very good at it. To her surprise, her husband first took over command of the Virginia militia and then became commander of the American Continental Army in 1775, when the Revolutionary War broke out. She took his appointment in stride and is quoted as saying:

**IN THEIR WORDS**

> "Our happiness or misery depends upon our disposition and not our circumstances."

## Taking an active role

Unlike many officer wives of the time, Martha decided to assume an active role in the war and not just stay behind on her plantation. She would travel with George and his army and spent almost half of the next five years with her husband and his soldiers. When she was home alone, she did a great job managing Mount Vernon by herself. She even added two wings to the mansion.

**FIRST LADY LORE**

George felt that Martha's presence was so important for him and his soldiers that he asked Congress to foot her travel bills. Congress happily agreed to do so.

## Becoming a war hero

Martha Washington became a national hero when she decided to travel with her husband during the Revolutionary War to join him for his winter camps. Thousands of people would flock to her just to be able to see her. Newspapers wrote stories about her travels and how important it was for George Washington and the troops to have her with them. For this reason, Martha became an important part of the Revolutionary War. Spending five of eight years on the front, she sacrificed as much as everybody else in the fight for independence and became an American heroine.

In 1777–1778, Martha spent the brutal winter with her husband and his soldiers at Valley Forge, Pennsylvania, about 20 miles northwest of Philadelphia. Her husband and about 12,000 soldiers had set up winter camp there to protect Congress, which was in session in New York City at the time. The troops suffered horrible conditions. To help morale and the horrible physical conditions soldiers were in, Martha would not only host dinners for the officers but also help the regular foot soldiers, taking care of the wounded.

In addition, Martha was a master seamstress and put her skills to good use sewing socks and mending clothing for the freezing soldiers. Although she wasn't knitting fancy tapestry and doing embroidery as most proper ladies did in the 18th century, she was doing important work and literally knitted thousands of socks. Soon, she became a house mother and foster mother to young officers and regular troops.

Martha even encouraged other officers to bring their wives and daughters to come and visit and help out. She managed to entertain at Valley Forge, despite the freezing cold and lack of food, and impressed French and German officers fighting for George Washington in the American army. When the Marquis de Lafayette met her, his impression was that Martha had amazing charm and truly must love her husband, because she sacrificed so much spending harsh winters with him and his soldiers.

**REMEMBER**

Martha's son, Jack, who had enlisted in the Revolutionary Army, died in 1781 in Yorktown of typhus. She outlived all four of her children.

Finally, in 1783, the Revolutionary War ended, and Martha was able to return to her beloved Mount Vernon.

# Going First: From Lady Washington to First Lady

It wasn't a dream of Martha's to be First Lady. She enjoyed living quietly with George at their Mount Vernon estate in Virginia. Unlike Abigail Adams or Dolley Madison (see Chapter 4), Martha didn't enjoy getting involved in politics or constantly hosting parties.

However, Martha had been raised to be a Southern elite woman, and this involved hosting social events. Even though this was not one of her favorite parts of the job she was very good at it and after retirement, she and George continued to host hundreds of people at Mount Vernon.

After the Revolutionary War had been won, Martha wanted to return to the quietness of Mount Vernon, but again her fate was to be different. Instead of enjoying the quiet life on her plantation in Virginia, George Washington became president in 1789, and Martha had to move to the temporary capital of New York City. She was quite unhappy about the move, preferring to stay at Mount Vernon. When asked about her new position as First Lady (see Figure 3-2), she stated:

FIGURE 3-2:
Martha
Dandridge Custis
Washington.

Source: Library of Congress, Prints & Photographs Division,
Reproduction number LC-DIG-bellcm-25569
(digital file from original)

IN THEIR
WORDS

"I never go to the publick place — indeed I think I am more like a state prisoner than anything else, there is certain bounds set for me I must not depart from."

In a letter, Martha wrote that she had expected that she and George would be left to grow old in solitude and tranquility together at Mount Vernon and called the change of course a disappointment. In fact, it was not until George was 65 and Martha 66 that they were able to go back into retirement.

When Martha Washington first arrived in New York City, the nation's first capital, people didn't know how to refer to her. Some called her Lady Washington, while others referred to her as The Presidentress.

The term First Lady of the United States (FLOTUS) is held by the hostess in the White House, usually the president's spouse. This was not always the case. After George Washington became president in 1789, people did not know what to call his wife. Should it be Marquise Washington, Mrs. President, or just Presidentress. All of these titles sounded aristocratic and with the country just having won a war of independence against Great Britain nobody wanted to sound aristocratic or British. A title needed to be created that was plain and democratic. So, people just called her Lady Washington. The official title of First Lady was then coined at Dolley Madison's funeral by President Zachary Taylor in 1849. By the late 1850's the title became more commonly used and Harriet Lane was called the First Lady in the Land and Julia Grant and Lucy Hayes later received the same title. This helped to make the title more popular, and today the term has been fully accepted and its use is widespread.

## Learning her way

In 1789, Martha undertook an 11-day trip to New York City from her home in Virginia, to meet up with newly elected President George Washington. When she arrived, she was celebrated like a queen. There were fireworks, a 13-gun salute, and people shouting, "Long Live Lady Washington!" At this point, she knew that the presidential spouse had a public role to play in American society. On their way to their rented house on Cherry Street in New York City, people even lined the streets and chanted her name.

George Washington had printed in the local newspaper in New York City when his calling hours would be. In other words, he told the public when to come and visit him. If people just wanted to come to pay their respects, they could do so Tuesday and Friday afternoons between 2 and 3 p.m.

As First Lady, Martha hosted formal dinners for Members of Congress, foreign diplomats, and members of the wealthy elites in New York City every Thursday and then public receptions for the common people each Friday. Anyone of good standing, meaning that they had to be decently dressed, could attend. This included not only politicians and the wealthy but also the average American.

## Starting traditions

In 1790, the capital was moved to Philadelphia. Martha was happier there, making more friends, but she still missed Mount Vernon.

Early presidential wives not only served as hostesses but were also a link to Congress, foreign diplomats, and the American people. Custom directed that a lady had to return all the calling cards left by other ladies. Therefore, if the wife of a new member of Congress left her card at the presidential mansion, the First Lady had to return the call, meaning she had to visit the Congressman's wife. Martha returned each visit usually within three days. This function was important because it was not only expected but could be used to establish good will with members of Congress.

Other functions were to represent the president at public events when the president wasn't available or to accept gifts on his behalf. For example, on several occasions when President Washington was ill, Martha attended church on his behalf, and when the City of New York wanted to give him a fancy carriage as a gift, he didn't accept it but Martha did.

Martha soon realized that in the role of First Lady, she could participate in the president's role as Head of State. In this function, she could represent the United States both domestically and also internationally, by hosting foreign diplomats in the White House.

## Taking sides

George Washington's second term turned out to be a major disappointment for Martha. Their good friends James Madison, Alexander Hamilton, and Thomas Jefferson started political infighting within the administration, and the two-party system developed as a result. She started to dislike Jefferson for his attacks on Washington's policies and was afraid that the stress of the presidency would kill her husband.

**FIRST LADY LORE**

The infighting between her friends and George brought Martha closer to John and Abigail Adams, and soon Abigail became a good friend. In fact, Abigail became such a good friend to Martha that she always sat to the right of her at the dinner table. Whenever someone else tried to sit in Abigail's chair, Martha would ask them to choose another chair.

# Hosting the World in Retirement

One of the happiest days in Martha's life was when George Washington decided to forgo seeking a third term. She was finally able to retire to Virginia in 1797 (see Figure 3-3). However, retirement wasn't all relaxation. George took care of his massive plantation that had grown to 8,000 acres, and Martha hosted hundreds of visitors yearly. Hosting about 600 strangers each year who just stopped by to see George Washington and say hello was a big undertaking. Martha had to feed them, and often they stayed overnight. To make matters worse, George Washington usually left early, and she had to entertain her guests. But, Martha did this with grace and a continued sense of pride for her husband. She had become the perfect hostess.

**FIGURE 3-3:**
Martha Washington in retirement.

Source: Library of Congress, Prints & Photographs Division, Reproduction number LC-DIG-pga-01370 (digital file from original print)

**TECHNICAL STUFF**

Mount Vernon became almost a second presidential mansion after Washington left office. Thousands of people, including diplomats from all over Europe, flocked to it to see George and Martha.

George Washington died two years later, and Martha was once again a widow. Martha burned all their correspondence. She didn't want anyone else to know about her husband's feelings, fears, and opinions of colleagues. Historians found only two letters hidden in her desk after she died. One was from her husband written after he accepted the offer to become the Commander of the Continental Army. In the letter, George wrote:

**IN THEIR WORDS**

"My dearest, I had to accept this. My honor required it. But please, my dear Patsy, don't be angry with me."

Washington then went on to explain his reasons for accepting the offer and why he needed her support.

FIRST LADY LORE

After George Washington died, Martha couldn't sleep in their bedroom anymore. Instead, she slept in a room in the attic.

Martha was devastated by George's death. The love of her life was gone. All of her children had passed, and she was ready to go, too. She said after George died:

IN THEIR WORDS

"It's over. My life is just waiting now."

Every day, Martha walked to George's tomb on Mount Vernon and prayed. She was counting the days until she could be reunited with the love of her life. In 1802, Martha came down with a severe fever, which killed her at the age of 70 on May 22, 1802. Both George and Martha were buried in a tomb at Mount Vernon.

TECHNICAL STUFF

George Washington was the only founding father and president to free his enslaved people. He had appreciated freed blacks (former enslaved people) fighting for him in the Revolutionary War, and this changed his mind on slavery. Martha felt otherwise. She felt slave holding was normal and the way society was and should be structured.

The Washington's established the tradition of bringing enslaved servants with them. This practice ended with the Taylor administration in 1850.

# Chapter **4**

# Setting Precedents

The role of First Lady was still being shaped by the women who filled it after Martha Washington. All three ladies discussed in this chapter, Abigail Adams, Martha Jefferson, and Dolley Madison, continued to set precedents for future First Ladies. While Martha Washington (see Chapter 3) focused on being a charming hostess for White House affairs, Abigail Adams was politically outspoken, impacting policy making. She was the first First Lady to have more than a ceremonial role. Dolley Madison combined the two traits. She was one of the most gracious White House hostesses who also wasn't afraid to speak her mind. On a sadder side, Martha Jefferson established the precedent of wives who passed before their husbands became president still being referred to as First Lady.

## Abigail Smith Adams (1744–1818)

Abigail Smith Adams (see Figure 4-1) was born on November 22, 1744, in Weymouth, Massachusetts. Her mother was a descendant from one of the oldest and most prominent families in Massachusetts, the Quincy family. Her father was a minister who had graduated from Harvard University. He was responsible for most of Abigail's schooling, and early on she was an avid reader, familiarizing herself with the great works of the day. She also fell in love with writing, which resulted in almost 1,200 letters to her husband, John Adams, which gave historians a glimpse of not only political life in the late 18th century but also her political influence on the future president.

*Source: Library of Congress, Prints & Photographs
Division, Reproduction number LC-DIG-hec-13515
(digital file from original negative)*

Abigail was introduced to John Adams by her sister's fiancé. John Adams at the time was a Harvard-educated lawyer. He was infatuated with her right away, being impressed with her intelligence, and the two got married in a ceremony presided over by her father on October 25, 1764.

Abigail was the first politically active First Lady. She was well educated, articulate, and intelligent. She often discussed political issues with her husband before he made his decisions. She was very influential in policy making and wasn't afraid to discuss politics with her husband.

REMEMBER

Abigail has the distinction of being one of two First Ladies who was married to a president and gave birth to a future president. The other one was Barbara Bush.

Abigail was one of the first feminists in American history. She fought for equal rights for women as early as the late 18th century. In a 1776 letter she sent to John Adams while he was attending the second Continental Congress, which was working on the Declaration of Independence, she wrote:

IN THEIR
WORDS

I desire you would remember the ladies and be more generous and favorable to them than your ancestors. . . . Do not put such power into the hands of the husbands, . . . Remember that all men would be tyrants if they could. . . . If particular care and attention is not paid to the ladies, we are determined to foment a rebellion, and will not hold ourselves bound by any laws in which we have no voice, or representation.

Abigail was also opposed to slavery. She called slavery antithetical to Christian principles of doing onto others as we would have others do onto us.

## Becoming a revolutionary

Abigail and John Adams had five children, with four surviving into adulthood. Her oldest son and future President John Quincy Adams was born in 1767. John Adams became active in politics, was an advocate for independence from England, and became a delegate to the Continental Congress after the Boston Tea Party in 1773 (see later in this section). He was gone for long periods of time, and during that time, Abigail managed their property and business affairs. Both she and her husband were raised in a culture of civic virtue where the public good takes precedence over self and thus were willing to sacrifice being together. However, the two stayed in touch by literally writing thousands of letters to each other during their lifetimes. Overall, 1,160 letters have survived to this day, and the most famous one is the one Abigail wrote to John while he was serving in the Second Continental Congress and was working on the Declaration of Independence.

**FIRST LADY LORE**

More than 2,000 of Abigail's letters to family and friends in which she discussed the major events of the Revolutionary War have been preserved. The revolution changed her from a naïve traditional woman to a worldly opinionated woman on par with her husband. Her letters also show that she was opposed to slavery and a very religious women, because in her letters she consistently references the Bible.

**TECHNICAL STUFF**

The British Parliament passed the Tea Act in 1773. This act allowed the British East India Company to take over the American tea business. Disgusted, the colonists responded with the Boston Tea Party, where people disguised as Indians boarded three British ships and dumped 342 crates of tea into the Boston harbor. Parliament responded with the so-called Intolerable Acts, closing Boston harbor and repealing many basic Colonial rights, including the right to local self-government.

**REMEMBER**

Abigail became a revolutionary herself. She melted pewter spoons to make bullets for the minutemen, American patriots fighting the British military.

## Living life abroad

After most of Massachusetts had been liberated from the British by 1776 and the Declaration of Independence, which John Adams helped edit, was signed in March of 1776, John Adams was sent to England in 1777 as a diplomat. Abigail raised their children, ran the family farm, and managed the couple's finances by herself for almost seven years. Abigail finally joined her husband after six years of separation and then went with him to France after he had been appointed U.S. minister to

France. Between 1784 and 1788, she lived with her husband in both France and England.

Back then, Congress didn't provide funding for running a diplomatic residence, and being minister almost ruined the Adams family. The couple had to pay for the expected social events held in their London and Paris homes out of their own pocket.

Abigail was happy to return home in 1788, and after John Adams was elected Vice President of the United States, she moved with him to New York, the first capital of the United States, and later Philadelphia after the capital moved. In Philadelphia, she became close friends with Marth Washington and hosted formal dinners every Wednesday for members of Congress and foreign dignitaries.

In 1794, her health began to decline, and she moved back to Massachusetts. She and John corresponded almost daily by letters discussing both national and local politics.

## Becoming First Lady

After John Adams became President of the United States in 1797, he urged Abigail to move back to the capital still in Philadelphia. She took up the role of hostess, receiving visitors to the presidential mansion and held dinners attended by lawmakers and foreign diplomats.

She had become America's second First Lady. Her functions included supervising a large staff and planning formal dinners in the President's mansion.

Being president was similar to being a diplomat. Back then, presidents received a very low presidential salary but still were expected to entertain. This imposed a great financial burden on not only the president but the whole family. For an average July 4th celebration, the Adamses had to buy 200 pounds of cake and two ¼ casks of wine and rum to entertain all members of Congress and their families.

## Turning into Mrs. President

Informally, Abigail discussed policy options with John Adams and gave him frequent advice. Soon, the political elite in Washington referred to her as an informal cabinet secretary.

Abigail was frequently called Mrs. President because of the influence she had over John. She discussed important problems with him, helped draft official letters, and basically became a minister without portfolio. For this reason, Abigail became a heroine for women who believed in women's rights.

Abigail supported John's policies, including the controversial Alien and Sedition Acts (see nearby sidebar). She believed that her husband and family were unfairly attacked by the press, which made libelous statements, and she believed that the press needed to be punished.

At the same time, Abigail was the first First Lady to attempt to manipulate the media to shape public opinion toward her husband and family. She planted stories in the Boston newspapers by sending them selected letters and news stories that she approved of.

## THE ALIEN AND SEDITION ACTS

The Alien and Sedition Acts were passed at the urging of President Adams and consisted of four separate acts designed to silence any opposition to his rule:

- The Naturalization Act made it more difficult to become a U.S. citizen. It mandated living in the country 14 years instead of 7 to acquire citizenship.

- The Alien Act allowed the government to deport foreigners who were considered a threat to the United States.

- The Alien Enemies Act allowed the government to imprison foreigners who were considered a threat to the United States.

- The Sedition Act made it a crime to criticize the federal government. Criticizing the president or Congress was punishable by imprisonment and fines up to $5,000.

President Adams never enthusiastically enforced the first three acts, but he and his party used the Sedition Act to send reporters, newspaper publishers, and even a Congressman critical of him, his political party, and his family to jail.

When Jefferson became president, he repealed the Naturalization Act — the other acts expired in the early years of Jefferson's presidency.

## HOW THE WHITE HOUSE BECAME THE WHITE HOUSE

The story of the presidential mansions is an interesting one. The first president and his wife, George and Martha Washington, lived in two private houses consecutively in New York City, the country's first capital. The two buildings they lived in were just called the Executive Mansion. George and Martha Washington lived in these two houses from 1789 until December of 1790, when the capital was temporarily moved to Philadelphia. Martha and her husband now rented a mansion owned by the wealthy merchant Robert Morris until 1797. This new residence was referred to as the President's House. The residence in Philadelphia was supposed to be temporary until a new executive mansion could be built in the new capital of Washington, D.C. The new executive building was ready to be occupied by 1800 and then President John Adams moved in. After the building was finished, the sandstone walls were whitewashed giving the house its familiar white color. Quickly, people started calling the building informally the white house.

However, the name Executive Mansion became the official name until President Theodore Roosevelt changed the name to the White House in 1901.

## Moving to and hating Washington, D.C.

In 1800, the new presidential building in the new capital of Washington, D.C., was ready, and Abigail had to make the move from Philadelphia. She oversaw the move from the president's mansion in Philadelphia to the presidential mansion in Washington, D.C. She disliked the new and still unfinished building and hated the humidity in Washington, D.C., which aggravated her rheumatoid arthritis. In a letter Abigail refers to Washington, D.C., as one of the "very dirtiest hole I ever saw for a place of any trade or respectability of inhabitants." She could not wait to leave Washington, D.C., and was not too upset that John lost reelection to Thomas Jefferson in 1800.

## Living out her life

After John Adams's term as president ended, the couple moved back to Quincy, Massachusetts, and lived there the next 17 years together.

However, tragedy struck the Adams family repeatedly in the period from 1800 to 1817. Three of Abigail's children died by 1817 and so did all of her sisters. In 1818, Abigail contracted typhoid fever at the age of 73. She died at home on October 28, a few weeks before her 74th birthday.

REMEMBER

Abigail Adams was so beloved in Massachusetts that her pallbearers included the governor of Massachusetts and the president of Harvard University.

IN THEIR WORDS

Abigail's son and future president John Quincy Adams wrote the following about his mother: "My mother's life gave the lie to every libel on her sex that was ever written."

## Becoming famous after her death

Abigail Adams left us letters, so we have a good record of her life. She actually provided the best record of a woman's role during the American Revolution and the early years of the U.S. government. Her letters, covering the period of 1762 until 1801, were published by her grandson in 1840 and became a bestseller. Her collected letters actually went into four editions in the 1840s alone and are still available for purchase today.

Charles Francis Adams, her grandson, summed up her life best, writing,

> She was a farmer cultivating the land and discussing the weather and the crops; a merchant reporting prices current and the rates of exchange and directing the making up of invoices, a politician speculating upon the probabilities of war, and a mother . . . and in all she appeared equally well.

# Martha Wayles Skelton Jefferson (1748–1782)

Martha Wayles (see Figure 4-2) was born on October 19, 1748, in Charles City County, Virginia. Nicknamed "Patty" by her parents, she grew up wealthy. Her parents, Martha Eppes Wayles and John Wayles, were prominent figures in Virginia's society. Martha was educated by private tutors and studied literature, dance, and French. Her father was an attorney and prominent slave trader who owned several plantations.

At the young age of 18, Martha married Bathurst Skelton, an attorney, who died within two years of them being married. Being a widow at the age of 20, she was courted by many young gentlemen, including Thomas Jefferson, who was also an attorney. They met while Thomas was serving in the Virginia House of Burgesses, Virginia's colonial legislative assembly. Martha lived only a few blocks away in the house she had inherited from her husband. By the time they met, Martha had not only become a widow but also recently lost her only child.

**FIGURE 4-2:**
Martha Wayles
Skelton Jefferson.

Source: C-Span / National Cable Satellite Corporation / Public Domain

**REMEMBER**

Thomas Jefferson decided to pursue Martha with what she loved most: music. They played music together and sang songs, and Thomas even gave her a piano as a gift. Martha fell in love with Thomas while they played music together. She played the harpsichord, and he played the violin.

The two got married on January 1, 1772, and then the couple moved to Thomas's estate called Monticello, which he had designed himself. When Martha married Thomas, the future president received a plantation and a large number of enslaved people as part of her dowry. After Martha's father's death in 1773, Thomas received even more property, including enslaved people, so he then owned 187 enslaved people, making him the second largest slave owner in Virginia.

**FIRST
LADY LORE**

Among the enslaved people Thomas received when marrying Martha was his future mistress, Sally Hemings, who was fathered by Martha's father, John Wayles.

**TECHNICAL
STUFF**

According to colonial law, a widowed woman's property automatically became the property of her new husband.

The next 10 years proved to be hectic. Thomas Jefferson was involved in the American Revolution, being a delegate to the Continental Congress in 1776 and writing the Declaration of Independence the same year. In 1779, he was elected the governor of Virginia. Martha became the First Lady of Virginia.

**FIRST
LADY LORE**

Martha started brewing her own beer while married to Thomas Jefferson, producing 170 gallons in the first year alone.

# Dying too soon

While Thomas Jefferson was active in politics and open rebellion, Martha stayed home raising their six children. Martha fell ill and became an invalid. Thomas turned down a job in France to stay with his ill wife. In June of 1781, Martha and Thomas got lucky when they managed to escape their estate, Monticello, after the British had attacked it. However, the strain of fleeing the British and bearing so many children made Martha very sick. She died on September 6, 1782, at the age of 33. Thomas went into mourning and never married again.

FIRST
LADY LORE

Martha made Thomas promise her never to marry again. She had many unpleasant experiences with stepmothers while she was growing up and didn't want her children to grow up with a stepmother.

IN THEIR
WORDS

Thomas Jefferson said the following after Martha's death:

> "Martha was the cherished companion of my life, in whose affections . . . I have lived . . . the last ten years of my life in uncheckered happiness."

REMEMBER

Of the six Jefferson children, only two survived into adulthood. They were Martha and Mary Jefferson.

# Becoming First Lady after her death

Thomas Jefferson became president in 1801, almost 19 years after his wife had died. Not having a spouse who could fulfill the social functions, such as hosting parties, that the presidency required, his daughter Martha (see Figure 4-3) became the Lady of the House, taking the place of her mother on several occasions. When she wasn't available for the festivities, Thomas would ask family friend Dolley Madison to preside over them.

TECHNICAL
STUFF

With Martha Jefferson a tradition was established of referring to a spouse of a president, who had died before her husband became president, as First Lady, if the president never got remarried.

REMEMBER

Dolley Madison excelled at planning and throwing parties, which became a good foundation for her future role as First Lady (see the next section).

After Thomas Jefferson retired from politics in 1809, he invited his daughter to live with him at his estate, Monticello. Thomas died in 1826, and both he and Martha are buried at Monticello.

**FIGURE 4-3:**
Martha Jefferson
Randolph,
daughter of
Thomas and
Martha Jefferson.

Source: Library of Congress, Prints & Photographs Division,
Reproduction number LC-USZ62-25769 (b&w film copy neg.)

Thomas Jefferson burned all the letters Martha wrote to him as was common practice then, with the exception of four letters. He wanted to keep their relationship and marriage private. Although there are no contemporary images of Martha Jefferson, she was described by family and friends as graceful, pretty, and very smart.

# Dolley Payne Todd Madison (1768–1849)

Dolley Payne (see Figure 4-4) was born on May 20, 1768, in Guilford County, North Carolina. Her parents, who were devout Quakers, had moved to North Carolina from Virginia to live in a Quaker settlement. They soon returned to Virginia, and Dolley grew up on the family's plantation. In 1783, her father John Payne freed his enslaved people and sold his planation and Dolley, who was 15 years old, and the family moved to Philadelphia to start a starch business.

Dolley was well educated. She had attended various Quaker schools and had received private tutoring. Her grandmother taught her about the finer things in life, such as fine food and fancy clothing. After her parents' business failed, the family started to run a boarding house, and Dolley became the cook. In 1790, she abided by her father's dying wish and married a Quaker lawyer from Philadelphia, John Todd. She was happily married and had two children. However, in 1793, a yellow fever pandemic struck Philadelphia and killed her husband and one of her children. Dolley was now a widow with one young boy. As a widow, however, she inherited her husband's property and was well off.

**FIGURE 4-4:**
Dolley Payne
Todd Madison.

Dolley was a very eligible young widow, and soon several young men pursued her. Her acquaintances included Aaron Burr who had stayed in her family's boarding house. It was Burr who, instead of pursuing Dolley himself, introduced her to James Madison, who was a member of the House of Representatives and was already known nationwide as one of the founding fathers, having written parts of the Constitution. He was 18 years older than Dolley, but the two hit it off, and James's close friends, George and Martha Washington, immediately liked her. Dolley was friendly and fashionable and loved music and dancing. In other words, everybody liked her because she was fun to be around.

The two married on September 15, 1794. After James retired from Congress in 1797, the couple moved to Virginia where James owned a large plantation known as Montpelier.

## Moving forward with charm and popularity

James Madison's retirement didn't last long. In 1801, the new President Thomas Jefferson called him back to the capital to serve as his Secretary of State. Dolley was delighted to return to the national scene, and with Thomas Jefferson being a widower, she would occasionally serve as his hostess for social functions at the White House.

In addition, Dolley started to entertain in her own home. Politicians and foreign diplomats couldn't wait to get an invitation to her events. Soon her home became the place to be in Washington, D.C. She would organize regular Wednesday afternoon parties, and everyone wanted to be invited.

**FIRST LADY LORE**

Dolley started her own fashion trend. She enjoyed wrapping scarves around her head, and the admiring public soon called it the "Dolley Turban" (see Figure 4-5).

**FIGURE 4-5:** Dolley Madison wearing her signature turban.

*Source: Unknown Source / Wikimedia Commons / Public Domain*

By 1808, Dolley had become one of the most popular women in the United States, well known and beloved by the American people. Her popularity helped get her husband elected in the 1808 presidential election, and by 1809, Dolley Madison was the new First Lady of the United States.

Dolley proved to be a major asset in James Madison's campaign for the presidency. After he won the presidency, his opponent Federalist Charles C. Pickney stated, "I might have had a better chance had I faced Mr. Madison alone."

**REMEMBER**

As First Lady, Dolley preferred to serve American food at White House dinners. She, therefore, looked for recipes all over the United States to serve authentic American cuisine at state dinners instead of foreign food, such as French food.

Members of Congress liked Dolley Madison so much that they had a reserved seat for her in the House of Representatives. She could come and go as she pleased.

## Blazing the trail for future First Ladies

After Dolley Madison became First Lady, she changed some traditions associated with the presidency. She organized the first inaugural ball for her husband, a tradition that lives on to this day. Second, she was able to secure more money from Congress for the presidential mansion. Therefore, she was able to hire a chef, increasing the number of guests invited to the White House for parties and expanding the guest list. Suddenly, not only members of Congress or foreign diplomats could attend but also well-known artists, writers, and even newsmakers were invited.

Because presidents brought their own furniture and took it back with them, the White House was basically empty every time a president left office. Therefore, Dolley spent a quarter of Congress's money to create and furnish the East Room in the White House to host more social events. In addition, Dolley went out and visited all of the Congressmen's families who had moved to Washington and invited them to the White House.

Dolley went to debates in Congress and watched Supreme Court arguments. This allowed for other women to accompany her, and Dolley even organized little groups of women going to Capitol Hill to watch policy making,

Dolley Madison entertained in drawing rooms. Drawing rooms were rooms specifically designed to entertain guests. Today, we call them living rooms.

Dolley's get-togethers were informal and nonpartisan; everybody had access to her and the president and could freely talk and discuss the issues of the day. Dolley treated everybody the same, be they political enemies or friends. Through her use of the drawing rooms, Dolley created networks with politicians, foreign dignitaries, and high society in Washington, D.C. Her use of social settings allowed for opposing sides to come together, which in turn helped her husband's political agenda. As an added benefit, Dolley was able to lower tensions in Congress, because members of Congress could meet in her drawing rooms, discuss issues outside the halls of Congress, and, after good food and wine, settle issues amicably.

## Saving a painting

In 1812, war with Great Britain broke out. President Madison fled the city, but Dolley remained in the White House to evacuate it. She remained there until the last possible minute, evacuating many precious items, including a famous painting of George Washington by Gilbert Stuart (see Figure 4-6). She even saved notes on the Constitutional Convention, cabinet papers, and the White House silver. This act saved many irreplaceable items in U.S. history, because as soon as the British arrived in Washington, D.C., they burned down the White House and the Library of Congress. The White House was totally destroyed by the British and had to be rebuilt. The Madison's never moved back in. Instead, they leased a large house a few blocks away, and Dolley started entertaining right away.

**FIGURE 4-6:**
The famous George Washington painting, saved by Dolley Madison.

This act turned Dolley into a national heroine. When she returned to Washington, D.C., thousands of people flocked to the streets to greet her.

**IN THEIR WORDS**

When asked whether she had saved George Washington's portrait, Dolley Madison said: "Our kind friend, Mr. Carroll, has come to hasten my departure, and is in a very bad humor with me because I insist on waiting until the large picture of Gen. Washington is secured, and it requires to be unscrewed from the wall. This process was found to be too tedious for these perilous moments; I have ordered the frame to be broken, and the canvass taken out it is done, and the precious portrait placed in the hands of two gentlemen of New York for safe keeping."

## THE STORY OF A MISSPELLED NAME

The story of Dolley Madison's first name is a strange one. Everybody referred to her as Dolley Madison until her grand-niece Lucia B. Cutts published a book in 1886 entitled "The Memoirs and Letters of Dolly Madison." With the book, she set the precedent of spelling her name, Dolly. Nobody questioned her because she was a relative of Dolley's. Lucia further claimed that Dolly was the abbreviation for Dorothea and that she was named after the granddaughter of the famous Virginia governor Alexander Spotswood.

Many businesses soon began marketing products under the name Dolly Madison. The Dolly Madison Bakery for example was started in 1937. The image the company used to market their products portrays Dolley in her famous turban but obviously her name was changed to just Dolly. The bakery is most famous for their Zingers snack cakes still sold today even though the bakery has been bought out by Hostess Brands.

Then in 1958 it was discovered in some of James Madison's papers that the name of his wife was spelled Dolley. This discovery made the front page of the *New York Times*. Already having trademarked their products, American businesses were not about to change the name and so they just stuck with Dolly.

So, yes, the correct spelling of her name was Dolley Madison, but often she is just referred to as Dolly Madison.

**FIRST LADY LORE**

Dolley Madison became so popular that businesses used her name and image to market their products. Soon, items such as ice cream and cigars had her name attached to them.

## Becoming the first lady named First Lady

President Madison decided to abide by the precedent George Washington set of serving only two terms and retired in 1817. He and Dolley moved back to Virginia, and Dolley continued to host her parties for local and state notables. She enjoyed her life in retirement until James Madison died in 1836. A widow for the second time in her life, Dolley returned to Washington, D.C., in 1837 to pay off her son's debts.

Her son, Payne Todd, had accrued lots of debts and had been in debtor's prison twice. For this reason, she had to sell her planation in Virginia. With the money from the planation, she paid off his debts and bought a house right across from the White House in Washington, D.C., where she continued to host crowded receptions. As soon as she returned, people flocked to her, and she soon became a hostess and social affairs advisor to President Martin Van Buren, whose wife had died before he became president. She helped him with social events, such as planning White House parties. She would do the same for Letitia Tyler, the wife of President John Tyler, who was disabled, and later on even advised First Lady Sarah Polk, who wasn't familiar with the process of hosting White House social events.

REMEMBER

Dolley Madison lived a long and fulfilling life and died at the age of 81 in 1849. When she died, President Zachary Taylor noted: "She will never be forgotten because she was truly our First Lady for half a century." With this statement, he coined the term *First Lady* for future presidents' wives.

FIRST
LADY LORE

Dolley Madison enjoyed taking snuff, even though it was considered unladylike at her time. She used her habit for good purposes. As the story goes, when Speaker of the House Henry Clay wanted to go to war against Great Britain, at a time when President Madison wasn't yet ready to do so, Dolley invited him over to discuss the issue, and the two dipped snuff together, and Henry Clay later became a close ally of President Madison. One of Dolley's friends is even quoted as saying, "The snuff box has a magic influence."

# Chapter **5**

# Continuing to Set an Example

This chapter looks at three First Ladies who contributed in some form to the way First Ladies behave and are judged today. Elizabeth Monroe loved and was beloved by the European aristocracy. She embodied what other nations perceived a First Lady of the United States should look and act like. However, when she came back to the United States from Paris, where her husband served as minister, she brought a formality to the White House similar to European royal courts and soon curtailed her social activities. For example, she didn't believe that it was her obligation to visit all the wives of the members of Congress, as had been tradition, and she disliked large parties. She was shy and reserved as a First Lady, participating only in smaller social events. Many First Ladies who followed her adopted her style.

Louisa Adams faced other problems. She wasn't born in the United States, and to make matters worse, her mother was English. Even though she was an American citizen by birthright because her father was American, her mother being English was used against her and her husband, John Quincy Adams, especially when she became First Lady. Louisa, like Elizabeth Monroe, was a hit in Europe and was well liked in Russia and Prussia, but she had a tough time connecting with the average American.

Rachel Jackson grew up a country girl like most Americans at that time but was never able to play the role of First Lady, because she died a few months before her husband was sworn in. She also faced bitter personal and political attacks from her husband's political enemies, being called a bigamist and even a whore. All of this contributed to her heart problems, and her husband blamed her death on his political enemies for the rest of his life.

# Elizabeth Kortright Monroe (1768–1830)

Elizabeth Kortright (see Figure 5-1) was born on June 30, 1768, into a wealthy New York family. Her father, Lawrence Kortright, was a wealthy merchant and had benefited greatly from British rule. Not surprisingly, he was a supporter of the crown and even a member of the British Tory Party. The Tory Party was and still is the major British conservative party. Lawrence was opposed to the American Revolution and wanted America to remain a part of the British Empire.

**FIGURE 5-1:**
Elizabeth
Kortright Monroe.

*Source: Library of Congress, Prints & Photographs Division, Reproduction number LC-USZ62-25771 (b&w film copy neg.)*

Elizabeth met James Monroe when she was 17, and they got married the same year. James had fought for the American side in the American Revolution and lived in New York City, where he was serving as a member of the Congress of Confederation. Despite different political views and different financial backgrounds, James wasn't very wealthy, coming from a middle-class family, the two fell in love and got married in 1786. A year later, the couple moved to Virginia, James's home state.

The Congress of Confederation was the national legislature of the United States, created in 1781. It met in New York City for most of its existence and had no real power. All power remained with the states. It was replaced with the Congress of the United States in 1789.

## Going abroad and saving an American hero's wife

In 1794, James Monroe was asked to serve as a diplomat in France, and Elizabeth went with him to Paris. The couple went to France at a time when the terror of the French Revolution was at its height. At that time, 1,500 people had been executed alone in the summer of 1794. The Marquis de Lafayette, an American war hero, had been able to flee France, but his wife and children had been captured and were awaiting execution. The French government had already executed the Marquis de Lafayette's mother and other relatives, and his wife and children were next. The Monroes knew that they had to act to save the family. Elizabeth's husband James had known the Marquis de Lafayette since the time of the American Revolution and considered him a family friend. In addition, the Marquis de Lafayette was a close friend of George Washington's and had fought with the American Army against the British during the Revolutionary War.

Elizabeth and James, therefore, decided to do their best to save Madame de Lafayette and her two children. Although James couldn't get officially involved because he was an American diplomat, Elizabeth, acting as a private citizen, could. She decided to visit Madame de Lafayette and her two children in prison in France. First, she bought a carriage — prohibited then in Paris because it was a sign of wealth — and then went to the prison. Suddenly, she was surrounded by large crowds that hadn't seen carriages in quite some time. They wanted to know who was inside this carriage and who was being visited. The whole event turned into a public spectacle, making everybody aware of Madame de Lafayette's predicament.

Prison officials were in a quandary. An obviously important woman was trying to visit an important prisoner. They relented and let Elizabeth see Madame de Lafayette. When Madame Lafayette saw Elizabeth, she broke down in tears. It turned out that she had been scheduled to be executed the same afternoon. When French officials were told of Elizabeth's visit and how the Marquis de Lafayette was a personal friend of the American diplomat, they decided they would release Madame de Lafayette to promote better French-American relations. Without Elizabeth's visit, which came at great risk for her, Madame Lafayette and her children would have been executed that day. Elizabeth continued to enjoy her time in Europe, and she even befriended and socialized with Napoleon while in France.

# Embracing European life

After returning home, in 1798, James Monroe won the governorship in Virginia, and Elizabeth became the First Lady of Virginia. She stayed out of politics and was content to raise her two daughters. However, President Jefferson asked James to go back to France to help negotiate the Louisiana Purchase. Elizabeth again accompanied him. By now, she is was a hero in Parisian circles for freeing Madame de Lafayette, and the French elites referred to her as *La Belle Americaine* or "the beautiful American." The Monroes remained in Europe until 1807, and Elizabeth enjoyed the good life. She was treated like a member of the European aristocracy and regretted having to go home in 1807.

REMEMBER

During her trips to Europe, Elizabeth observed and appreciated formal old-world (European) style and values. She enjoyed wearing expensive dresses, up to $1,500 per dress, which would be about $30,000 today, and started wearing fine jewelry, usually crucifixes similar to those worn by the French and Spanish aristocracy.

TECHNICAL
STUFF

## DEAL OF THE CENTURY!

France acquired the Louisiana Territory in 1682 and gave it to Spain in 1762. France reacquired the territory in 1802. President Jefferson sent his friend James Monroe, the former governor of Virginia and future president, to Paris to attempt to buy the port city of New Orleans from France.

The French shocked Monroe by offering to sell the whole Louisiana Territory for a measly $15 million. Jefferson happily accepted and signed the treaty setting the terms for purchase. On December 20, 1803, the Senate approved the purchase, and the United States doubled in size overnight. Jefferson and Monroe successfully added 828,000 square miles to the country. The territory included what would become parts of Wyoming and the following states:

| | | |
|---|---|---|
| Arkansas | Colorado | Iowa |
| Kansas | Louisiana | Minnesota |
| Missouri | Montana | Nebraska |
| North Dakota | Oklahoma | South Dakota |

# Going home and being miserable

After returning to the United States, James Monroe served in the Virginia state legislature and became governor of Virginia one more time. In the beginning, Elizabeth was content being at home, deeply in love with her husband and totally devoted to him. However, secretly, she longed for Europe. Then things got worse.

In 1811, President Madison appointed James Monroe Secretary of State, and Elizabeth had to move to Washington, D.C. With the position of Secretary of State being the springboard to the presidency at this time, it's no surprise that James Monroe was elected president in 1816, and Elizabeth became the First Lady. Unlike Dolley Madison (see Chapter 4), Elizabeth didn't enjoy entertaining much, and she preferred to be by herself. While Dolley Madison visited just about everybody who mattered in Washington, D.C., Elizabeth preferred to have people come to her. Instead of larger social events, Elizabeth preferred smaller, more intimate gatherings. This especially angered the wives of members of Congress and diplomats because they weren't allowed to attend unless the First Lady was in attendance. The rule was simple: "No women guests in the president's house in the absence of a hostess." So if Elizabeth didn't invite women or didn't show up, women weren't allowed at White House events. It got even worse during James's second term, when Elizabeth disappeared from the public for months.

Even though Elizabeth was good friends with Dolley Madison, the two were totally different. Dolley enjoyed large crowds and enjoyed visiting people. Elizabeth preferred to stay home with her children and grandchildren. She enjoyed very small receptions and small dinners and then was social and well liked. However, she despised large gatherings or visiting people. This resulted in scandal because all the wives of Congressmen arriving in Washington, D.C., expected a visit from not only the wives of cabinet members but also from the First Lady herself. When this didn't happen, the wives of these Congressmen began to boycott Elizabeth's few social events, which in turn resulted in Elizabeth having even fewer social events. Her reputation began to suffer, and people turned against her.

To make matters worse, Elizabeth was seen as an alien, un-American, because she fell in love with France. She always acted like a member of the French aristocracy, spoke French to her children, and even bought French furniture for the White House, because she believed that it was important for the United States to be illustrative of a great country. She even served French food at social gatherings, unlike Dolley Madison who had made it a point to serve only American food at official state dinners.

In addition, Elizabeth enjoyed expensive dresses and even wore rouge and makeup, which was considered immodest and improper in the United States. The average American objected to this. She was, therefore, not a political figure like Abigail Adams but had flair about her with a sense of fashion and beauty. Today, many historians refer to her as the Jackie Kennedy of the 19th century.

Elizabeth Monroe had two daughters. Her older daughter Maria was the first presidential child to have a wedding in the White House in 1820. Elizabeth by then had serious health problems, suffering from rheumatoid arthritis and epilepsy. Often her second daughter Eliza had to take her place. For this reason, Eliza planned her sister's wedding in 1820. She decided to make it a small private affair. However, about 600 influential Washingtonians expected to be invited to the first White House wedding. When this didn't happen, Elizabeth took the blame, and it just reinforced her reputation of being reclusive and anti-social.

After James Monroe decided not to run for a third term, abiding by the two-term tradition established by George Washington, Elizabeth moved back to Virginia in 1825. The couple was in debt, because back then public officials, be they elected politicians or diplomats, didn't get paid well. Despite money problems, Elizabeth enjoyed her last years and passed away on September 23, 1830, at the age of 62.

President Monroe burned all correspondence with Elizabeth after he left the presidency. He wanted to protect their privacy, and therefore historians today have no firsthand evidence about Elizabeth's thoughts, beliefs, and political feelings.

# Louisa Johnson Adams (1775–1852)

Louisa Catherine Johnson (see Figure 5-2) was born on February 12, 1775, in Nantes, France. Her father, Joshua Johnson, who had been the American consul to London, was no longer welcome at this point in England because he was a supporter of the American Revolution. So he went to France for a brief period of time. Louisa's mother, Catherine Nuth, was a member of the British upper class and spared no expense educating her three daughters.

When John Quincy Adams arrived in England in 1794 to ratify the Jay Treaty, he was 28 years old and already an accomplished diplomat. John Quincy met Louisa for the first time when he was invited for dinner at the Johnson house. Both became enamored with each other quickly. They shared a love for literature. Louisa had written poems and theater plays herself, and both spoke French fluently. Even though both loved each other, the marriage almost didn't happen when John Quincy found out that Louisa's father was quite poor and not a large plantation owner as he had thought. However, their love was strong enough to overcome this obstacle, and they got married on July 26, 1797, in London. Soon after their marriage, John Quincy's father, John Adams, was elected President of the United States and appointed his son Ambassador to Prussia.

**FIGURE 5-2:**
Louisa Johnson
Adams

*Source: Library of Congress, Prints & Photographs Division, Reproduction number LC-USZ62-14438 (b&w film copy neg. of cropped image)*

**TECHNICAL STUFF**

The Jay Treaty, named after Chief Justice John Jay, made the United States repay prerevolutionary debt to Great Britain. In turn, the British paid for damages caused by the British Navy having seized American ships. In addition, the British agreed to abandon British forts located in the American northwest.

**FIRST LADY LORE**

Louisa Adams has the distinction of being the first foreign-born First Lady (Melania Trump became the second in 2017). She was born in London to an American father, but her mother was English. Therefore, she was an American citizen by birthright but was often considered a foreigner not only by the average American but also by her own mother-in-law, Abigail Adams. John Quincy Adams was so afraid that his mother would try to block the marriage that he sent the letter revealing his intention to marry Louisa so late that it didn't arrive in time for the Adams family to prevent his marriage.

**FIRST LADY LORE**

The couple was received well in Prussia and became a favorite of the Prussian King Frederick Wilhelm III. He liked them so much that he prohibited traffic on the street where they lived after their son had been born. The king wanted to make sure that the streets were quiet and nobody would wake the newborn. This allowed the new parents to rest comfortably.

REMEMBER

John Quincy Adams was deeply in love with his wife. She fit in perfectly with the European aristocracy and was well liked. However, his mother, Abigail Adams, despised her and called her a half-breed who would likely bankrupt her son with her extravagant wishes.

In 1801, the couple moved back to the United States, and John Quincy practiced law in Boston and later served as a member of Congress. During this time, Louisa, now 26 years of age, and Abigail Adams never got along. It's tough to like someone who publicly called you a half-breed. However, former President John Adams started to like her, and the two developed a deep friendship.

## Living an adventure

In 1809, Louisa's life changed again. President Madison appointed John Quincy Adams as Ambassador to Russia, and the couple had to leave their two oldest children behind to be raised and educated in the United States. Louisa, John Quincy, and her youngest son, only two years old, moved to St. Petersburg, the capital of Russia. St. Petersburg was quite primitive at the time. The water supply was poor, roads were rough, and it was tough to find a place that could keep you warm during the cold winter nights. Many diplomats refused to bring their wives along for this reason, and Louisa didn't have a lot of women to socialize with. Then Louisa got pregnant and had a daughter in 1811; unfortunately, the little girl died a year later.

In 1814, John Quincy had to suddenly leave Russia to negotiate the peace treaty with Great Britain that would end the War of 1812. Suddenly, Louisa was alone in Russia with her young son. She had to plan and undertake a long dangerous trip from Russia to France, where the treaty was being negotiated, during the winter time. The trip took 40 days and took her through rural Russia and Prussia and across the Alps. She later wrote that often she wouldn't sleep at night, afraid of being murdered. She was able to bring only three servants along, whom she had just hired and didn't know well, and one turned out to be a convicted criminal. When she finally reached France, she was right in the middle of a popular uprising with Napoleon recently having returned to power. After being reunited in France, things began to look up in 1815 when John Quincy Adams became the Ambassador to England. Louisa was able to move to London and be reunited with her two older sons.

REMEMBER

At first Louisa was shocked that her husband would allow her to undertake such a dangerous trip by herself. She was even more surprised that he allowed her to make all the travel arrangements. She had never been given that much responsibly in her marriage before. The successful and dangerous journey elevated her in her husband's eyes, gave her a lot of self-confidence, and even impressed her mother-in-law, who started to treat her better.

FIRST
LADY LORE

Louisa was a favorite of Tsar Alexander of Russia. He considered her his favorite dancing partner.

# Becoming First Lady

Louisa and John Quincy enjoyed their time in London, but then in 1817, newly elected president James Monroe appointed John Quincy Adams Secretary of State, and the family had to move back to the United States. Louisa despised Washington, D.C., as soon as she saw it. It wasn't a fitting capital like London or Paris or even Berlin. The White House had no indoor plumbing, and cows and sheep grazed close by. There wasn't even security at the White House, and anybody could just walk in uninvited.

IN THEIR
WORDS

"There is something in this great, unsocial house which depresses my spirits beyond expression," Louisa said of the White House.

Even worse, it was expected that wives of cabinet members would make social calls on all the wives of the members of Congress. Louisa refused for the first years to do so, but by 1819, she became fully engaged in Washington's social business.

Louisa Adams became quite politically ambitious for her husband. She had been around many powerful people in Europe and expected her husband to become a powerful politician himself. Therefore, beginning in 1819, she changed her tune and started to do whatever was necessary to help him become president. Be it tea parties, or visiting the wives of congressmen or giving political advise, Louisa decided to do what she could to see John Quincy become president of the United States.

Louisa knew that her husband would be in line for the presidency after President Monroe retired and that her role would be to help him secure support. Being despised by the Washington elite wouldn't be very helpful. She started to host weekly tea parties that hundreds of people attended. Suddenly, she became popular and well liked. In addition, Louisa started to visit the wives of members of Congress, going to as many as 25 houses a day and spending about 30 minutes with each wife.

REMEMBER

Back then, there were no movies or television shows or the internet to entertain people. The most common form of entertainment was attending parties and dinners. For this reason, hosting social events provided people with not just social but also political support.

REMEMBER

Louisa was a very talented musician, playing both the harp and the piano. However, after becoming First Lady, her husband asked her to stop, believing that a First Lady shouldn't perform for others.

# Seeking the election of 1824

After John Quincy Adams decided to run for president, Louisa threw a ball in honor of General Andrew Jackson, who was widely considered to be the front-runner for president in 1824. She invited hundreds of people, about 900 showed up, and her party for Jackson, held in January of 1824, was the event of the year for the Washington elites. It was a big success and considered a brilliant strategic move because at the party both John Quincy and Louisa tried to talk Andrew Jackson out of running for president. However, Jackson had already made up his mind and ran for the presidency after all.

**TECHNICAL STUFF**

President Monroe was the first president in 16 years to retire without naming a successor. This complicated matters in the 1824 election. Four men, all from the same political party, the Democratic-Republican Party, ran for the presidency. They were John Quincy Adams, General Andrew Jackson, the Speaker of the House Henry Clay, and the Secretary of the Treasury William Crawford.

All four of the men received Electoral College votes in the election, but no one received a majority. Jackson won the popular vote but received only 99 Electoral College votes out of a possible 261. Adams came in second with 84 Electoral College votes. Crawford finished third, and Clay came in fourth.

With nobody receiving a majority in the Electoral College, the House of Representatives had the constitutional right to pick the new president. Clay, who despised Jackson, threw his support behind Adams, helping him win the presidency. Adams, in turn, appointed Clay Secretary of State. Jackson and his followers cried foul. For the first time in U.S. history, the candidate who won the popular vote lost the election. This put a shadow on Adams's presidency from the beginning, and Andrew Jackson's supporters would do their best to not only undermine President John Quincy Adams but to also attack his wife. Jackson's supporters accused her of spending too much furnishing the White House, acting like European royalty, and not being a real American.

**FIRST LADY LORE**

To make sure that her husband would win the vote in the House of Representatives and be elected president, Louisa held a tea party for almost 500 people, including 67 Congressmen, who would vote on the presidency the next morning, on February 8, 1825. John Quincy won the vote in the House of Representatives and thus the presidency. Nobody really knows how many Congressmen changed their votes and supported Adams because of the party, but many historians believe that without the tea party, John Quincy Adams would not have become president. Louisa was now the First Lady of the United States.

Louisa worried about the safety of her husband after he became president. His enemies wouldn't just call him a Yankee Aristocrat with a foreign wife, but out of spite, Jackson's supporters blocked just about every bill or policy President Adams proposed, regardless of merit. Therefore, the years as First Lady were hard on Louisa, and today John Quincy Adams's presidency is considered a failure.

As First Lady, Louisa changed how she handled her duties. She decided to be similar to Elizabeth Monroe, being more formal and reserved and not holding many public events in the White House. She also stopped attending many public functions. In other words, she stopped being sociable. The main reason were the constant attacks by Andrew Jackson's supporters and her husband's unsuccessful presidency. She was quite content when John Quincy Adams lost reelection in 1828. Finally, she was able to leave Washington, D.C.

Family tragedy struck after John Quincy lost the 1828 presidential election to Andrew Jackson. In 1829, their oldest son fell off a ship and drowned. Many people speculated that he didn't fall but possibly died by suicide, because he was a heavy drinker with a lot of gambling debts. In 1834, their second oldest son, an alcoholic, died at age 31, leaving his wife and two children to be cared for by Louisa and John Quincy.

## Going back to Washington, D.C.

In 1830, John Quincy Adams decided to reenter politics. He was elected back to Congress. Even though Louisa wasn't pleased, she went back to Washington, D.C., because she loved her husband. She became one of the most popular party givers in the capital, even rivaling Dolley Madison. Her European style, dresses, and manners made her one of the most popular hostesses in the capital.

In 1848, John Quincy suffered a stroke in the House of Representatives and died in the halls of Congress. Louisa was with him when he died, and she suffered a stroke shortly afterward. She lived four more years and then died of a heart attack on May 15, 1852, at the age of 77.

Louisa left behind a large collection of writings, diaries, poems, and correspondence, and therefore historians know quite a bit of her life.

**FIRST LADY LORE**

Louisa Adams was addicted to chocolate. Her sons had to bring her chocolates by the barrel.

## Rachel Donelson Jackson (1767–1828)

Rachel Donelson (see Figure 5-3) was born in Halifax County, Virginia, on June 15, 1767. Her father was a member of the Virginia legislature, a militia leader, and a land surveyor. Being the daughter of a Virginia legislator had its perks. As a young child, Rachel was able to meet George Washington and Thomas Jefferson, fellow Virginians. As soon as she turned 12, her family moved to the frontier, back then

Eastern Tennessee, to settle in one of the very remote areas of the United States. They were among the earliest white settlers of the area, and it took a 100-mile river trip to get there. There was no official schooling available, but Rachel learned how to read and write from her parents. Most of her time, however, was spent working the land of the new community.

**REMEMBER**

Rachel was different from any of her First Lady predecessors. She wasn't born in a large city or on a big plantation. She wasn't born into wealth and educated by private tutors. Instead, she grew up on the American frontier. She had no opportunities to be well educated and to become a proper lady.

Five years later, Rachel's family moved to Kentucky; they left Tennessee because of the constant conflict with Native Americans. While in Kentucky, she met her first husband, Lewis Robards, who came from a wealthy prominent family. They were married in 1785, but Robards turned out to be a very jealous and abusive husband. In 1790, Rachel decided that she couldn't take the abuse anymore and fled to the wilderness in what is now Tennessee. Her husband, in turn, started divorce proceedings.

# Meeting Jackson

Rachel met Andrew Jackson after moving to Tennessee. He was a young lawyer in Nashville and stayed at one of her mother's rental homes in the area. Rachel's father asked Andrew to accompany Rachel on a trip to Mississippi where one of her sisters lived. Andrew agreed, and on that trip, he fell in love with her.

As soon as Andrew came back to Nashville, he found out that Rachel's husband Lewis Robards had filed for divorce, and he assumed that the divorce was finalized. So he immediately returned to Mississippi to ask Rachel to marry him. She agreed, and they got married in 1791 and lived a happy life — until they found out that Lewis had never completed the divorce proceedings. He never signed the paperwork. He then refiled for the divorce and claimed adultery. This time, the divorce proceedings went through, and Lewis and Rachel were officially divorced in September 1793. Andrew Jackson and Rachel then got remarried in 1794.

People made fun of and judged Rachel for the rest of her life. However, she and Andrew were happy. Andrew was sent to Congress after Tennessee became a state in 1796. Andrew was well liked and well respected in Nashville. He bought an estate he called the Hermitage and served as both a judge and the head of the Tennessee state militia.

REMEMBER

Andrew Jackson had quite a temper. Whenever someone accused his wife of committing adultery or being a bigamist, he'd get into a fist fight with them or even duel them for his wife's honor. In 1806, Andrew actually shot and killed Charles Dickinson in a duel after he called Rachel a bigamist and accused Andrew of cheating on a horse race bet.

Andrew and Rachel Jackson weren't able to have any children. Therefore, in 1809, they adopted a nephew, Andrew Jackson Jr.

Fighting in the War of 1812 against the British, Andrew became a national hero after winning the battle of New Orleans in 1815. Afterward, he became the governor of the new Florida Territory in 1821 after successfully fighting the Seminole Indians.

REMEMBER

In 1812, the United States and Britain went to war. Britain aligned itself with several Native American tribes that were also hostile to the United States. One of these tribes, the Creek, massacred 250 settlers in the Mississippi Territory. Andrew Jackson organized a militia and went after the Native Americans. He found them in 1814. As a gesture of goodwill, he let all the women and children go free. Then he attacked the men, killing more than 800 Creek warriors. Later, he forced the Creek to sign a treaty with the U.S. government, ceding more than half of present-day Alabama to the United States.

TECHNICAL
STUFF

President Madison appointed Andrew major general in 1814 and sent him south to defend New Orleans. Andrew organized one of the most unique militias in U.S. history. He recruited frontiersmen, pirates, slaves, Frenchmen, and whomever else he could find. When the British launched a frontal assault on January 8, 1815, Andrew was ready. In the battle of New Orleans, Andrew Jackson's militia killed more than 2,000 British soldiers, while losing only 8 men. Andrew Jackson was a national hero.

While Andrew was off fighting the British and Native Americans, Rachel stayed home on their plantation. On a few occasions, she joined her husband in New Orleans and Florida, but she enjoyed her home life at the Hermitage and helped raise 13 children, mostly nieces and nephews. She wasn't afraid of getting her hands dirty helping out with farm work, and in the evening she relaxed by smoking her pipe.

FIRST
LADY LORE

The Jacksons adopted an Indian infant boy after a battle in which Andrew Jackson killed his family.

## Almost becoming First Lady

In 1823, Andrew Jackson was elected to Congress and subsequently decided to run for the presidency. Even though he won the popular vote and the most Electoral College votes, he didn't receive an absolute majority in the Electoral College. Therefore, the House of Representatives decided the election. As soon as John Quincy Adams won, Andrew Jackson created his own political party and started to focus on the 1828 presidential election.

Rachel wasn't very happy with her husband's presidential ambitions. She knew her opponents would try to use her and her divorce scandal against her husband. In addition, she had grown up on a farm, enjoyed the quiet rural life, and despised socializing and formal parties that were the norm in the capital.

She was correct. Her husband's political opponents went after her viciously. They called Rachel a whore, adulteress, and a bigamist, even though she had been married to Andrew Jackson for 36 years by then. And, they claimed that both Rachel and Andrew were unfit for the presidency because he was married to a woman with loose morals. In addition, they made fun of her Tennessee accent and for smoking a pipe.

IN THEIR
WORDS

Rachel Jackson despised the Washington elites. She is quoted as saying, "I had rather be a doorkeeper in the house of God than live in that palace in Washington."

By 1828, when Jackson finally won the presidency, Rachel had become ill. After the election, she knew that she was dying and so was looking for someone to replace her in the White House to fulfill the role of First Lady. She tutored her niece, Emily Donelson, in becoming a proper replacement for her as First Lady. She taught Emily how to host parties properly and how to converse like a proper lady. Rachel was thus the first First Lady to prepare a younger substitute for the job of First Lady.

Rachel never made it to Washington, D.C., to serve as First Lady. She died December 22, 1828, of a heart attack, about three months before her husband became president. Andrew Jackson blamed his political opponents for her death, believing that the continuous slanderous campaign against her had killed her.

**FIRST LADY LORE**

Rachel Jackson was buried in the white satin gown she had planned to wear for inauguration.

After Rachel was buried at the Hermitage, Andrew Jackson put the following inscription on her tombstone: "A being so gentle and so virtuous, slander might wound, but could not dishonor."

Andrew Jackson subsequently allowed his niece Emily Donelson to play the role of First Lady. She performed well in the role until the Peggy Eaton affair happened (see the nearby sidebar). Jackson was so upset with Emily over her role in the affair that he replaced her with Sarah Yorke Jackson, the wife of his adopted son.

## SCANDAL: THE PEGGY EATON AFFAIR

Senator Henry Eaton was a good friend of Andrew Jackson. After Andrew won the presidency in 1828, Henry Eaton became Secretary of War in 1829. Henry had been a boarder at an inn, owned by Peggy Timberlake's father. There were rumors of Henry and Peggy having an affair, even though Peggy was married at the time. Then, Peggy's husband died by suicide, and Peggy was single again. Instead of going into mourning and waiting for a year, as custom dedicated, Peggy decided to marry Henry Eaton. For this reason, the wives of many cabinet members, including the vice president and Emily Donelson, ostracized Peggy. All of this reminded Andrew Jackson how Washington society had treated is late wife. He was furious and replaced Emily Donelson. Andrew clearly saw Peggy Eaton as a surrogate for Rachel and tried to protect her.

Interestingly, the Eaton affair also resulted in Andrew Jackson and Martin Van Buren becoming close friends. Van Buren, Andrew's Secretary of State, was one of the few who treated Peggy well and befriended her. Van Buren, of course, later became vice president and then president of the United States.

# 3

# Leading Up to a Civil War

Find out how Hannah Van Buren became First Lady after she died. Understand why young substitutes covered for First Ladies Anna Harrison and Letitia Tyler during this part of U.S. history. And see how Julia Tyler became the youngest First Lady to date.

Uncover the life of one of the most influential First Ladies, Sarah Polk, who wasn't afraid to express her opinion and became a major influence with her husband.

Discover why some First Ladies — Margaret Taylor, Abigail Fillmore, and Jane Pierce — never wanted the job. On the flip side, see how Harriet Lane, niece to President James Buchanan, exceled at her role as First Lady.

Examine the life of Mary Todd Lincoln and how she became a drag on her husband's career.

# Chapter 6

# Calling in a First Lady Substitute

his chapter takes a look at the four First Ladies during the period of 1837 until 1847. These First Ladies were mostly replaced by young and model-like presidential hostesses. Reasons were manyfold. One First Lady died before her husband won office. Another never made it to Washington, D.C., because her husband died one month into the presidency. A third was disabled by a stroke and became the first First Lady to die while in office. The fourth and last one was just too young and inexperienced and was in office for less than one year.

Instead of having a First Lady to perform her official functions, which usually meant organizing presidential social affairs, such as hosting dinners or throwing a ball, two daughters-in-law stepped in. They were Angelica Van Buren and Priscilla Tyler. They were both young and beautiful and not very interested in politics. Angelica Van Buren had her in-law, former First Lady Dolley Madison, tutor her on the role of hostess and help out if needed, and Priscilla Tyler was a successful actress, well known and admired for her beauty.

These First Lady substitutes weren't very worldly, lacked etiquette, and weren't well educated, but they were the perfect presidential hostesses. As the next chapter shows, several First Ladies in the 1850s selected substitutes so that they wouldn't have to bother with a First Lady's social obligations. They either claimed illness or grief for allowing someone else to perform their functions and fulfill the expectations set by their predecessors. This new version of First Ladies, and especially the young hostess substitutes, had none of the experiences as their predecessors and were therefore not very influential in American history.

# Hannah Hoes Van Buren (1783–1819)

Hannah Hoes (see Figure 6-1) was born in Kinderhook, New York, on March 8, 1783, into a loyalist family. Her father was a staunch supporter of the British Empire and opposed American independence. She and Martin Van Buren grew up together in a very small, tight-knit Dutch immigrant community. In fact, they were first cousins — the only presidential couple who were first cousins. Both Hannah and Martin spoke Dutch and belonged to the local Dutch Reformist church. The Van Buren and Hoes families were close and socialized together often. This is how the two grew close and fell in love.

**FIGURE 6-1:**
Hannah Hoes
Van Buren.

Source: Library of Congress, Prints & Photographs Division,
Reproduction number LC-USZ62-25776 (b&w film copy
neg. of cropped image)

Hannah married Martin Van Buren, who had become a local lawyer, in a secret ceremony on February 21, 1807, when she was 23 years old. Five years later, Martin was elected to the State Senate in New York, and the two moved to Albany, the capital of New York State. They had five children; one died in infancy, and the other four sons lived long and healthy lives. Hannah was a modest and very religious wife who was happy to stay home and raise her sons.

Not a lot of information is available on Hannah because Martin left her out of his 800-page autobiography and didn't mention or discuss his marriage much after she passed. One of Martin Van Buren's colleagues in the Senate and close friend gave one of the few descriptions of Hannah. He said, "Hannah was a woman of sweet nature but few intellectual gifts, who had no ambitious desires." Her niece called her "modest, even timid with a loving gentle disposition."

Hannah was very religious but not very interested in politics. After giving birth to her fifth child, Hannah contracted tuberculosis and died on February 5, 1819, at the age of 35, 18 years before Martin became president. Martin never remarried and moved with his four surviving children, all grown sons, into the White House after he was elected. For this reason, there was no hostess in the White House, and very few social events were held. This changed when his oldest son Abraham married Angelica Singleton, an in-law of Dolley Madison. Dolley Madison had actually played the role of matchmaker between the two, and for this reason, both Angelica and Dolley Madison served as White House hostesses during the Van Buren presidency. Angelica Van Buren (see Figure 6-2) served as the White House hostess from 1838 to 1841.

**FIGURE 6-2:** Angelica Van Buren, daughter-in-law of Martin Van Buren.

*Source: Library of Congress, Prints & Photographs Division, Reproduction number LC-DIG-hec-03158 (digital file from original negative)*

# Anna Tuthill Symmes Harrison (1775–1864)

Anna Tuthill Symmes (see Figure 6-3) was born in Flatbrook, New Jersey, on July 25, 1775. Her father was a local judge and war veteran who had served as a colonel in the Continental Army during the American Revolution. Anna's mother died when she was four, and she was therefore raised by her grandparents on Long Island in the state of New York. There, she had a wonderful upbringing, she received a good public education, and she enjoyed life.

**FIGURE 6-3:** Anna Tuthill Symmes Harrison.

Source: Library of Congress, Prints & Photographs Division, Reproduction number LC-USZ62-25778 (b&w film copy neg.)

Anna grew up comfortably and wealthy. She enjoyed the life of a lady, often shopping for fancy clothing in New York City, and then suddenly her father decided to move west to Ohio. He founded his own city, which he called North Bend. The town still exists today, with a little over 600 people living there. Presidents William Henry Harrison and Benjamin Harrison are buried there. Back then, Ohio was considered a part of the American frontier, mostly unsettled, full of dangers, with some federal forts here and there. Anna met William Henry Harrison in Ohio — present-day Cincinnati area — after he had assumed command of Fort Washington, close to her home in North Bend. The two fell in love quickly, but her father disapproved, because he considered being in the military too dangerous and the pay too low. He wanted Anna to marry a preacher or farmer. For this reason, when he left town for a few days, the two eloped and got married on November 25, 1795.

Anna became a frontier woman and had ten children. In addition, she became a teacher, not just for her own children but also her neighbor's children because no schools or teachers were yet available on the American western frontier.

**FIRST LADY LORE**

Anna Harrison was the first First Lady to receive a public education. All First Ladies up to this point had been educated at home by parents or private tutors.

Anna and William next established a small farm next to her father's estate. Her father finally accepted the marriage. Anna spent most of her life at North Bend, running the family farm and raising their ten children.

**TECHNICAL STUFF**

In 1812, war broke out with Great Britain. When William Henry Harrison was governor of the Indiana Territory, he always blamed the British for inciting the Shawnee Indians and was ready to go after them. As brigadier general in the U.S. Army, William won major battles in the War of 1812. He liberated Detroit, Michigan, from British occupation, and defeated the British Army and then the rest of the Shawnee in the famous Battle of Tippecanoe. He made sure that the British didn't invade from Canada, and this further enhanced his reputation. By 1814, everybody in the United States knew about the great "Indian fighter."

Anna was alone most of the time, with William fighting wars against the British and Native Americans. In 1815, William resigned from his military command and moved back home to spend time with Anna and his children. Politics intervened. In the next few years, William served as governor of the Indiana Territory, a member of the U.S. House of Representatives, and in the U.S. Senate. He was even appointed ambassador to Colombia but was recalled by President Andrew Jackson in 1829. Finally, in 1830, he decided to retire and spend the rest of his life on his farm with his wife.

Because of his military exploits, William was well known and beloved nationwide. For this reason, the newly established Whig Party decided to run him for president in 1836. He did well but didn't win, but the Whig Party was so impressed with him that they renominated him in 1840. This time he won, thanks to his new and innovative campaign style.

**TECHNICAL STUFF**

President William Henry Harrison's lasting legacy is the way he won in 1840. For the first time in U.S. history, a presidential candidate didn't talk much about issues — he ran a race based solely on his image and his campaign slogan was "Tippecanoe and Tyler, too." William gave the United States its first image campaign. The image campaign has been used ever since.

**IN THEIR WORDS**

Anna was 65 when William got elected president, and she was very unhappy about him winning the presidency. She is quoted as saying, "I wish my husband's friends had left him where he is, happy and contented in retirement." However, William did win the 1840 election, and Anna, who was ill in early 1841, decided not to travel to Washington, D.C., for the inauguration. She decided to wait a few weeks to get better and for the weather to get warmer in the capital. She handed her First Lady duties temporarily to her daughter-in-law Jane Irvin Harrison.

REMEMBER

Jane never had a chance to perform very many First Lady functions because she served as a substitute only for a little over four weeks. William caught pneumonia after his inaugural address and died on April 4, 1841.

TECHNICAL STUFF

William Henry Harrison gave the longest inaugural address in U.S. history. He talked for almost two hours in freezing rain, without a coat and a hat. He caught a cold, which turned into pneumonia and killed him on April 4, 1841. He was the fourth oldest president (68) to ever win office, and he holds the distinction of serving the shortest term of any president in U.S. history. Anna holds the distinction of being the only First Lady to never perform any First Lady duties.

On the day she was supposed to travel to the capital to be with her husband, Anna was notified that her husband had died. All Anna could do was stay home and wait for his body to arrive. She buried him on their family farm and then decided to stay in her home in North Bend until 1858 when her house burned down. She was 83 years old and had to move in with her last surviving son John Scott Harrison. Anna died at the age of 88 on February 25, 1864.

FIRST LADY LORE

Anna Harrison was the first presidential widow to receive a pension. Because William had died in office, she received $25,000 appropriated by Congress. In addition, she was given the franking privilege, which allowed her to send mail for free within the United States for the rest of her life.

REMEMBER

Anna is the only First Lady who had a grandson, Benjamin Harrison, become president of the United States (he was inaugurated as the 23rd president in 1889).

# Letitia Christian Tyler (1790–1842)

Letitia Christian (see Figure 6-4) was born on November 12, 1790, on a plantation in New Kent County, Virginia, the same county Martha Washington was born in. Her father was a wealthy merchant, and she grew up comfortably. Early on, she was taught about domestic responsibilities, including raising a family and running a plantation. She met John Tyler around 1811 after Tyler's father had been elected governor of Virginia in 1809. Her father, Robert Christian, was an acquaintance of the Tyler family, and her brother was a classmate of John's at the College of William and Mary. They fell in love right away and got married on February 29, 1813, after John had briefly served in the War of 1812. While John pursued a career in politics, Letitia stayed home and raised a family. She had eight children, one of which didn't survive into adulthood.

**FIGURE 6-4:**
Letitia Christian
Tyler.

*Source: Library of Congress, Prints & Photographs Division,*
*Reproduction number LC-USZ62-25779C (b&w film copy neg.)*

# Being the wife of an absent politician

John Tyler became addicted to politics, so Letitia stayed home running the family plantation and raising all the children. The Tyler's had between 30 and 35 enslaved people and had a tendency to move frequently. Letitia pleaded with John to get out of politics, and he did quit twice, in 1821 and 1836, but always got back in.

**IN THEIR
WORDS**

Letitia told John, "Come home, stay out of it, I want you here."

John Tyler had other ideas. He served as a delegate to the Virginia legislature and then became a member of the U.S. House of Representatives. Then, in 1825, he became governor of Virginia. In 1829, he was selected to be U.S. Senator. All the while, Letitia was at home running the plantation. Often, she saw her husband only once every six months.

To Letitia's and John's great surprise, John was selected to be the vice presidential nominee for the Whig Party, which had named William Henry Harrison as its presidential candidate in 1840. The Whigs had figured they needed to put a Southerner on the ticket and told John not to talk about slavery, which he supported, during the campaign. John, therefore, made few campaign appearances and didn't talk much.

While John was climbing up the political ladder, Leticia's health was declining. She suffered a stroke in 1839, which left her partially paralyzed. Because of this, John had decided to remain on his plantation after he won the vice presidency in

1840. Back then, vice presidents had no real function, and they weren't expected to move to the capital to fulfill their few obligations. Then President William Henry Harrison died, and John Tyler was sworn in as president of the United States. Now the family had to move to Washington, D.C.

## Allowing Priscilla Tyler to step in

Being partially paralyzed, Letitia presided over her responsibilities from her second-story bedroom in the White House. Even though she was accustomed to hosting social events at the Tyler plantation, Letitia wasn't able to fulfill this role as First Lady and therefore selected her daughter-in-law Priscilla Cooper Tyler for the role of unofficial hostess.

Priscilla had been a famous actress and was the daughter of a famous actor. She was young and pretty and easily played the role of a lifetime: First Lady. With a little help from Dolley Madison, who was still around in Washington social circles, Priscilla became a charming hostess and was well liked by the Washington elites. Priscilla arranged state parties and dinners. She gave two formal dinner parties a week, one public reception every other weekend, and a public party for the average American that attracted thousands to the White House once a month. This proved to be quite expensive for the Tyler family because, back then, Congress was very stingy with money and most presidents paid for parties out of their own pocket.

The only time Letitia Tyler appeared in public was at her daughter Elizabeth's wedding, which was held in the White House on January 31, 1842. Letitia died on September 10, 1842, at the age of 51 after suffering a second stroke and was buried at the planation in Virginia where she had been raised.

IN THEIR
WORDS

Priscilla Cooper Tyler said the following of Letitia: "Letitia Tyler is the most unselfish person you can imagine. . . . Mother attends to and regulates all the household affairs and all so quietly that you can't tell when she does it."

FIRST
LADY LORE

Letitia Tyler didn't leave her room in the White House but kept up with current affairs discussing political issues with family and friends. She spent her time sewing and enjoying her family. Letitia was the first First Lady to die in the White House.

John Tyler remarried in 1844. His second wife, Julia Gardiner (see next section), was 30 years younger than him, which caused quite a stir in Washington, D.C. He fathered another seven children with her, bringing his total to 15 children. This is the most children any U.S. president has ever had.

# Julia Gardiner Tyler (1820–1889)

Julia Gardiner (see Figure 6-5) was born to a wealthy and prominent New York family on May 4, 1820. Her father was a lawyer and state senator in New York State, and her mother, Juliana McLachlan, was the heiress to a major Scottish brewery. The Gardiners were so rich that they even owned a whole island in Long Island Sound that one of their ancestors had purchased from the Algonquin Indian tribe. The family still owns Gardiner island to this day.

**FIGURE 6-5:**
Julia Gardiner
Tyler.

*Source: Library of Congress, Prints & Photographs Division, Reproduction number LC-USZ62-25781 (b&w film copy neg.)*

Julia was raised on her family's estate in East Hampton and received a private education. Later, she attended an exclusive private school in Manhattan. When she was 19, she appeared as a model for an ad for a local department store in a New York newspaper, which was considered scandalous back then. A young unmarried woman shouldn't be publicly exposed like this. Not surprisingly, her parents disapproved of this, and so they took her on a lengthy trip throughout Europe to take her mind off modeling. On this trip, Julia began to appreciate the customs of the European aristocracy, which she would later duplicate in the White House.

**FIRST
LADY LORE**

Julia Gardiner was known as the Rose of Long Island.

# Becoming the youngest First Lady, briefly

In 1842, Julia's parents took her on a trip to Washington, D.C., where she met President John Tyler and his family for the first time. He was recently widowed, his wife having died two months earlier. The two noticed each other, but nothing more happened. Instead, Julia became friends with his daughters and often socialized with them. In 1843, President Tyler invited the Gardiner family to ride on a new steam frigate, the U.S.S. *Princeton.* Suddenly, a large navy gun exploded on the warship, killing Julia's father, David Gardiner, and the Secretary of State, Abel Upshur. Julia was devastated, and President Tyler did his best to console her. While she spent more time with him, the two slowly fell in love; however, she rejected his first marriage proposals. After a while, she relented, and the two got secretly engaged. After receiving the blessing from Julia's mother, President Tyler and Julia were married in New York City on June 26, 1844. She was 24 years old at the time, and John Tyler was 54.

REMEMBER

John Tyler's daughters were shocked that their father had married a friend their own age. Over time, they got used to their former friend being their father's wife, but they refused to call her mother or stepmother. Instead, they referred to her as their sister.

Despite being one of the youngest First Ladies in the White House, Julia was one of the most socially adept First Ladies. She loved holding receptions, giving dinners, hosting formal balls, and proved to be a skilled entertainer in the eight months she presided over the White House. The Washington elites loved her, as did the press. Some in the media even referred to her as the lovely Lady Presidentress and called her the most accomplished woman of her age.

Julia, who had admired the European aristocracy, attempted to replicate some of their traditions. For example, she insisted on having finer horses than the Russian Ambassador and had a group of young ladies, all dressed in white, surround and follow her at official functions. Soon the ladies were referred to as the vestal virgins. Julia brought the waltz and the polka to the White House and even had waltzes named after her. She also contributed to the way social occasions in the White House were conducted. She turned them into more formal European-type affairs, with guests being announced and orchestras playing in the background. She loved to entertain and dance. One of her lasting legacies is the custom of having "Hail to the Chief" played whenever the president is introduced on formal occasions.

By the fall of 1844, it had become clear that President Tyler wouldn't get renominated by any political party, killing his chances for reelection. He therefore dropped out of the race and endorsed Democrat James Polk for president.

As one of her last acts as First Lady, Julia threw a grand finale ball in honor of her husband. Three thousand people attended, consuming more than 100 bottles of champagne.

TECHNICAL
STUFF

Like President Tyler, Julia was a big supporter of allowing Texas into the Union. So she lobbied in early 1845 for the annexation of Texas. She appeared at congressional debates and disseminated her husband's proposal to approve the admission of Texas into the Union via joint resolution and a simple majority vote, instead of a two-thirds vote in the Senate. She did her best and used her charm to rally lawmakers behind her husband's proposals. Texas finally was admitted into the Union on March 1, 1845, a few days before President Tyler left office.

## Going home to Virginia

John and Julia Tyler moved to Virginia to John's estate, which he called Sherwood Forest. There, Julia raised seven children. Julia, like her husband, became an outspoken supporter of states' rights and slavery. She even went as far as to write a lengthy defense of slavery that was published in the *Richmond Enquirer.* In the defense of slavery, she argued that Black enslaved people on the plantations of the South were better treated than the common workers in the factories up North or even England.

IN THEIR
WORDS

In a response to the English Duchess of Sutherland who had criticized slavery, Julia wrote: "You need to take care of business at home; you've got people from the lower classes there who are starving."

## Dying a Confederate

During the 1850s, former President John Tyler became more and more involved in politics one more time. Before 1861, he tried his best to help preserve the Union. However, after listening to Abraham Lincoln's inaugural address, he decided that the Union was over, backed the Confederacy, and openly urged secession. Later that year, the people of Virginia elected him to the Confederate House of Representatives. He died of a stroke in early 1862, shortly before he could assume the office.

Julia was now alone trying to run a massive plantation. Her youngest child was only two years old, and then the Civil War broke out. She felt unsafe in Virginia and tried to move back to Long Island, New York. The North agreed that she could come home if she swore allegiance to the North and condemned secession and slavery. She refused. Instead, she decided to enter New York State illegally. She booked passage on a ship to Bermuda with her whole family and then illegally entered New York State from Bermuda.

In New York, Julia continued to be a vocal supporter of the Confederacy. Because of this, her family cut her off, and by the time the Civil War ended, Julia was almost broke. Finally, in 1881, after a long battle with Congress, which refused to pay her a pension because her husband had renounced his U.S. citizenship during the Civil War, she started to receive a federal pension of $1,200 annually for being a widowed First Lady.

By then, Julia had moved back to Richmond, Virginia, where she was welcomed with open arms in the former Confederacy. People referred to her as the ex-Presidentress, and Julia often discussed what she referred to as the "holy southern cause." She stayed there until her death on July 10, 1889. She was buried next to her husband in the Virginia capital.

# Chapter 7

# Acting Like a President

arah Polk was one of the most accomplished and powerful First Ladies in American history. She definitely had influence with her husband and, thus, policy making. She and her husband, President James Polk, were truly part-ners throughout his political career. She shared an office with him, was his personal unpaid secretary, and wasn't afraid to express her political opinions publicly, even over state dinners. This shocked many, because having a woman discuss politics publicly was unheard of in the middle of the 19th century. Future president Franklin Pierce even said that he'd rather talk politics with Sarah than her husband.

Both men and women of the time not only tolerated Sarah's political behavior but also respected her for it. People valued her ideas and judgment. They considered her more than a pretty social creature, hosting social events at the White House. For the American public, she was both an elegant, even queenly, First Lady and a thinking woman whose ideas needed to be respected.

## Sarah Childress Polk (1803–1891)

Sarah Childress (see Figure 7-1) was born on September 4, 1803, in Murfreesboro, Tennessee. She came from a wealthy family, growing up in a life of luxury. Her parents, Joel and Elizabeth, were plantation owners and innkeepers. Her father believed that women should be as well educated as men and, being wealthy, was able to provide Sarah with the best possible education at that time. First, Sarah was tutored at home, and then she attended a private school for girls in Nashville. Later, at the age of 13, she was sent to the best school for girls in the South — Salem Female Academy in North Carolina. The academy not only provided the best possible education for girls but also allowed for missionary work. Attending the school allowed Sarah to be well read, familiar with not only religious scholars but also major political philosophers and both American and European history.

**FIGURE 7-1:**
Sarah Childress Polk.

*Source: Library of Congress, Prints & Photographs Division, Reproduction number LC-USZ62-25782 (b&w film copy neg.)*

**TECHNICAL STUFF**

Salem Female Academy in North Carolina still exists today. It's now called Salem College and is one the few private liberal arts all-female institutions of higher education left in the United States.

# Becoming a Politician-Er, Wife of One

Sarah met James Polk while he was the clerk for the legislature in Tennessee. Future president Andrew Jackson, who was a close friend to both families, brought them together. Allegedly, Jackson told James after he met Sarah, "This is who you need as a wife." James and Sarah got married on January 1, 1824, after James had been elected to the state legislature. The two never had any children, which is believed to have been on purpose because James wanted a political career, and

Sarah had no interest in being a stay-at-home mom. Instead, she became his political companion and even his campaign manager for his congressional and gubernatorial campaigns.

**FIRST LADY LORE**

Sarah Polk was a true political animal. When James Polk asked her to marry him, she said she would only if he became a politician. He did, running and winning a seat in the Tennessee state legislature, and she subsequently agreed to marry him.

From the very beginning, Sarah considered household tasks secondary to being involved in her husband's career. She even boarded with him in Washington, D.C., while he was a member of Congress. This, of course, meant that she had no household to run but could focus fully on his political career. Even though she had volunteered to stay in Tennessee after James got elected to the House of Representatives, he asked her to come to the capital to be with him.

**IN THEIR WORDS**

James Polk encouraged Sarah not to be a stay-at-home wife, telling her, "Why? If it (the house) burns down, we can live without it."

Sarah Polk was fortunate to become First Lady at a time when women became more active in politics in the United States. Women were involved in the Great Petition Campaigns, where they collected thousands of signatures to send to Congress to advocate for or oppose certain policies. For example, in the abolition movement, women worked on petitions, collecting signatures, to ask Congress not to annex Texas because the movement was afraid Texas would become a slave state and to end slavery in the District of Columbia.

As First Lady, Sarah made the White House more formal again; guests had to be well dressed, and dinners consisted of multiple courses. She was very pious; there was no dancing in the White House, and she also forbade the serving of hard liquor to cut down on the number of drunken guests. At the same time, although she didn't drink herself, she did have wine and brandy served at state dinners. She believed the presidency needed to be respected, and the White House should become a respectable place.

## Getting into politics

James Polk was a big President Jackson supporter and was elected to the House of Representatives in 1825. While he quickly became an influential Congressman, Sarah decided to stay behind in Tennessee for one year. However, being bored, she quickly decided to follow her husband to Washington, D.C. In 1826, she moved to the capital to further his political career.

Sarah was very active during James's congressional career. She studied the issues of the day and discussed them with him. She went over his speeches for him and even discussed with him political maneuvers during his congressional and gubernatorial campaigns. A newspaper editor in Nashville referred to her as "Membress of Congress" because of the active role she played in her husband's congressional career.

During his second term, President Jackson made sure that James Polk became Speaker of the House of Representatives in 1835. After the House selected James to be the Speaker, his opponents made fun of him, accusing him of not having a mind of his own, because he was so loyal to President Jackson. They insulted James by using terms like *slave* and *servant* to describe him. Sarah didn't mind. She knew the way to the presidency was through President Andrew Jackson.

James Polk left Congress in 1839 to become governor of Tennessee, making Sarah the First Lady of Tennessee. She got bored quickly by state politics and wasn't happy about the meager $2,000 salary. By 1844, the Polks were ready to return to Washington, D.C. James made it known that he wanted to be considered for the vice presidency. The Democratic front-runner was former president Martin Van Buren who wanted to run again after losing in 1840. However, he and most Northern Democrats opposed the annexation of Texas, while the Southern and Western wing of the party, still led by former president Andrew Jackson, supported it. Therefore, they wanted a different Democratic presidential nominee.

For this reason, former president Andrew Jackson endorsed his loyal friend James Polk rather than Martin Van Buren for the presidency. After several unsuccessful ballots at the Democratic National Convention, the delegates realized that Martin Van Buren wouldn't receive the necessary votes to win the Democratic nomination. The only alternative was James Polk.

In the presidential election of 1844, James Polk subsequently won the presidency, and Sarah moved back to the capital as First Lady.

IN THEIR
WORDS

In 1844, Henry Clay, her husband's opponent for the presidency, bragged about how his wife could make butter and was a great housekeeper, implying that Sarah could do neither. Sarah responded in the following way: "If I should be so fortunate as to reach the White House, I expect to live on twenty-five thousand dollars a year, and I will neither keep house nor make butter."

## Becoming a "working" First Lady

Sarah Polk was a big contrast to Julia Tyler as First Lady. Sarah was a devout Presbyterian and preached adherence to the Sabbath, not allowing any social activities on Sundays. She didn't drink or dance and was very modest. At the presidential inaugural ball, for example, the dancing stopped when she entered.

In the White House, Sarah became actively involved in her husband's daily activities. She was his assistant and his communications director; she reviewed and read newspapers for him and then summarized the news. She even edited some of his speeches. Members of the cabinet were aware of her importance and started to address messages and letters to both the president and her.

Most First Ladies up to this point had stayed out of the public eye. Even Abigail Adams had discussed and consulted her husband on politics in private. Not Sarah Polk. She was an independent woman who wanted to share in her husband's political career publicly. She became his advisor, helped him with speeches and letters, and was indispensable to him as his secretary, political counselor, nurse, and emotional resource.

**IN THEIR WORDS**

President Polk once said: "None but Sarah knew so intimately my private affairs."

Sarah Polk was a fierce reader. She constantly ordered new books to read, and especially if she had invited an author to dinner, she would try to read their work so that she could discuss it with them as soon as they arrived for dinner.

**FIRST LADY LORE**

Some were unhappy with Sarah's influence over James Polk. Vice President George Dallas, for example, said, "She is certainly mistress of herself and I suspect of somebody else also." Whenever confronted with these sentiments, Sarah would say that she was just assisting her husband to protect his health.

When it came to conducting official White House hostess business, Sarah was less involved. Because the Polks were very wealthy, they could easily afford to be the First Couple and make changes to the White House and its staff. Back then, presidents had to provide their own furniture and pay for most of the parties they hosted with their $25,000 salary. This was a money-losing proposition, and many early presidents left the White House poorer than when they entered it.

Sarah was able to reorganize the White House staff, using the family's enslaved people. This was quite common because all Southern Presidents, beginning with George Washington had brought enslaved people with them to work in the White House as servants. She even bartered for bargains. She'd have her staff ask for discounts from local businesses and then allowed these businesses to display the presidential seal when conducting business.

**FIRST LADY LORE**

Sarah Polk was the first First Lady to serve Thanksgiving dinner at the White House.

In addition, the White House got central heat and gas lighting during the Polk presidency. Sarah, however, insisted to have one room, the yellow oval room, lit with candlelight in case the new gas lights went out. When this happened a couple of times, the candlelit room proved to be invaluable.

## Being advised by a former First Lady

Sarah received a lot of advice and help from former First Lady Dolley Madison on how to run the White House and be a proper hostess. Sarah, in turn, made sure that Dolley was always invited to her social functions. To be able to become the perfect hostess, Sarah had become very close to the former first lady, and Grande Old Dame of Washington, D.C., and Dolley mentored her and gave her fashion advice, not that Sarah needed it. Sarah had grown up with the finest clothing made of silk and satin and bought expensive clothing from Paris as First Lady. Sarah Polk knew how to dress well and act like a lady, while being a politician at the same time.

REMEMBER

Sarah, right away, changed a First Lady tradition: She decided not to return calls by wives of the members of Congress. She believed she had more important things to do, such as advising a president, than visiting hundreds of women in the capital.

## Fearing for her husband

Sarah Polk was very much concerned with her husband's health. James Polk had been sickly all his life but was a workaholic. She was afraid that he'd literally work himself into an early grave. Therefore, Sarah often helped him out with his work, first as a Congressman and later in the White House. For example, she'd go through James's papers and letters and mark the ones that were important and needed attention right away. This cut down on his work, and he got more sleep, which she insisted on.

Although not a lot of letters between them are left for historians to study, because they were always together and therefore didn't write many letters to each other, a few of them do deal with Sarah's concern for James's health.

IN THEIR
WORDS

Sarah wrote the following in her letters: "It is only the hope that you can live through the campaign that gives me a prospect of enjoyment," and "let me beg and pray that you will take care of yourself and do not become too much excited."

Sarah was also fiercely protective of James's political health. Whenever she believed that someone had insulted him or spoke out against his policies, she'd ban them from all presidential social events. For example, she banished former president Martin Van Buren form the White House after he had criticized James's policies during the Mexican-American War.

## Helping make policy

Sarah was a good conversationalist, and a good hostess, even though she didn't attend the theater or sporting events because of her religious beliefs. She freely expressed her opinions to everybody who'd listen. Once in a while, she even forgot to eat because she was involved in a political discussion during a state dinner. Sarah was widely admired for her opinions and good judgment, and many compared her very favorably to Abigail Adams.

Sarah supported the Mexican–American War and the concept of Manifest Destiny (see nearby sidebar). She held White House receptions for veterans, attended sessions of Congress, and even lobbied members of Congress for the war effort. She'd never use the phrases "I believe" or "I support" when talking to Congressmen but would always say "the President believes" to make sure Congressmen knew that she was representing the president's view.

**TECHNICAL STUFF**

# MANIFEST DESTINY

The term *Manifest Destiny* was coined in the summer of 1845 by journalist and diplomat John Louis O' Sullivan, who supported annexing Texas. It referred to the belief that it was natural for the United States to extend its geographical borders to the Pacific.

Expansionists in all political parties used the concept of Manifest Destiny to justify the acquisition of California, the Oregon Territory, and later Alaska. By the 1890s, the doctrine had gained new force and support. Many expansionists were pushing for the acquisition of islands in the Pacific and the Caribbean.

President Polk, like Sarah, believed in Manifest Destiny. He knew that the United States could become a great power in the world only if it expanded to the Pacific Ocean. He first attempted to buy California from Mexico. In late 1845, he offered Mexico $25 million. Mexico, however, refused his offer. By early 1846, all of Polk's attempts had failed. He concluded that only war could accomplish his goals. In April of 1846, the Mexican-American War broke out, and in 1847, when U.S. troops captured Mexico City, the war was over.

Polk ran the war himself, working 18-hour days and clashing with his generals. After arguing with some of his generals, Polk became so paranoid that he trusted only himself to do the job.

With the Mexican army ill-equipped and poorly led, the war was over quickly. Even though the United States lost 13,000 troops, only 2,000 of them actually died in battle. Most were killed by disease.

In early 1848, Polk forced Mexico to sign the Treaty of Guadeloupe Hidalgo. This harsh and insulting treaty added New Mexico, Arizona, California, Nevada, and Utah to the United States, as well as parts of Colorado and Wyoming.

When it came to domestic politics, Sarah Polk proved to be quite traditional. She opposed women's suffrage, believing that voting rights are unnecessary for women. She also supported slavery, believing that slavery was necessary for the Southern economy to survive.

# Going into Retirement Alone

By the time Sarah Polk left the White House, she was one of the most admired and respected women in the United States. She was widely considered to be a role model for young women.

President James Polk, however, literally had worked himself into an early grave. By the time he left office in March of 1849, his work habits had taken a toll on his frail body. Constantly being sick, along with his habit of working 12 to 18 hours a day, caused his immune system to weaken. Three months after leaving office, James caught cholera and died. Sarah (see Figure 7-2) had to move by herself into the mansion they had built in Tennessee for their retirement, which they had called Polk Place. She lived there another 42 years and turned their home into a shrine to Polk's presidency.

**FIGURE 7-2:** Sarah Childress Polk in mourning.

Source: Artist George Dury / Wikimedia Commons / Public Domain

**FIRST LADY LORE**

After her husband's death, Sarah Polk wore black for the rest of her life, a whopping 42 years.

**REMEMBER**

Polk Place became an important political stopping point for state and national legislators before and after the Civil War. In 1860, Sarah sold her Mississippi plantation, including all her enslaved people, and declared herself neutral in the upcoming conflict between the Union and the Confederacy, though she privately supported the Confederacy. During the Civil War, she welcomed both Northern and Southern military leaders to her home. Soon, Polk Place was considered neutral territory, and neither side, North or South, violated its sanctity throughout the Civil War.

Sarah Polk died on August 14, 1891, in Nashville, Tennessee, at the age of 88.

IN THIS CHAPTER

» Peeking into Margaret Taylor's
somewhat private life

» Checking out Abigail Fillmore's tenure
as First Lady

» Seeing the shadow of Jane Pierce's
time in the White House

» Studying one of the best — from
Democratic Queen to First Lady:
Harriet Lane

Chapter **8**

# To Be or Not to Be First Lady

In this chapter, we explore the lives of four First Ladies. Two of them, Margaret Taylor and Jane Pierce, didn't want to be First Lady and resented their husbands for becoming president. They refused to perform their First Lady roles, citing health and personal tragedy, and allowed their daughter and family friend, respectively, to take over and fulfill the all-important hostess role in the White House. A third, Abigail Fillmore, was more interested in acquiring a library for the White House than being a First Lady. The fourth, Harriet Lane, wasn't even married to a president but turned out to be one of the best First Ladies in American history, usually ranking as one of the top First Ladies in the 19th century.

## Margaret Smith Taylor (1788–1852)

Margaret, more commonly known as Peggy, Smith (see Figure 8-1) was born on September 21, 1788, in Calvert County, Maryland. Her father, Walter Smith, was a Revolutionary War veteran, and the family was very well off. She was educated in a private finishing school in New York City and could have easily had a life of luxury. She chose differently. In 1809, Peggy traveled to Kentucky to visit her sister, and there she met Zachary Taylor, a lieutenant. She was 21 at the time, and they soon got married on June 21, 1810.

**FIGURE 8-1:**
Margaret Smith
Taylor.

## Having a family and traveling America

Zachary's father gave the couple a farm as a wedding gift, and Peggy soon had a daughter, Ann. Peggy and Zachary had six children together — five daughters and one son — but only four lived into adulthood. However, soon it became clear that Zachary's military career wouldn't allow him to spend much time on the family farm. Peggy had to make a decision: stay on the farm and see her husband once in a while or travel with him to his various assignments. She chose the latter and moved all over the American southwest for the next 15 years. In 1820, the family was hit with a fever that killed two of her children and came close to killing Peggy. She recuperated and became semi-invalid.

Having five daughters, Zachary didn't want any of them to marry military men because of the harsh lifestyle it meant for them. As fate would have it, all of them did.

**TECHNICAL STUFF**

Their youngest daughter, Sarah, fell in love with a young lieutenant by the name of Jefferson Davis. Jefferson Davis, of course, would become the president of the Confederate States of America in 1861. Sarah married Jefferson and moved with him to his plantation where she contracted malaria and died three months later.

While Zachary was fighting in the Mexican-American War, Peggy lived in their mansion in Baton Rouge, which they had bought in 1840. She enjoyed Southern culture and became a prominent member of Louisiana society. For this reason, Peggy was very unhappy when Zachary accepted the presidential nomination for the Whig Party and then won the presidency. She was 60 years old and didn't want to move again. She said:

"My husband's nomination is a plot to deprive me of his society and to shorten his life by unnecessary care and responsibility."

Zachary supported slavery in the existing slave states — he believed that the Southern economy would collapse without slave labor. At the same time, he opposed expanding slavery into new states.

## Preferring to remain private

Peggy became First Lady after Zachary Taylor was elected president in 1848. Peggy didn't do much as First Lady, maybe because her health was declining and she was getting old, or more likely she just didn't enjoy politics and being First Lady. She didn't like any publicity and didn't want her husband to become president. She had embraced the tough frontier life, traveling with Zachary to his many assigned posts, and just wanted to enjoy a quiet life on her plantation.

Peggy followed her husband to the capital and lived in the White House but kept a low profile as First Lady. She was very private and left the White House only to go to church. She delegated all hostess functions to her daughter Mary Elizabeth Bliss, who went by Betty. She was energetic, beautiful, and a perfect hostess. Betty became a surrogate First Lady and presided over social functions. Peggy would receive visitors upstairs, claiming she was in ill health, and occasionally join her husband for dinner parties. She wasn't covered by the media and appeared in only a few official documents. She avoided being photographed and didn't sit for portraits. She even covered her face with a handkerchief while her husband was dying in 1850 so nobody could see her face and draw it.

Some of Peggy's biographies mention that during the Mexican-American War she prayed for her husband's safe return and vowed to shun fashion and society if he returned safely. This was another reason besides her dislike of politics and her health, of why she refused to participate in the White House social life.

Zachary Taylor died of cholera in 1850. Peggy became the first First Lady to serve during the death of a president.

The new president, Millard Fillmore, immediately turned all the First Lady functions over to his wife, Abigail. President Fillmore offered Peggy to stay in the White House as long as she wished, but she moved out within two days. She spent only 15 months as First Lady and really didn't perform any functions.

**IN THEIR WORDS**

Peggy's grandson, who she raised, said of her: "[She was] a strict disciplinarian, intolerant of the slightest breach of good manners."

Peggy Taylor lived only two more years after her husband died. She died August 14, 1852, in East Pascagoula, Mississippi, at the age of 63.

# Abigail Powers Fillmore (1798–1853)

Abigail Powers (see Figure 8-2) was born on March 13, 1798, in Stillwater, New York. Her father, Lemuel Powers, was a Baptist minister, who died while Abigail was very young. Her mother took the family and moved to a small Baptist enclave in Western New York, which was considered the frontier. It was cheaper to live there than being closer to New York City. Abigail was taught by her mom using her dad's extensive library. Abigail fell in love with books and reading.

**FIGURE 8-2:** Abigail Powers Fillmore.

*Source: Library of Congress, Prints & Photographs Division, Reproduction number LC-USZ62-1776 (b&w film copy neg.)*

By the age of 16, Abigail became a school teacher in New Hope, New York. During her time as a teacher, it was quite common for schoolchildren of all ages to be taught in one room. Students showed up after they'd finished work or their chores for the day, and only then could school start.

## Tutoring the (future) president

When she was 21, Abigail had a student, Millard Fillmore, who was a young mill worker. He had recently been laid off work and had decided to go back to school in 1819 to better himself. He was only two years younger than her. Abigail saw potential in him and inspired him to go on with his education, making Millard ambitious.

Millard wanted to get more education to be successful in life, so Abigail began to tutor him privately. Not surprisingly, the two fell in love and got married on February 6, 1826. Abigail continued to teach school while Millard became a clerk to a lawyer. After passing the bar examination, Millard opened a small law firm in East Aurora, New York.

REMEMBER

There were no law schools at the time. Lawyers studied law as clerks to an established lawyer and then took a bar exam. As soon as they passed the exam they could practice law.

While Abigail continued to teach, Millard's law firm was a success. Soon they were able to move into a large house in Buffalo, New York, and Millard became involved in politics. In 1828, he won a seat in the New York state assembly and then was elected to the U.S. Congress in 1832. Abigail enjoyed her comfortable life; she was social, played music, and privately advised her husband. Publicly, she assumed the role of a perfect hostess.

In 1849, Millard Fillmore became vice president of the United States, and Abigail moved to the capital with him. Her health began to deteriorate, and she asked her daughter Mary Abigail to take her place when it came to hosting and attending formal events.

## Becoming First Lady by default

President Taylor died in 1850, and suddenly Abigail was the First Lady of the United States. When she and Millard moved into the White House, they were shocked at how primitive the building was. Abigail bought a stove right away — meals were prepared over an open fire. She asked Congress for more money to spruce up the place. She especially wanted a library in the White House, a sign of sophistication. Congress agreed and gave Abigail $2,000. With that money, Abigail created a small library, a place where she could read, study, listen to and play music, and entertain close friends. Abigail was especially interested in books by female authors to highlight their works. The room she picked for her library later became the president's workspace, called the Yellow Oval Room. The library today is on the first floor in the White House in a room that was originally a laundry room.

**REMEMBER**

Abigail Fillmore was the first of the nation's First Ladies to work outside the home and then to continue holding a job after getting married. Abigail was highly educated on the issues of the day and discussed them privately with her husband and friends. She had an insatiable curiosity and desire to learn, not just reading books but also teaching herself into late adulthood. For example, she taught herself to speak fluent French.

Abigail suffered from a chronic sore ankle, the result of a broken foot or ankle which did not heal properly, which made standing for long times quite difficult for her. Despite this, she endured hours of shaking hands and presided over many dinner parties and receptions. Abigail was an elegant first lady and enjoyed wearing expensive dresses. She was educated, witty, and funny, but she always had to have her 18-year-old daughter Mary Abigail around for moral support and as a possible backup if she decided to leave a function early.

**FIRST LADY LORE**

The Fillmores were sober and religious people. They banned drinking and smoking at the White House, and their parties and receptions were usually not very fun to attend.

Millard didn't get renominated, and his tenure as president was brief. Abigail had fallen ill by 1852. She insisted on attending the inauguration of the new president Franklin Pierce, which was held outside in Washington, D.C., in March of 1853. It was cold and snowy, and Abigail caught a cold that turned into pneumonia from which she died on March 30, 1853, at the age of 55. Abigail's legacy is her small library in the White House, which still exists today.

# Jane Means Appleton Pierce (1806–1863)

Jane Means Appleton (see Figure 8-3) was born on November 19, 1806, in Hampton, New Hampshire. Her father was a well-known minister, the reverend Jesse Appleton, who was also the president of Bowdoin College. With her father an academic, Jane was well educated and raised in a very strict religious household. When her dad died in 1819, her mother moved the family to Amherst, New Hampshire. There, Jane met Franklin Pierce, who had graduated from Bowdoin College and came from a prominent political family.

## Living not so happily ever after

Jane and Franklin were exact opposites. She was introverted and very religious; he was young, good looking, and liked to drink and party. Jane's family disliked Franklin because he wasn't wealthy and wanted to pursue a political career, which they disapproved of. Therefore, the couple dated for several years before getting married. Finally, in 1834, after Franklin had won a seat to the U.S. Congress, they decided to get married.

The two weren't happily married. Franklin was always away in Washington, D.C. After he became a Congressman, Jane refused to move with him permanently to the capital. Instead, Jane had decided to stay with relatives when she found out that she was pregnant. She refused to have their child raised in Washington, D.C., a place she associated with a sinful life. Therefore, Franklin was alone for most of his congressional career and partied hard, drinking way too much. Soon he was an alcoholic. Then tragedy struck. Jane gave birth to a little boy who died after three days.

Franklin's career, on the other hand, took off. He was selected a U.S. senator in 1837. Jane was very unhappy, saying:

**IN THEIR WORDS**

"Oh how I wish he was out of political life."

A few years later, Franklin decided to give in to his wife's wishes. He retired from politics in 1842, and went back to practicing law. Then tragedy struck again. Their second son died of typhus at the age of four in 1843.

## Retiring, or not

Now, it looked like Franklin was staying home for the rest of their lives. He turned down the offer to become attorney general in the Polk administration and refused to run for governor of New Hampshire. He even promised Jane that he wouldn't stand for the presidency for the Democratic Party.

Then the Mexican-American War broke out, and Franklin volunteered to fight. He came back a hero and was asked to resume his political career. So Franklin approached some of his political friends and let it be known that he was interested in the presidential nomination. Suddenly, he became the presidential nominee in 1852. When Jane heard the news that Franklin had been nominated as candidate for the Democratic Party, she actually fainted. Both Jane and their last surviving son, Benjamin, told Franklin that they wanted to stay in New Hampshire. Franklin lied to Jane, telling her that he never pursued the nomination and would very likely lose the election. Jane told everybody that she prayed that her husband would lose. He didn't, and Jane Pierce became the First Lady of the United States.

**TECHNICAL STUFF**

In 1852, the Democratic Party was split. On one side were the Southern Democrats favoring slavery; on the other side were the Northern Democrats, who opposed the extension of slavery. Not surprisingly, the party couldn't agree on a candidate for the presidency. Franklin Pierce proved to be the ideal compromise candidate, a Northern Democrat who didn't oppose slavery. On the 49th ballot, he received the nomination.

Then tragedy struck for a third time. On January 6, 1853, the Pierce family was traveling form Concord, New Hampshire, to Boston, Massachusetts, by train. The train ran off the tracks, and while both Franklin and Jane were unharmed, they had to watch their 11-year-old son Benjamin being struck in the head by a piece of metal, which killed him instantly.

By the time she became First Lady, Jane started to believe that Franklin's political career had led to her son's death, and she resented him greatly for it. For most of her tenure as First Lady, she was depressed, isolated herself from people, and even used mediums to try to talk to her dead son.

# Refusing to be a First Lady

Jane never recovered from the tragedy of losing her son Benjamin. She believed that God had given the Pierce family a sign for Franklin to stop being involved in politics. She withdrew from all social functions in the White House and turned to mediums instead. She held séances to try to contact the spirit of her dead son.

The inaugural ball was canceled, and the Pierce presidency had almost no social activities. Jane skipped Franklin's inauguration and spent most of her time as First Lady in her room. Soon people referred to her as the shadow in the White House. Locked away, Jane wrote letters to her dead son and went into a deep depression. The few social events that did take place were hosted by her aunt Abigail Kent Means. The White House became a morbid place.

Jane opposed slavery, while Franklin tolerated it. This was one issue Jane felt strongly about, and in 1856, she intervened to help Dr. Charles Robinson, who was an abolitionist. He had been detained in Kansas and was facing the death penalty. After Jane heard of the arrest, she talked to Franklin. To please his wife, Franklin ordered Robinson released from prison, thus saving his life.

In 1856, Franklin Pierce didn't get renominated, officially ending his political career. Jane was sick with depression and tuberculosis, and the new president James Buchanan felt bad for her. For this reason, he arranged for the Pierces to take a long trip to Europe. He supplied them with a government ship, the U.S.S. *Powhatan,* which took them all the way through the Caribbean on to Europe. The hope was that Jane would recover from her depression and other ailments. Jane started to feel better, especially on the Portuguese island of Madeira. She wrote the following to her sister.

"I can't believe who I was when I was in the White House. I am a completely different person."

However, by 1860, she started to feel bad again, and the couple returned home. They bought a farm in Concord, New Hampshire, but then Jane got worse. Therefore, Jane spent her last years mainly living with her sister in Massachusetts who took care of her. Jane never recovered and died on December 2, 1863, of tuberculosis, in Andover, Massachusetts. She was 57 years old. Franklin buried her in Concord, New Hampshire, next to her sons. Franklin Pierce lived almost six more years and was buried in 1869 next to his wife.

Famous author Nathaniel Hawthorne and Franklin Pierce were classmates at Bowdoin College and became best friends. Hawthorne wrote Pierce's campaign biography in 1852, and in it he introduced Jane. He presented her as being in delicate health and her health as the reason for Pierce's decision to not accept the attorney general nomination from President Polk. That characterization by

Hawthorne solidified the public view of Jane as sickly. Later Hawthorne wrote a letter during the first year of Pierce's presidency wishing that Pierce had a different wife.

After Nathaniel Hawthorne died in 1864, Franklin found himself all alone. He found solace in the bottle and died a bitter man in 1869.

# Harriet Lane (1830–1903)

When James Buchanan became president in 1857, he proved to be the only bachelor president the United States would ever have. Therefore, he asked his niece, Harriet Lane (see Figure 8-4), to step in and fulfill First Lady functions. Harriet was well educated and well traveled, and she proved to be a wonderful hostess in the White House. She was well liked and respected by the Washington elites and turned the White House into a fun place one more time after years of sorrow during the Pierce administration.

**FIGURE 8-4:**
Harriet Lane.

Source: Library of Congress, Prints & Photographs Division, Reproduction number LC-USZ62-25788 (b&w film copy neg.)

**REMEMBER**

James Buchanan was the only president in American history who was single not only while being president but for all his life. After asking his niece Harriet to fulfill First Lady duties, she was officially recognized as the First Lady of the United States despite not being married to the president.

While practicing law, Buchanan fell in love and became engaged to be married, but his fiancée broke their engagement over what Buchanan called a minor disagreement. She died by suicide shortly thereafter. Buchanan never recovered from her suicide.

## Growing up in politics

Harriet Lane was born on May 9, 1830, in Mercersburg, Pennsylvania, and was raised in a well-to-do family. Her father was Elliot Tole Lane and her mother, Jane Buchanan, future president James Buchanan's sister. Both of her parents died young, her mom while Harriet was only nine and her father, when she was 11. For this reason, James became her guardian and raised her. He soon became the father figure in her life and sent her to an exclusive private school for girls in Lancaster, Pennsylvania. Next, he moved her to Washington, D.C., where he was a U.S. senator. In the capital, Harriet attended another private school, Visitation Academy in Georgetown.

James Buchanan's political career began to take off. First, he became the secretary of state in the Polk administration, and then President Pierce appointed him minister (ambassador) to England. Buchanan decided to take Harriet, then 23, along, and she spent the next few years in England. She loved mingling with the European aristocracy and even met Queen Victoria. The queen took a liking to the young American, and she became a court favorite. Queen Victoria even gave her the title of "Wife of an Ambassador" so that she could partake in the diplomatic activities of the day. Suddenly, young Harriet had become a part of the Diplomatic Corps in Queen Victoria's court.

Harriet went back to the United States in 1856 when James was getting ready to run for president. Her job was to be socially helpful to her uncle. Harriet had been trained in the art of socializing and also listening and observing. Her job was to attend and give parties and listen for any kind of political clues that could make or break a political career in Washington, D.C.

Harriet was young and beautiful, a fashionable dresser, and she knew how to listen to and converse with people and loved to dance. Soon, she became popular, and even the American press began to notice her and report on her. She created her own fashion style, favoring low-cut gowns, which was considered risqué in the 1850s. By the late 1850s, Harriet had become one of the most popular First Ladies in American history. She rivaled Dolley Madison in popularity, and the press began to call her the "Democratic Queen."

## Becoming a single First Lady

As soon as James Buchanan was elected president, Harriet took care of the social aspects of his presidency. She had been very impressed with some of the customs of the English court and introduced them to the United States. For example, she wore white dresses, filled rooms with roses for the fragrance, and hired English catering companies. Harriet began to host fancy dinners and parties. She gave two dinners a week with 40 guests each.

Harriet even took care of seating arrangements, which was tough back then with the country so split over the question of slavery. You didn't want to put two political enemies next to each other at the dinner table because that could result in verbal or physical fights. Harriet herself never took sides on political issues publicly and became a friend to all and made no political enemies. To help out her uncle, Harriet read the daily newspapers to him and summarized important points. She was well aware of the political issues of the day.

Harriet loved the arts and was the first First Lady to invite artists to dinner and organize musical performances on a regular basis in the White House. Soon the American public started to refer to her as the "First Lady of the Land."

**REMEMBER**

Harriet was well liked and was so beloved that the U.S. government named a naval ship in her honor, the *Harriet Lane* (see Figure 8-5). Ironically, the *Harriet Lane* was the first Union Navy vessel to fire a shot when Confederate forces attacked Fort Sumter in South Carolina, starting the American Civil War. Later the ship was captured by Confederate forces in 1863 off the coast of Galveston, Texas, and was used by the Confederate Navy.

THE UNITED STATES REVENUE CUTTER "HARRIET LANE."

**FIGURE 8-5:**
The *Harriet Lane*,
U.S. naval ship.

*Source: Library of Congress, Prints & Photographs Division, Reproduction number LC-USZ62-48021 (b&w film copy neg.)*

**FIRST LADY LORE**

**FIRST LADY LORE**

To this day, only two other First Ladies had naval ships named after them. They were Martha Washington and Eleanor Roosevelt.

While in England, Harriet made friends with English aristocratic women who were involved in social reform activities. So she decided that she should do the same. As soon as she became First Lady, Harriet got involved in several social reform activities, or good causes as we call them today. Examples include prison reform, public education, and healthcare for Native Americans. Harriet was the first person to be interested in Native American well-being after a group of Native American chieftains visited the White House. Native Americans appreciated her help and referred to her as the "Great White Mother." Some even named their daughters Harriet after her.

In 1860, she served as the Prince of Wales, future King Edward's royal escort in Washington. He at the time was the highest-ranking foreign official to ever visit the United States. This event was of enormous importance because it finally signaled an end to English-American hostilities, and the United States and Great Britain began cordial relations, which turned into a special relationship in the 20th and 21st centuries.

## Living her own life

After Abraham Lincoln won the presidency in 1860, President Buchanan and First Lady Harriet Lane were celebrated by a crowd of over 4000, right before they left the capital. James Buchanan and Harriet Lane went back to Pennsylvania. In 1866, at the age of 35, Harriet finally got married. She had rejected many marriage proposals earlier in her life, but she finally accepted one from Henry Elliot Johnston, a wealthy banker from Maryland. She moved to Baltimore, but tragedy struck when both of her sons with Henry died of rheumatic fever. Because of this tragedy, Harriet and Henry founded the Harriet Lane Home for Invalid Children, which became a part of the pediatric care facility at John Hopkins University Hospital in 1972.

After Henry died 15 years into their marriage, Harriet went back to Washington, D.C. She became a second Dolley Madison, constantly being invited to White House parties. Soon, no party in Washington, D.C., was a party without her. She began to work on establishing a gallery of art, and when she died in 1903, she donated her collection of art, including paintings, sculptures, and historical memorabilia. Her collection became the foundation for what is today the National Collection of Fine Arts at the Smithsonian.

Harriett Lane died of cancer on July 3, 1903, in Narragansett, Rhode Island, and today is considered to be among the best First Ladies this country has ever seen, even though she was never married to a president.

# Chapter 9

# Living a Life of Tragedy

M ary Todd Lincoln is one of the most written about and also one of the most infamous First Ladies in American history. Her life was one of ambition and personal tragedy. Mary Lincoln, as she preferred to be called, was better educated and socially more sophisticated than her husband and was a major reason for her husband's successful political career, culminating in him being elected president in 1860. Then due to personal and political tragedies, she became a political liability to him, and today the academic community is split on her tenure as First Lady. She wasn't the first First Lady to influence a president, but she was the first First Lady to be self-serving, petty, and unpredictable. Some consider her one of the better First Ladies, while others believe she was one of the worst. The truth is probably in the middle.

## Mary Todd Lincoln (1818–1882)

Mary Todd (see Figure 9-1) was born December 13, 1818, in Lexington, Kentucky. Her parents, Robert Smith Todd and Eliza Parker, were well off and considered local aristocracy. Her father was one of the leading businessmen in Kentucky and owned enslaved persons. He was able to provide Mary with a top-notch private education and a wonderful social life. She enjoyed horseback riding, dancing, and wearing the finest clothes. However, even at a young age, she showed signs of depression and a split personality. She was happy and then suddenly started crying for no reason. Many believe that she suffered from bipolar disorder.

## Moving away from home

After her mother died, Mary's father remarried, and Mary and her new stepmother didn't get along. Her stepmother considered herself above the Todd family
and mistreated the children. Mary tried to excel to please her stepmother, studying horseback riding and sewing, but she grew moodier by the day. As soon as
Mary turned 14, her father enrolled her in a boarding school outside of Lexington,
Kentucky, where she learned about politics and history and how to speak French.
Her step-grandmother, who was fond of French culture and the great French philosophers of the time, tested her on these subjects on the weekends when she got
to go home. In addition, Mary was often able to discuss politics with family friend
Henry Clay, an American statesman.

When she turned 16, Mary moved to Springfield, Illinois, to stay with her married
sister to get away from her stepmother. Her sister had married into a prominent
Illinois political family, which provided Mary with more opportunities to talk politics with the local gentlemen. Mary enjoyed Springfield, which was the capital of
Illinois, because it had a great social scene. She was young and beautiful, and
many young gentlemen, including Stephan Douglas, who beat Abraham Lincoln in
the Senate race in 1858 and later ran against him in the 1860 presidential election,
pursued her.

Mary met Abraham Lincoln for the first time in 1840 at a dance, when he asked her to dance with him.

## Meeting Lincoln

**FIRST LADY LORE**

According to Mary, Abraham actually approached her and said, "Miss Todd, I want to dance with you in the worst way." Mary would later say that that is exactly what he did — he danced with her in the very worst way.

The two were an odd couple. She was five foot two, and he was six foot four. She came from one of the most prominent families in Kentucky; he was born in a log cabin. However, opposites do attract, and the two fell in love. Abraham Lincoln was a state senator but not well off, and the Todd family was very unhappy when the two became engaged. They considered him beneath her and the family. However, both loved politics, and Henry Clay, one of the Todds' neighbors, proved to be a great matchmaker. To the great shock of everybody, the couple got into a fight and the wedding was called off. Mary was crushed, but Abraham soon came back and began to pursue her again. They finally got married on November 4, 1842.

**FIRST LADY LORE**

Abraham thought it was really funny to introduce the two as "the long and the short of it." Mary didn't think it was funny.

In 1846, Abraham Lincoln was elected to the U.S. House of Representatives. He served one term and then went back to practice law in Springfield. Mary hated Washington, D.C., at the time. She called it a swampland full of disease. To make matters worse, the other Congressmen's wives, who considered her backward because she was from Kentucky, didn't treat her well. Ironically, Mary was better educated and more sophisticated than most of them. The experience didn't deter her from wanting to go back to D.C. in the future, but she decided that if she went back, it would be to live in the White House.

Back in Illinois, the couple had four sons together and lived a good life. Abraham made average money for a lawyer, but Mary inherited money from both her father and grandfather in the 1850s to supplement his income.

**TECHNICAL STUFF**

Abraham Lincoln ran for the U.S. Senate in 1858 in Illinois as a Republican. His opponent was none other than Stephen Douglas, the Democrat who had also courted Mary. The campaign became an instant classic, because of the Lincoln-Douglas Debates. Lincoln challenged Douglas to seven debates, which attracted many voters (more than 15,000 people attended one debate) and national newspaper coverage. By election time, Abraham Lincoln was a household name, not only in Illinois but throughout the United States. He lost the Senate race to Stephen Douglas, even though he received more popular support. At the time, the state legislature picked the U.S. senator, and the Democratically controlled Illinois legislature chose Stephen Douglas.

In 1860, now-famous Abraham Lincoln decided to run for president. Mary was happy and provided him with much-needed help. One of her life goals, to live in the White House, was about to come true.

## Making a president

Without Mary, Abraham Lincoln wouldn't have become president. She constantly pushed him to do better and pursue higher office. She was responsible for him becoming more refined in politicking and less gruff, as she called him.

Throughout his political career, Mary pushed Abraham, making sure he wouldn't give up after a political defeat, especially after losing the Senate race in Illinois in 1858. Abraham's law partner John Stuart once said, "His wife made him president, she had the fire, will, and ambition. Lincoln's talent and his wife's ambition did the deed."

Mary became Abraham's campaign manager; she scheduled interviews for both of them and advised him on his competition. She even arranged tours of their home to interested voters. After he got nominated for the presidency, Mary wrote letters to campaign supporters. After he won the presidency, Abraham said, "Mary, Mary, we are elected."

Mary was also there when Abraham faced personal issues. For example, he suffered from bouts of depression, and she was always there to help and console him.

By 1861, it looked like Abraham and Mary Lincoln would be the new power couple in the White House and that Mary was destined to become one of the most memorable First Ladies in history. That she did, but not in the way she had expected. As soon as she became First Lady in 1861, she turned into a liability for President Lincoln, and most of this was of her own making.

# Failing as First Lady

In February of 1861, after Abraham had been elected president, Mary moved to Washington, D.C., with their three sons. Her fourth son, Eddie, had died of tuberculosis in 1850. She was looking forward to becoming a hostess in the White House, planning parties and dinners. Mary was well educated, well spoken, and lively, and she loved to dance — all characteristics expected of a First Lady.

At first, Mary received favorable media coverage, her parties were well received, and the press even complimented her on redecorating the White House. She received the nickname "Republican Queen," which she enjoyed.

**REMEMBER**

However, things changed quickly when the start of the Civil War changed Mary's political and personal life. The country was split, the Confederate states had seceded, and the press after a while not only considered Mary a Southern sympathizer but also extravagant and wasteful. Her brothers decided to fight for the Confederacy, and rumors started that there was a spy in high places in the White House, namely Mary, and that Mary was a traitor who was subsequently banned from the White House. None of that was true. Mary actually supported the abolitionist movement and was the first First Lady to invite Black people to the White House.

**REMEMBER**

Mary, together with her freed African American seamstress Elizabeth Keckley, raised money for freed slaves in Washington, D.C.

Then, after she celebrated the first Union victories of the Civil War to show the country that she wasn't a Confederate supporter, the Confederacy considered her a traitor. She just couldn't do right by anyone.

To her chagrin, as soon as Abraham Lincoln won the presidency, her influence over him disappeared. President Lincoln was concerned with war, and she had no more impact over policy making. So she decided to shop instead.

## Spending like crazy

President Lincoln often called Mary his child wife because she expected to be spoiled and have lots of money spent on her. He did his best to spoil her, often going into debt, but after he became president, he didn't have time to do so. He was fighting a civil war instead. Mary decided to continue her spending spree on her own, racking up massive amounts of debt, often without telling her husband. While the press had once called her the Republican Queen and complimented her for redecorating the White House and for her beautiful, very expensive dresses, times had changed. It seemed almost obscene to spend massive amounts of money on decorations and clothing while the country was fighting a bloody civil war and people were suffering.

When Mary spent $26,000 on White House furniture and decorations, going $6,000 over the budget Congress had allotted, people started to turn against her, calling her a shopaholic.

To justify her extravagant expenditures, Mary said: "The people scrutinize every article that I wear with critical curiosity. The very fact of having grown up in the west subjects me to more searching observation. To keep up appearances, I must have money, more than Mr. Lincoln can spare for me."

Mary loved to shop. Once she bought more than 300 pairs of gloves in just four months. Another time, she spent $27,000 on trivial things in 1864 alone.

When their son Willie died in 1862, Mary disappeared for more than a year. There were no more social events or musical performances at the White House, but Mary kept spending like crazy on mourning attire and special jewelry. The public perceived her spending as frivolous. What about the average Americans who had lost sons in the war? They couldn't afford to spend monies on these items. Soon, Mary was $27,000 in debt, with Abraham making only $25,000 a year. To make matters worse, she threw temper tantrums to get whatever she wanted. Soon, President Lincoln was afraid that his wife would do something to disgrace him.

By the time Abraham Lincoln decided to run for reelection, the Lincolns were in so much debt that Mary knew that her husband needed to win reelection to pay her debt. However, he wasn't aware of how much she owed. As soon as he got reelected, Mary immediately went on another shopping spree, buying jewelry for herself and silverware for the While House. Often, people would allow her to buy on credit to get access to the White House, such as a meeting with the president and asking him for favors.

## Changing moods

Mary couldn't control her temper, and everybody in the White House walked on egg shells so as not to offend her. She knew exactly what she was doing. Whenever she threw a temper tantrum, she knew she'd get whatever she wanted.

Mary had a tendency to threaten merchants when she wanted goods someone else had already bought or when dresses weren't ready on time. Her dressmaker reported that she'd kick and scream, and even lie on the floor screaming, if a dress wasn't ready on time.

Mary Lincoln did contribute in her way to the war effort. She visited soldiers and even wrote letters for them if they were unable to do so. However, there was no press surrounding her trips to field hospitals, so nobody knew about it. If the public had known about her efforts, it may have helped their perception of her.

# Enduring tragedy

Mary watched three of her children die and then had to sit and watch her husband be assassinated next to her. Not surprisingly, the grief over her losses coupled with suffering from depression and likely bipolar disorder pushed her over the edge.

## Losing her children and brothers

In 1862, Abraham and Mary's son Willie died. Mary went into a deep depression and locked herself in her room. It got so bad that Abraham almost had her hospitalized. She started holding séances to try to connect with her dead son, which further undermined her reputation and the way people looked at her. Many thought that she had gone crazy. Her only joy left was her son Tad, who was a fun-loving kid always playing in the White House.

On top of this, more family tragedy struck. Her three brothers died fighting for the Confederacy.

## Watching the assassination of Abraham Lincoln

Abraham Lincoln got reelected in 1864, the Civil War ended in 1865, and Mary started to get a little better health-wise. The future suddenly seemed brighter. Abraham had won the Civil War, got reelected, and was considered a hero in the North. However, everything changed on April 14, 1865.

Mary and Abraham had enjoyed a wonderful day together. They had gone on a carriage ride and then decided to go see a play, which was one of Mary's favorite things to do. They opted for the play *Our American Cousin* at Ford's Theatre in Washington, D.C. Around 10:00 p.m. during the play, a proslavery supporting actor named John Wilkes Booth entered the presidential box and shot Abraham Lincoln in the back of the head. Mary screamed, "The president has been shot!" and passed out.

Mary wasn't allowed to stay at her husband's side while he was dying. She was too hysterical. Instead, their son Robert was at his father's side when he died the next day.

President Lincoln had premonitions about his death. In dreams, he saw himself as a corpse and heard people say, "Lincoln is dead."

Abraham's assassination destroyed Mary. She was so distraught that she couldn't attend the funeral. She left the White House five weeks later and went back to Illinois. She started to have more mental problems and spent money like crazy trying to forget her sorrows. Suddenly, she was in enormous debt. Often when Mary got up in the mornings, she had thoughts about suicide, stating the following:

"Tell me, how can I live without my Husband any longer? This is my first awakening thought each morning, and as I watch the waves of the turbulent lake under our windows I sometimes feel I should like to go under them."

# Going On After Abraham's Assassination

Mary was 47 when Abraham was shot. Her son Tad always had a learning problem, a speech impediment, and disciplinary issues. She decided that a trip to Europe would help both of them, and she also planned to enroll Tad in a school in Germany for discipline. To pay for some of the trip, she asked Congress for more compensation than Congress had allocated to pay to a presidential widow. It took years for Congress to decide how much and whether to pay Mary, so she went further into debt.

The trip to Europe went well, and Tad went to school in Frankfurt, while Mary went to fashionable spas and enjoyed mingling with the European elites.

In 1871, Congress decided to give Mary a pension, $3,000 per year (later increased to $5,000 annually), and she went back to Illinois. Suddenly, Tad got very sick. The doctors couldn't figure out what was wrong with him, and he died on July 15, 1871, at the age of 18. The cause of death was listed as either tuberculosis, pneumonia, or congestive heart failure. Nobody really knows what killed him.

Mary collapsed mentally. She began to live an illusional world, and her only remaining son, Robert (see Figure 9-2), decided in 1875 that she had to be committed to a mental institution.

Mary and Robert had already been feuding, because she didn't like the woman he picked for his wife. Robert petitioned a judge to have her committed into his care. During the hearing, she had to sit and listen to witnesses discuss her spending habits and spiritual attempts to reach her dead son.

During the hearing, it was discovered that Mary had started to sew her life savings into her clothes. This didn't help her case.

After getting custody of Mary, Robert had her committed to Bellevue, a private mental institution for wealthy and famous people. Mary had her private room and her own attendant. She was able to walk the grounds freely but couldn't wait to get out. Robert visited her weekly, but she never forgave him for what he did to her.

Mary constantly plotted how to get out. She secretly, with the help of her older sister and a Congressman, arranged for a newspaper interview. She talked for two hours to a reporter who then published the interview and publicly stated that Mary was clearly sane and didn't deserve to be committed. Mary asked a judge for a hearing to be held so that she could be released to live with her sister. A new hearing was granted, and Mary was found sane and was released in September of 1875.

Instead of moving in with her sister, Mary immediately moved to France. She enjoyed living in France for four years but then had a bad fall, which partially paralyzed her. In addition, Mary suffered from cataracts, which almost blinded her. So she decided to return home in 1880. She was physically and mentally unsound.

## KEEPING POLITICS IN THE FAMILY

Mary and Abraham's son Robert made quite a career for himself. He served as secretary of war for both the Garfield and Arthur administrations. Later, he was named ambassador to Great Britain during the Benjamin Harrison administration. He died in 1926, at the age of 82, after a successful and lengthy career in politics and business.

Mary lived two more years with her sister in their Springfield home and died of a stroke on July 16, 1882, in Springfield, Illinois, at the age of 63. She never reconciled with Robert. The following quote by Mary Lincoln best sums up her tragic life:

**IN THEIR WORDS**

"In grief, words are a poor consolation — silence and agonizing tears are all that is left the sufferer."

# 4

# The Civil War, Reconstruction, and Becoming a World Power

## IN THIS PART . . .

Discover how the role of First Lady changed from traditional to the new woman, with bios on Eliza Johnson, Julia Grant, Lucy Hayes, and Lucretia Garfield.

Check out the nuances of First Ladies Ellen Arthur, Frances Cleveland, Caroline Harrison, and Ida McKinley.

Uncover how Edith Roosevelt set up her own little spy network in Washington, D.C., how Helen Taft pushed her husband to become president, and how there were two First Lady Wilsons.

Explore how the role of First Lady continued to evolve, from Florence Harding's independent streak to Grace Coolidge's more traditional path to Louise Hoover's devotion to public service.

# Chapter **10**

# Reconstructing a Country

This chapter presents a diverse group of first ladies. Their husbands have to deal with the legacy of the Civil War and Reconstruction, and by the time Lucretia Garfield becomes First Lady the process of reconstruction is finally over.

Eliza Johnson didn't want to be First Lady and rarely made any public appearances. She couldn't wait to go back home to Tennessee. Julia Grant loved being First Lady. Her husband was an admired war hero, and she loved to spend money and be admired by the country. Lucy Hayes was treated different by the press and the American public because she was college educated, was involved in civic causes, and knew politics better than most men at the time. She was President Rutherford Hayes's partner and was accepted as such. Lucretia Garfield was an educated, independent, and strong-willed woman who often clashed with her husband. She would have been a great First Lady; however, an assassin's bullet killed her husband and cut her tenure as First Lady to just about six months.

# Eliza McCardle Johnson (1810–1876)

Eliza McCardle (see Figure 10-1) was born on October 4, 1810, in Leesburg, Tennessee. She was the only child of shoemaker John McCardle and his wife, Sarah. Eliza's dad died when she was very young, and her mother supported the family by sewing quilts and making sandals. Soon Eliza began to help her mother. She attended a local Rhea Academy for girls, which ended at about the eighth-grade level.

**FIGURE 10-1:**
Eliza McCardle
Johnson.

Source: Library of Congress, Prints & Photographs Division,
Reproduction number LC-USZ62-25821
(b&w film copy neg. of cropped image)

## Meeting and helping her husband

Eliza McCardle first met Andrew Johnson when she was only 14 years old. Andrew had just arrived in Greenville, Tennessee, coming from North Carolina. He was poor and uneducated, and he had only a small wagon full of belongings and an old horse. Despite all of this, Eliza fell in love with him quickly, and the two got married.

**FIRST LADY LORE**

The story goes that when Andrew Johnson arrived in Greenville, he needed directions. So he turned to the first person he encountered. That person was Eliza. She stood there with some friends, and he asked her for directions. After providing him with information, she turned to her girlfriends and told them that she just met her new boyfriend.

Andrew Johnson never went to school and started working for a tailor when he was only ten years old. Eliza did her best to educate him, helping him learn how to properly read and write and do rudimentary math. Andrew appreciated her and always used his humble upbringings to improve the lives of the less fortunate.

Greenville was looking for a tailor when Andrew arrived, and he was able to open a shop right away. They were married on December 17, 1827, and lived in the back of their shop. Eliza was 16 years old, and Andrew was only 18.

FIRST LADY LORE

Eliza Johnson was the youngest of all the First Ladies to marry.

## Staying in Tennessee as Johnson's career grows

Soon, Andrew's tailor shop became a favorite place for people to meet to discuss and debate politics. In other words, it became a hangout for debating societies in Greenville, and Andrew discovered his oratory skills. People in Greenville liked Andrew Johnson, and he was elected to the Greenville town council, thus starting his political career. By the time he was 26, he was the town's mayor.

Eliza stayed out of politics and raised their children. By 1834, Andrew had become mayor, and they had four children — two girls and two boys. Then in 1835, Andrew was elected to the Tennessee legislature, and eight years later, he was elected to the U.S. House of Representatives. He served until 1853. Eliza decided not to move to Washington, D.C., with him but stayed in Tennessee. Andrew visited her frequently, but she ran the household, raising their children and becoming a very good businesswoman. Soon, the Johnson family owned several rental properties and could even afford to have a few enslaved people. In the early 1850s, Eliza got sick, likely with tuberculosis, and became disabled for the rest of her life. One of the reasons she avoided Washington, D.C., was that the climate was better in Tennessee for her condition.

In 1853, Andrew returned home to Tennessee to serve as governor, and then he became a U.S. Senator in 1857.

As a member of Congress, Andrew was an advocate for poor whites, having been one himself. He had five enslaved people and held a staunch pro-slavery view. Despite these views, he continued to be an ardent supporter of the Union, aggressively campaigning to keep the Union intact. When the Southern states seceded from the Union in 1861, Andrew Johnson was the only Southern senator to stay in Washington, D.C.; he didn't recognize the legitimacy of the Confederacy.

Eliza stayed in Greenville, in Eastern Tennessee, which was loyal to the Union. Then things changed, and Confederate supporters took over Eastern Tennessee. Northern sympathizers were ordered to pack up their stuff and leave the region. Eliza was allowed to leave and go up North to join her husband.

**REMEMBER**

On August 8, 1863, Andrew Johnson freed his enslaved people. They all stayed on as paid servants and took his last name. One of the former enslaved men, Sam, wrote to Andrew Johnson, who was a U.S. Senator in Washington, D.C., at the time, and asked for a loan to buy a piece of land that Andrew owned. Andrew said no to the loan but gave Sam the land for free.

**FIRST LADY LORE**

After Tennessee joined the Confederacy, Eliza and her daughter Martha started preparing food for pro-Union guerillas in the hills of Tennessee.

In 1862, Andrew became the military governor of occupied Tennessee, and his job was to restore the state so it was ready to rejoin the Union. He did a great job and in 1864, President Lincoln selected him to be his vice-presidential running mate.

## Becoming a recluse in the White House

Eliza arrived in Washington, D.C., after her husband had become vice president in March of 1865. She brought the whole Johnson clan with her. This included her two daughters, two surviving sons, and five grandchildren. (Eliza's fifth child, a son named Charles, died fighting in the Civil War on the Union side. He was an assistant surgeon.) She basically became the first grandmother in the White House. She took the bedroom right across from her husband's office and read daily newspapers and then clipped important stories from the newspapers and presented them to her husband.

**FIRST LADY LORE**

After Andrew Johnson became vice president during Abraham Lincoln's second term and then president after Lincoln was assassinated, Eliza was terrified that her husband was next in line to be assassinated because he was a Southerner who had advocated for and supported the North.

Eliza loved reading newspapers and everything political. She read her husband's speeches and even helped him write some. Every day, she clipped out the best stories and gave then to Andrew so he could talk about them.

Being ill and considering herself to be an invalid, Eliza took a room on the second floor of the White House to meet family and friends but rarely left it. She read, sewed, and played with her grandchildren.

Eliza greeted guests after state dinners. Because she didn't have the fortitude to both eat dinner and make polite conversations afterward, she chose the latter and came down for coffee and to talk to everybody.

The press called her a myth because they never got to meet and talk to her. Her only public statement to the press was: "My dears, I am an invalid."

Eliza was seen publicly only two times in three years. She attended a reception for Queen Emma of Hawaii and served as hostess for a children's ball in 1868 shortly before her term as First Lady ended.

## Being revered for being frugal

When the Johnsons moved into the White House, the whole building was in disarray. It had become an embarrassment for the United States. There was mold on the carpets, and many rooms had lice in them. Congress acknowledged this and gave the Johnsons $30,000 to clean up the mess. Eliza and her daughter, Martha, started to redo the White House. Both women were very thrifty, and they refurbished furniture instead of buying new; they had carpets cleaned instead of buying new carpets; and they put up golden décor and paneling instead of expensive wallpaper. To save money on milk and butter, the Johnsons even got two cows and kept them on the White House lawn. The country that had just suffered through a bloody and expensive war loved the Johnsons' frugalness. The average American thought that the Johnsons were just like them — poor and not wasting any money.

**IN THEIR WORDS**

Eliza's daughter, Martha, once said: "We are plain people, from the mountains of Tennessee, called here for a short time by a national calamity. I trust too much will not be expected of us."

**REMEMBER**

Eliza's daughter Martha one day went to the attic in the White House to look for old stuff to be refurbished. Instead, she found portraits of past presidents. They immediately framed them and put them up as decorations. They are still there today for the American public to see in the Transverse Hall in the White House.

## Avoiding impeachment

The last few years in the White House were unhappy for Eliza. President Johnson was impeached by the U.S. House of Representatives and survived removal by only one vote in the U.S. Senate. Eliza mostly stayed in her room during impeachment proceedings, reading newspapers and clipping out articles about Andrew. She showed him the good ones before he went to bed and the bad ones in the morning. She wanted to make sure that he slept well and didn't get too agitated before bed. Her daughter Martha Johnson Patterson, the wife of Tennessee Senator David C. Patterson, took over serving as hostess fully.

After being informed that her husband her been acquitted, all Eliza said was, "I knew it."

Wanting to get rid of Andrew Johnson, because he supported a more lenient treatment of the former Confederate states, the Republican leadership passed the Tenure of Office Act in 1867. The act prohibited the president from dismissing any federal officials without the consent of the Senate. Congress easily overrode Andrew's veto of the act.

Andrew Johnson then rashly dismissed his secretary of war, Edwin Stanton, who was close to the Republicans. When the Senate refused to remove Stanton under the Tenure of Office Act, Andrew declared the act unconstitutional and removed Stanton anyway. The Republicans used the issue to start impeachment proceedings against him.

In the House, impeachment was a foregone conclusion. Andrew Johnson was impeached on 11 counts, with the central issue being the violation of the Tenure of Office Act. In the Senate, a conviction was less certain. Many senators believed that the Tenure of Office Act was unconstitutional in the first place, and the Supreme Court later agreed and finally declared the act unconstitutional in 1926. When the vote was tallied, 7 Republicans had crossed party lines and joined all 12 Democrats in the Senate by voting against convicting and removing the president (The final tally was 35 for conviction, 19 against.) Johnson had survived being removed by one vote since it takes a two-thirds vote to impeach.

## Remaining together to the end

In 1869, at the end of Andrew's term, Eliza was happy to leave Washington, D.C., and looked forward to retirement back in Tennessee. They restored their almost-destroyed home in Greenville, and Andrew went back to politics. He was elected back to the U.S. Senate in 1875 and was received well in the chamber. However, soon afterward, he died of a stroke in July of 1875. Eliza moved in with her daughter but died seven months later on January 15, 1876, at the age of 65.

Andrew Johnson was the only president in U.S. history to be elected to the U.S. Senate after serving as president.

The Johnson's marriage was a true love story. They were married 48 years; they were soulmates; and then they died six months apart. Eliza and her family to this day are considered one of the most well-liked families to ever have lived in the White House, because they were gracious, down to earth, and lived like the average American.

# Julia Dent Grant (1826–1902)

Julia Dent (see Figure 10-2) was born on January 26, 1826, on a plantation near St. Louis, Missouri. She attended a private boarding school near St. Louis and was a member of the wealthy slave-holding plantation elite in Missouri.

**FIGURE 10-2:**
Julia Dent Grant.

*Source: Library of Congress, Prints & Photographs Division, Reproduction number LC-USZ62-101867 (b&w film copy neg.)*

## Being at odds with family on slavery

Julia's brother attended West Point and was a roommate of Ulysses S. Grant. After he graduated in 1843, Ulysses was stationed near St. Louis and often visited his former roommate's family at their mansion that locals referred to as White Haven. He was invited over for dinner one night and met Julia, who was 18 at the time and home from boarding school. Suddenly, his weekly visits changed into daily visits, and soon the two fell in love.

The two became engaged in 1844, over Julia's father's objections, who didn't like Grant's anti-slavery views. However, before a family fight could occur, Ulysses was suddenly transferred and stationed in Louisiana and then Texas. Next came the Mexican-American War, and Ulysses fought heroically. While Ulysses was off fighting, Julia stayed home on her parents' plantation and patiently waited for him. He returned to Missouri in 1848 after the Mexican-American War had ended, and the two finally got married on August 22, 1848.

REMEMBER

The whole Grant family boycotted Ulysses's and Julia's wedding because he married into a slave-holding family.

REMEMBER

Ulysses Grant was opposed to slavery, and when he received an enslaved person from Julia's father, he set them free. Julia on the other hand had grown up in Missouri, a Western border state that did not join the Confederacy. She did consider herself a Westerner, but her family, except for one brother who fought for the North, supported slavery. Her father owned a small plantation with 18 enslaved people, and Julia was used to having enslaved people around her. Some of the older enslaved people she called auntie and uncle. Whenever she visited her husband on the battlefield, she brought an enslaved person along to take care of her children.

## Finding their way back to the battlefield

At first, when Ulysses was transferred to New York and then to Michigan, Julia traveled with him. Then he was stationed out west to the Oregon Territory. This was a very remote outpost and far too dangerous for Julia and her young child. So she returned home to Missouri to give birth to their second child. Ulysses was miserable by himself, and after his requests for being transferred were denied, he just quit the army in April of 1854.

Ulysses, who had been a soldier all his life, had a rough time becoming a civilian. Julia's father had given them a piece of land to farm, but Ulysses proved to be inept at farming. Next, he failed as a realtor, and then, having four children, he decided to move back to his family in Illinois and take a job as a clerk in the family's leather goods business. He wasn't good at that either, but because he was family, he couldn't get fired.

Then the Civil War started in 1861. Ulysses rounded up a group of local volunteers, requested a commission, and joined the fight on the Union side. He whipped the regiment into great shape, and his commanding officer was impressed, so he made him a colonel and sent him into battle.

Of course, this was to the great dismay of Julia's family who supported the Confederacy. Ulysses and his volunteers made an impression and soon he rose through the Union Army ranks. After he conquered Vicksburg, Mississippi, in 1862, he became the most famous of all the Union officers. President Lincoln was so impressed with Ulysses that he appointed him the commander of all the Union forces in 1864, and finally in 1865, Ulysses was the general who accepted the surrender of the Confederate forces led by General Robert E. Lee.

Julia traveled as much as she was able to, to see her husband and accompanied him frequently to the battlefield. She visited sick soldiers and hung out with his fellow officers.

# Loving the White House

The presidency came next. As soon as Julia became First Lady, she went to work. She doubled the number of the servants and personally became involved with her staff. She knew about them and their families and tried to help and provide advice if needed. Her employees loved working for her.

**FIRST
LADY LORE**

Julia was especially fond of one servant by the name of Henry Harris. He had a lot of children, and she wanted to make sure that the children were all provided for, so she forced him to take a part of his paycheck and invest it in Washington, D.C., real estate. He did and died a very rich man.

Julia was a wonderful hostess at the White House, hosting lavish parties and dinners. She believed that the White House had to become a model for the nation. She hired a well-known chef from New York and made sure her servants were properly dressed when serving guests. Some of her events actually contained 29 courses served with expensive French wine. Soon she was friends with all the Congressmen's wives and widely beloved in Washington, D.C. She in turn loved her role. There were only a few other First Ladies who loved being First Lady as much as Julia Grant.

**IN THEIR
WORDS**

Julia said of being First Lady: "My life in the White House was like a bright and beautiful dream."

**FIRST
LADY LORE**

Julia's daughter Nellie met and then decided to marry an Englishman by the name of Algernon Sartoris in the White House on May 21, 1874. Her parents objected because she was only 17. After they couldn't convince her to call off the wedding, Julia decided to make it the best wedding ever. She redecorated the East Room in the White House, and the wedding was held in front of about 250 guests. The press had covered the story intensely, and the people went crazy. Thousands lined the street to see the new couple. As a side note, the marriage wasn't a happy one. Nellie moved to England with her husband, and he turned out to be a drunkard and womanizer.

**FIRST
LADY LORE**

Julia started a family tradition where every evening, about half an hour before dinner, the whole family, including the president, would come to her room to share the day's events.

Julia loved being First Lady. She enjoyed entertaining and having weekly receptions open to the public. She loved being First Lady so much that she encouraged her husband to run for a third term in 1876, and after he declined, she pushed for him to run again in 1880. This time, he was ready for a third term, but he didn't get the Republican nomination.

After Julia found out that her husband had declined a third term, she went to pieces and started crying. She said, "You can't do this to me. I want it."

# Redirecting retirement through writing

After leaving the White House, the Grants went on a world tour for 28 months. Ulysses, who loved to travel, had decided to take Julia on a world tour to take her mind off not being First Lady anymore. They were treated like royalty in Europe, meeting with Queen Victoria and dining with the Emperors of Russia and Austria-Hungary. But they didn't stop in Europe. They traveled to the Middle East to visit the Holy Land and explored the Nile River by boat. They even went to Asia, visiting India and meeting the Emperors of China and Japan. Julia loved every minute of it. With this trip, the Grants established the tradition of post-presidency diplomacy.

After not receiving the nomination in 1880, the Grants moved to New York City. Then suddenly, he and Julia discovered that they were broke. Grant had allowed his son to invest his money, and when the investments turned sour, Ulysses was left penniless. At this point, a fan of President Grant decided to help out. His name was Mark Twain. He stepped in and suggested that Ulysses write his memoirs. Twain next helped Ulysses get a good deal with Webster and Company, one of the great publishing houses of the time that Twain co-owned. It took some time and effort to convince Ulysses to write his memoirs, but he finally relented so that he could provide Julia with enough money in her old age.

At first, Ulysses hated wring his memoirs, but then he started to enjoy it. He finished his autobiography a week before he died from throat cancer on July 23, 1885. (At times, he smoked more than 20 cigars a day.) His book, titled *The Personal Memoirs of U.S. Grant*, became one of the finest accounts of the Civil War. It was published the following year and was a big success.

The profits from the book allowed Julia to pay off all the family debt and have enough money left over to live a comfortable life for 17 more years. She died of kidney failure in New York City on December 14, 1902, at the age of 76. The book ended up making more than half a million dollars in royalties, is considered a classic, and is still in print today.

Julia Grant was the first First Lady to write her own memoirs. Her children encouraged her to do so because she had such a wonderful and interesting life. The idea was to not publish it but give it to the family so they could remember her and Ulysses. Then she changed her mind, after seeing her husband's memoirs sell so well, but no publishing house would publish her work. Nobody back then believed that a book written by a First Lady would sell. So her work remained unpublished in her family's hands. Finally in 1975, the family was convinced to publish her memoirs. The book *The Personal Memoirs of Julia Dent Grant* did well and is still available for sale.

# Lucy Ware Webb Hayes (1831–1889)

Lucy Webb (see Figure 10-3) was born on August 28, 1831, in Chillicothe, Ohio. Her parents were well off and devout Methodists. Lucy lost her father when she was two years old. He died of cholera trying to free enslaved people who he had inherited in Kentucky.

When Lucy was a teenager, her mother moved the family to Delaware, Ohio, so her brothers could study at Wesleyan College, one of the best private institutions of higher education at the time. While visiting her brothers at Wesleyan College, Lucy impressed several professors with her unusual intelligence, and they invited her to attend classes at the all-male college.

Lucy was 15 when she first met Rutherford Hayes on campus, but he was nine years older than her. He enjoyed her intellect but considered her too young to date her.

After Lucy's brothers graduated, the family moved to Cincinnati, Ohio, so that Lucy's brothers could study medicine. The move enabled Lucy to enroll in the Methodist all-female Wesleyan College there, and she graduated at the age of 18. Lucy excelled at rhetoric, the English language, and learned how to give speeches. All of this would come in handy later as First Lady.

FIRST
LADY LORE

Lucy Hayes was the first American First Lady to have a college degree.

While Lucy was studying, Rutherford Hayes also relocated to Cincinnati, hoping to have a better law career there. Cincinnati was a growing city with a lot of opportunities, and he believed he could be quite successful in the city. He was correct, his law career took off, and as an added bonus he met up with Lucy Webb again, who was now old enough to date, and the two soon fell in love. It was actually Rutherford's and Lucy's mothers, who were church friends, who set up the first date, believing the two were a good match. They were correct.

FIRST
LADY LORE

Lucy and Rutherford attended a wedding together in 1849, and Rutherford found a gold ring in his piece of wedding cake. Back then, the custom was to put a ring into a wedding cake and whoever found it was the next person to be married. Rutherford gave the ring to Lucy, and two years later at their own wedding, on December 30, 1852, she put it on his finger. He wore the ring for the rest of his life.

## Getting involved in civic causes

Lucy Hayes cared very deeply about several causes popular with the American public. First, she was an abolitionist, calling for the abolition of slavery; and second, she supported the temperance movement, believing in abstinence from alcohol. She convinced her husband to care about these causes, and soon he started to represent runaway enslaved people for free in Northern courts. Lucy and Rud, as she called him, were very happily married. They had eight children, and five survived into adulthood. At this point, Rutherford became active in Republican politics and campaigned heavily for Abraham Lincoln. Lincoln noticed and invited the Hayeses to travel with him for parts of the trip to Washington, D.C., where Lincoln was to be inaugurated.

When the Civil War broke, Rutherford volunteered for a three-year tour of duty, and he became the commander of the 23rd Ohio Volunteer Regiment. Lucy supported his choice to volunteer because she was a fervent abolitionist and often joined him after battles, while her mother took care of the children. While not with her husband, she volunteered to help out in battlefield hospitals where her brother, a surgeon, worked. Soon soldiers called her Mother Lucy.

In 1864, Rutherford got elected to the U.S. House of Representatives without even campaigning. He was still fighting in the Civil War. He served two terms and then was elected governor of Ohio. As the First Lady of Ohio, Lucy became involved in public education for the disadvantaged and worked for state funding of orphans whose parents had been killed in the Civil War.

Rutherford decided to retire from politics when his term as governor was up in 1872, and moved the family to Fremont, Ohio, to be close to his favorite uncle, who was in poor health. After his uncle passed, Rutherford became quite wealthy, inheriting a large amount of money and a large estate, which he and Lucy called Spiegel Grove. In 1875, the Republican Party decided to nominate Rutherford one more time for governor of Ohio. He easily won and was considered the front-runner for the Republican nomination in 1876 if President Grant decided not to run for a third term.

## Riding the bumpy road to the White House

The election of 1876 turned out to be the most controversial election in U.S. history — until the 2000 election, that is. The Democratic nominee, Governor of New York Samuel Tilden, won the popular vote by more than 200,000 votes. In the Electoral College, Tilden appeared to have won 203 electoral votes to Rutherford Hayes's 166.

Although all results showed that Samuel Tilden had won, the Republican Party disputed the outcome of the election. It claimed that Blacks had been denied the right to vote in many parts of the South, especially in South Carolina, Louisiana, and Florida. The election officials refused to accredit the Democratic electors in these three states. The officials instead had the three states give their electoral votes to Rutherford Hayes. Now the election was tied, with each candidate receiving 184 electoral votes.

Not surprisingly, chaos ensued in the capital. The Democrats controlled the House, and the Republicans controlled the Senate. The Republican Party knew that if the election went to the House, they would lose. So they recommended a bipartisan commission to study the election and certify the results. The Republicans arranged it so that the commission would ensure a victory for Rutherford.

The Democrats were furious and refused to attend the inauguration. The inauguration was held in secret because the Republicans feared for Rutherford's life. He received the title "His Fraudulency."

Lucy didn't discuss politics publicly but was fiercely protective of her husband. After receiving criticism for how he got elected, she told him in private:

"I keep myself outwardly very quiet and calm, but inwardly there is a burning venom and wrath."

## Improving lives as First Lady

When Lucy became First Lady in 1877, the media fell in love with her right away. This time, the press didn't talk about her prowess at hosting White House events or her elegance but focused on other qualities, such as having a First Lady who was educated and believed in social causes and meaningful reform. This signaled a shift for the media away from focusing on unimportant matters, such as a First Lady being pretty, young, and able to host parties, to someone who has her own mind and wants to improve the livelihood of many Americans. With the exception of three First Ladies (Abigail Adams, Dolley Madison, and Sarah Polk), most First Ladies in the early 19th century played the expected role of the president's wife, chief hostess, and leading fashion icon of the United States.

Lucy made it clear from the beginning that she wouldn't be a fashion icon or disappear from public view like other First Ladies had done. She collected receipts for clothing to show the country how frugal she was. The American public loved this new First Lady, and she soon became so popular that large advertisers used her image for marketing purposes, and her pictures graced many magazines.

**FIRST LADY LORE**

To celebrate their 25th wedding anniversary, Lucy threw a big fancy party. The party included an Easter egg hunt on the presidential lawn. It proved to be so popular that it was decided afterward that it needed to be held annually, and thus the tradition of the Easter Egg hunt on the White House lawn began.

As First Lady, Lucy Hayes worked for education for poor Americans and ethnic minorities such as Native Americans, Hispanics, and African Americans. She also worked for education for the disadvantaged.

**REMEMBER**

Lucy didn't support the suffrage moment. It wasn't very popular at the time. Instead, she was fully devoted to her husband's political career, and she wasn't considered a feminist.

## BECOMING A NEW WOMAN

The view of what a First Lady should be changed with Lucy Hayes. She was a college graduate and was widely labeled as a *new woman*. A new woman was defined as an educated woman who spoke out on public issues and participated in civic organizations or even politics at the local level. At this time, more women began to study, universities opened up to women, and many women became involved in civic organizations that were the predecessor to political organizations. Women's clubs were created throughout the United States. One of the largest and most powerful was the Women's Christian Temperance Union, founded in 1874, to oppose the sale and consumption of alcohol. Some women were even appointed to government positions and won local offices.

# Abstaining from alcohol

At the Hayeses' White House, all alcoholic beverages were banned. Rutherford and Lucy didn't drink and wanted to keep the support of a segment of the Republican Party, which advocated for the prohibition of alcohol. President Hayes was afraid of alcohol destroying families, because back then, alcohol was the major cause for bankruptcy, prostitution, and sexually transmitted diseases.

This disappointed many who were used to Julia Grant's parties where the champagne was flowing. At the Hayeses' White House, things were a little more boring. Soon, Lucy Hayes became known as "Lemonade Lucy" because lemonade and water were all that was served at White House functions. One guest stated, "The water flowed like Champagne."

REMEMBER

Lucy was involved in the temperance cause because her grandfather Isaac, an Ohio state legislator, opposed the sale and consumption of alcohol and had made a great impression on her when she was a young girl.

REMEMBER

Lucy Hayes was a very religious and moral woman. The couple got up every morning with prayers and concluded the day by singing hymns.

# Enjoying new technology

While the Hayeses were in the White House, the telephone was invented. Lucy loved new ideas and technologies, and so they had the first telephone in Washington, D.C. Another invention Lucy appreciated was the typewriter; she got one right away and loved to use it. Most important, during her tenure as First Lady, the White House received indoor plumbing.

At the same time, Lucy was very frugal when it came to beautifying the White House. Congress had given no money for the White House to be updated, so she put furniture over carpet holes to cover them, had old furniture refurbished, and even reversed curtains to cover the worn bottoms.

# Showing compassion

The following story is a great example of how nice and compassionate Lucy Hayes was:

> In 1879, an old 1812 veteran came to the White House to be honored and have his picture taken with the president. His uniform did not have his sergeant's stripes on it, because they were sent separately. The man was distraught, but Lucy calmed him down, got her sewing kit and sat on the floor and sewed the stripes onto his uniform. When the British Ambassador walked into the White House, he saw the American First Lady sitting on the floor helping out an old war veteran.

This wouldn't have happened in any other country. The ambassador, not Lucy, shared this story. For Lucy, it was the right thing to do, and she would have never bragged about it.

Lucy served as First Lady for only one term because Rutherford had pledged to serve only one term, and he kept his pledge. After President Hayes's term ended in 1881, he and Lucy moved back to Ohio. They spent the rest of their lives at Spiegel Grove, and Lucy was active in her two pet causes, education and helping homeless women. She died after suffering a stroke on June 25, 1889, at the age of 57.

**FIRST LADY LORE**

One of the great stories of the day was that when Lucy was buried at her estate Spiegel Grove in Ohio, thousands of people showed up, and when the procession went behind her house to her grave site, all her cows had assembled and lined up like soldiers giving her one last salute.

# Lucretia Rudolph Garfield (1832–1918)

Lucretia Rudolph (see Figure 10-4) was born on April 19, 1832, in Garrettsville, Ohio. Her father, Zebulon Rudolph, was a farmer, a member of the Disciples of Christ, and deeply religious. Lucretia first went to a local public school, where one of her classmates was James Garfield. Later, her father put her into Geauga Seminary in Chester, Ohio, where she studied Greek, Latin, algebra, natural science, geography, and music. In 1850, she transferred to Western Reserve Eclectic Institute in Hiram, Ohio, a school of higher learning, founded by the Disciples of Christ. Her father was actually one of the cofounders. It is here where she met James Garfield again.

James had returned from Cleveland, and his mother pushed him to finish school. Being a Disciple of Christ like Lucretia and her family, she wanted her son to attend Western Reserve Eclectic Institute. Both Lucretia and James excelled in school, and after graduating, Lucretia became a public school teacher, while James went to Williams College in Massachusetts. The two had become a couple and wrote each other on a regular basis.

## Staking independence

James Garfield was popular in college and started dating other women. He was unsure whether he should continue pursuing a relationship with Lucretia. She, at the same time, enjoyed her independence, making her own money, and didn't look forward to having to play second fiddle to a husband.

**FIGURE 10-4:** Lucretia Rudolph Garfield.

Source: Library of Congress, Prints & Photographs Division, Reproduction number LC-USZ62-25793 (b&w film copy neg. of detail)

**IN THEIR WORDS**

In a letter, three months before her marriage, Lucretia wrote the following: "My heart is not yet schooled to an entire submission to that destiny which will make me the wife of one who marries me."

After graduating from college, James went back to Ohio to teach at the Western Reserve Eclectic Institute, which had become Hiram College. The two decided to give it another try and got married on November 11, 1858, in Lucretia's parents' house. The marriage wasn't a happy one. James was unhappy with Lucretia continuing to work and being so independent. By 1860, James considered the marriage a mistake. The two rarely saw each other, with him being in the Ohio state legislature and Lucretia choosing to stay home to raise their children. Next, James left to fight in the Civil War.

## Making changes for each other

James and Lucretia Garfield spent only 20 months together in a close to five-year period from 1859 to 1863. Lucretia accepted the blame and began to change. Instead of continuing to be an independent woman, she began to subordinate herself to her husband. In March of 1860, she wrote her husband the following: "I am going to try harder than ever before to be the best little wife possible."

James had become a popular professor at Hiram College and soon became the college's president. When the Civil War broke out, James was made a colonel, and he recruited a group of soldiers, mostly his former students. They went to battle and did well, and by 1862, James Garfield was a war hero. He was subsequently elected to the U.S. House of Representatives in 1862.

In 1862, Lucretia found out that James had cheated on her and now wanted only a business relationship with her. Then their child, a daughter by the name of Eliza died in 1863 of diphtheria, and both decided to change. Lucretia became more docile, and James decided that his marriage was worth saving and that he wanted to become the best father possible.

Lucretia and James reconciled, went to Europe, and then bought a house in Washington, D.C., so that they were no longer separated. The two joined a literacy society and hosted book club meetings. Lucretia started to attend debates of Congress and became more involved in James's political life.

**FIRST
LADY LORE**

Lucretia loved to be social but only in small settings. She didn't feel comfortable in larger settings. As First Lady, she didn't hold large parties but rather had two parties with fewer people invited. This allowed for more conversation and a more intimate setting.

During the presidential elections of 1880, James Garfield conducted a front porch campaign, where people came to his house for rallies to hear him speak. This allowed Lucretia to always be present at his campaign rallies and to actively participate in his campaign. Soon she became an important part of his campaign. After winning the presidency, James even sent her to New York City under an alias, Mrs. Greenfield, to discuss cabinet positions with the local Republican power broker, Roscoe Conkling.

## Serving less than a year as First Lady

After becoming First Lady in March of 1881, Lucretia became sick with malaria in May. She decided to go to the beach town of Long Branch, New Jersey, to recuperate.

On July 2, 1881, President Garfield was waiting for his train at the Potomac and Baltimore railroad station on his way to New England for a political appearance and then to visit his wife, when Charles J. Guiteau, a deranged religious fanatic, shot him twice. One bullet hit his arm and the other went into his back, but neither bullet killed him — his doctors did that. While looking for the bullet in his back, the doctors turned a three-inch wound into a 20-inch wound, puncturing his liver in the process. The wound became infected, and James died on September 19, 1881.

FIRST
LADY LORE

One of the doctors treating President Garfield was a female doctor by the name of Susan Edson. Because she was a woman, she got paid only half of what the male doctors made. Lucretia was incensed when she heard this and demanded that she receive the same. After the First Lady's intervention, Dr. Edson received the same salary as her male colleagues.

REMEMBER

Before the assassination, President Garfield's assassin, Charles J. Guiteau, actually went to the White House to ask for a government job. He met Lucretia there and was impressed with her kindness toward him. After he didn't get a government job, he decided to kill President Garfield. He went to the train station to shoot the president in May of 1881, but saw Lucretia with him. So he decided to shoot President Garfield another day because he didn't want to endanger Lucretia.

Lucretia, still ill, hurried back to the White House after her husband was shot. She was at his side for the next three months. He was moved to Elberton, New Jersey, so that the whole family could be at his bedside.

During the months Lucretia took care of her dying husband, she became a national hero. The press focused on her continuously. Articles were published describing how calm, composed, and courageous she was. The press even praised her intelligence and strength. One newspaper actually called her the bravest woman in the universe.

FIRST
LADY LORE

Lucretia Garfield was the first presidential wife to attend her husband's memorial services.

Following the funeral, Lucretia moved back to Ohio. There on the family farm, she lived another 36 years mostly in seclusion. She spent most of her time preserving her husband's correspondence and papers. She actually set up her own James Garfield presidential library in her house.

She was now well off, with a public fundraising campaign collecting almost $360,000 and Congress paying her a $5,000 annual pension. So she decided that Ohio was too cold during the winter time and she bought a winter house in Pasadena, California. She was active there with the Red Cross when WWI broke out, and she participated in the Rose Parade. She died on March 1918 at the age of 85.

FIRST
LADY LORE

Lucretia was the first First Lady to keep a diary in the White House, and she didn't destroy any official papers or even private correspondence between her and her husband. For this reason, historians today have a great amount of information on the Garfields and the Garfield White House.

Her diaries show a feminist inclined woman, who however chose to conform to accepted standards to please her husband and save her marriage. As a public school teacher she fought for equal pay for female teachers and as First Lady she stood up to the temperance movement and started to serve wine in the White House again. We do not know how she would have continued to act as First Lady because she never had enough time in the White House to establish herself.

# Chapter **11**

# Getting Close to the 20th Century

In this chapter, I explore the legacies of First Ladies Ellen Arthur, Frances Cleveland, Caroline Harrison, and Ida McKinley. The four close out the 19th century and each contributed in their own way to their husband's presidency. Unfortunately, Ellen Arthur died before she had a chance to become First Lady, but without her constantly pushing her husband he would not have become president. Frances Cleveland accomplished a feat no one has since been able to accomplish — she was both the 23rd and 25th First Lady. Her husband won in 1884, lost reelection in 1888, but then staged a comeback and won one more time in 1892. She is also the first national celebrity First Lady and the first First Lady to get remarried after her husband, President Cleveland, died.

Caroline Harrison's legacy as First Lady was to transform the White House into a mansion filled with historically significant artifacts. In addition, she was responsible for installing electricity into the White House. Ida McKinley was college educated and interested in her husband's career. However, the "Belle of Canton, Ohio," lived a tragic life, full of personal and health tragedies, and spent most of her adult life confined to a rocking chair crocheting, knitting, and reading. She was the first First Lady to support women's suffrage, giving the movement a needed boost.

# Ellen Herndon Arthur (1837–1880)

Ellen Lewis Herndon (see Figure 11-1) was born on August 30, 1837, in Culpeper, Virginia. She was the only child of Elizabeth Hansborough and William Lewis Herndon, one of the most prominent couples in Virginia. Her father was a naval officer and steamship commander who had to move his family frequently for his job. He moved them to Washington, D.C., in the 1850s, where Ellen became an accomplished singer who sang in one of the most famous choirs of the time, St. John's Episcopal Church on Lafayette Square. Then they moved to New York City, and Ellen joined the exclusive Mendelssohn Glee Club.

**FIGURE 11-1:**
Ellen Herndon
Arthur.

Source: Library of Congress, Prints & Photographs Division,
Reproduction number LC-USZ62-25794 (b&w film copy neg. of
detail)LC-USZ62-17135 (b&w film copy neg.)

**FIRST
LADY LORE**

Because of her father's fame, Ellen got to meet many famous people and became well connected. She got to go to Abraham Lincoln's second inaugural in 1865, she attended the wedding of Nellie Grant in the White House (see Chapter 10), and she was friends with the parents of Theodore Roosevelt.

## Pushing her husband's political career

In New York, Ellen's cousin Dabney Herndon introduced her to his roommate, a young and up-and-coming lawyer by the name of Chester Arthur. He was active in politics in the Republican Party and seemed to be destined for a career in politics.

Then the following year (1857), Ellen's father died at sea in a storm. He had been in command of a merchant steamship that hit a pretty bad storm off the coast of North Carolina. He was able to evacuate many of the passengers but then went down with the ship himself. He became a national hero after this. Chester consoled Ellen during this time, and the two started dating and attending social and cultural events together in New York City. They got married on October 25, 1859.

Ellen was a very ambitious woman who pushed her husband to be successful in politics. She didn't like that politics kept them apart for long periods of time, but she was very socially ambitious and wanted to move up the social ladder as quickly as possible.

In 1861, Chester's political career took off. He became the engineer in chief of the state militia of New York, and then after the Civil War broke out, he became a brigadier general and quartermaster for the State of New York. In this position, he recruited and equipped the state militia. Chester was able to create a fighting force of more than 200,000 men. This turned him into a major figure within the Republican Party.

**REMEMBER**

When the Civil War broke out, Ellen sympathized with the South. Chester affectionately called her "my little rebel wife." When her cousin Dabney was captured fighting for the Confederacy, Ellen asked Chester to get him out of prison and he did.

Ellen enjoyed the good life in New York City. She lived in a fancy mansion, attended dinner parties, went on shopping sprees, and attended just about every cultural event in the city. She and Chester even had their own chef and butler.

While Chester was away working in the capital of New York, Albany, Ellen stayed at home raising their three children, though only two survived into adulthood.

## Missing out on being First Lady

In 1877, Chester went back to practicing law and then was a surprise vice presidential nominee in 1880, which Ellen didn't get to see. She had attended a benefit concert on January 10, 1880, and caught a cold after waiting for her carriage, and then she got pneumonia. Chester rushed home from Albany, but Ellen was already unconscious. She died on January 12, 1880, at the age of 42 in New York City.

When Chester Arthur became president, he didn't have a wife and his daughter Molly wasn't old enough (only ten at the time) to take over First Lady functions for him. So he rotated official White House hostess functions between the wives of cabinet members and even the wives of members of Congress. That didn't go well, so he often planned his own functions. Beginning in 1883, his sister Mary McElroy handled hostess functions. However, she was more of a part-time hostess because she lived most of the year in Albany, New York, with her family.

Ellen's death affected Chester deeply. He had fresh flowers put next to her portrait in the White House every day of his presidency. And at official White House dinners, the place next to him was always left vacant in memory of her.

# Frances Folsom Cleveland (1864–1947)

Grover Cleveland had known Frances Folsom (see Figure 11-2) since she was born on July 21, 1864, in Buffalo, New York, and had even given her parents a baby carriage as a gift. He and Frances's dad were law partners, and after her dad, Oscar, died in a horse carriage accident, when Frances was 11 years old, Grover stepped up and helped the family administer their estate. Frances grew up with Grover being a frequent visitor and affectionately called him "Uncle Clev."

**FIGURE 11-2:** Frances Folsom Cleveland.

Source: Library of Congress, Prints & Photographs Division, Reproduction number LC-DIG-ggbain-07366 (digital file from original neg.)

## Growing up with Uncle Clev

When Frances got older, Grover began to show interest in her, and while he was governor of New York, he and Frances, who attended Wells College in New York, started writing letters to each other. Grover even visited her at night at the college in an unmarked train. Frances, in turn, had a picture of Grover on her college room desk.

Frances, like Lucy Hayes and Lucretia Garfield (see Chapter 10), was well educated when she became First Lady, receiving a bachelor's degree in 1885 from Wells College. By the time she turned 21, she was a confident woman, and most people thought she was a lot older than she was.

## Turning the tides to husband

President Grover Cleveland was the second bachelor president in the history of the United States. (The first had been James Buchanan.) He became president in 1885 at the age of 48. Right away, the American public and the press asked who would be the White House hostess and, most important, when would the president get married and to whom.

President Cleveland's sister Rose Elizabeth Cleveland performed the role of White House hostess from 1885 until he got married in 1886. She was well educated, spoke several languages, and lectured on woman's rights. She didn't enjoy being the White House hostess but was good at it and considered the job a favor to her brother. After 15 months on the job, she got bored having to attend so many receptions. She was glad when her brother got married and left as quickly as she could.

When President Cleveland invited the widow Emma Folsom and her daughter Frances over for dinner, rumors started that he was interested in the widow Emma. He wasn't. He was actually interested in her daughter, Frances, who was 28 years younger than him.

Despite the Folsoms going on a European trip, the rumors continued. When they arrived back in the United States, Grover sent his personal secretary to meet them while they were still at sea and take them back by boat to avoid the media. The press went crazy and wouldn't stop reporting about the possible marriage between Emma and the president, but they got it all wrong. When the official presidential announcement came in 1886 that Grover Cleveland was about to get married, it wasn't to Emma, the mother who was his age, but to her daughter, Frances, who was 21 years old. They actually had gotten engaged before the Folsoms went on their European trip. The press received only a one week notice before the wedding, making Frances even more mysterious to the average American.

Grover Cleveland was the first American president to be married in the White House. The press covered the couple closely. They even followed them onto their honeymoon, and the couple had no privacy.

Frances Cleveland was and still is the youngest First Lady in the history of the United States. She was 21 when she became the First Lady of the United States.

When Frances married President Cleveland on June 2, 1886, famous American composer John Philip Sousa conducted the U.S. marine band at the wedding reception. See Figure 11-3 for a glimpse of their wedding.

**FIGURE 11-3:**
The wedding of Frances Folsom and President Grover Cleveland.

Source: Library of Congress, Prints & Photographs Division, Reproduction number LC-USZ62-5946 (b&w film copy neg.)

## Being the youngest First Lady ever

As First Lady (see Figure 11-4), Frances pursued a policy of nonengagement, refusing to get involved in politics. She received numerous requests to support certain causes, an example being the temperance movement, but she refused to get involved. Even though she herself didn't drink (she toasted at her wedding with mineral water), she didn't believe it was right for a First Lady to be involved in politics.

**FIGURE 11-4:**
Frances Folsom
Cleveland as
First Lady.

*Source: Library of Congress, Prints & Photographs Division, Reproduction number LC-USZ62-129836 (b&w film copy neg.)*

Frances held two receptions per week, including one for the public on Saturdays so that everybody who worked could attend. At one reception, she personally greeted more than 8,000 people. Soon, Frances, who was young and attractive, became more popular than her husband. Women imitated her hairstyle and lined up by the thousands to meet her during her Saturday receptions. She was so popular that her image appeared on many goods, ranging from tobacco products to soap and even to sewing machines. All of this was done without her consent because, back then, there were no advertising regulations.

Journalists followed Frances around to report on her and not on the administration. By 1888, she was so popular that she was put on campaign posters with President Cleveland. There were even Frances Cleveland clubs. However, President Cleveland still lost the 1888 election. The couple moved back to New York City, and Grover returned to his law practice.

**FIRST
LADY LORE**

In 1891, while Grover was practicing law in New York City, their first child, Ruth, was born. The media fell in love with her. A new candy bar, Baby Ruth, was named after her.

# Staging a comeback

After President Cleveland lost reelection in 1888, Frances was convinced that he would win in four years, and she told the staff:

> "I want you to take good care of all the furniture and ornaments in the house, and not let any of them get lost or broken, for I want to find everything just as it is now, when we come back."

She was right; they were back in 1892.

In 1892, Frances was even more popular, and her image was on campaign buttons and even plates and posters. During the 1892 campaign, Frances was so popular with the American public that the Republican Party attempted to smear her and Grover. They accused Grover of abusing her; to which, Frances replied, "These are wicked and heartless lies." "I can wish the women of our country no greater blessing than that . . . their husbands may be as kind, attentive, considerate, and affectionate as mine."

Frances's daughter Esther became the first presidential child to be born in the White House in 1893.

During her second term as First Lady, Frances scaled back her social calendar. She decided to do the absolute minimum when it came to hosting and holding receptions. She was afraid for her children's safety and increased the White House security staff from 4 to 27. Instead of allowing the press to take family pictures, she provided it with photos of her liking. This allowed her to keep the press away from her family.

To protect their privacy after they got married, Grover had purchased an old secluded house in Washington, D.C. Grover had the house remodeled and turned it into a mansion. Frances and Grover used the place for summer vacations and brief retreats from the White House. The house proved to be the perfect place to hide Frances and their children from the press and provide additional security for his family.

The Clevelands resided in a public place, the White House, for official business and then spent most of their time in a second private residence away from the press and possible crime.

# Getting remarried and caring about education

The Clevelands left the White House in 1897 and moved to Princeton, New Jersey. They often entertained the faculty of Princeton and became good friends with the president of Princeton University, future U.S. president Woodrow Wilson. President Cleveland died in 1908 at the age of 72. Frances was only 44. She continued to live in Princeton and was involved in fundraising activities for the university and her own alma mater, Wells College. In 1913, she got remarried to a Princeton archaeology professor by the name of Thomas J. Preston Jr. (see Figure 11-5).

**FIGURE 11-5:**
Frances remarried to Thomas J. Preston Jr.

Source: Library of Congress, Prints & Photographs Division, Reproduction number LC-DIG-ggbain-26039 (digital file from original negative)

The same year, Frances became the second vice president for the New Jersey Association for Anti-Suffrage. She held the position until 1920, when women received the right to vote in the United States. Frances did vote in 1920 but didn't believe women should have the right to vote. According to her, the right to vote for women was a silly unnecessary thing.

Frances also cared about the kindergarten movement in the United States and especially education for women. She was instrumental in the founding of Douglas College, which today is a part of Rutgers University in New Jersey.

Shortly before her death, President Truman invited Frances for a luncheon where she met Dwight. D. Eisenhower, who, not knowing who she was, asked her where she had lived in Washington, D.C. She responded, "in the White House." Frances Cleveland died in her sleep on October 29, 1947, at the age of 83, in Baltimore, Maryland.

Frances Cleveland was the first presidential widow to get remarried. The only other one is Jaqueline Kennedy Onassis (see Chapter 15).

**FIRST LADY LORE**

# Caroline Scott Harrison (1832–1892)

Caroline Lavinia Scott (see Figure 11-6) was born October 1, 1832, in Oxford, Ohio. Her father, John Witherspoon Scott, was a Presbyterian minister and a professor of sciences and mathematics at Miami University, Ohio. He founded the Oxford Female Institute, a college for women, where Caroline studied the arts, dance, and music. She received a degree in music in 1852 and later taught piano to students in Ohio and Kentucky.

**FIGURE 11-6:**
Caroline Scott Harrison.

Source: Library of Congress, Prints & Photographs Division, Reproduction number LC-USZ62-73641 (b&w film copy neg.)

Caroline's parents were well educated and big supporters of women's education. For this reason, Caroline supported female education for the rest of her life.

Her future husband, Benjamin Harrison, attended the university Caroline's father was teaching at and excelled in the natural sciences. He took a course in mathematics from her father and, after meeting Caroline, started to visit their house under the pretense to see her father. He really was there for Caroline. Both graduated in 1852 and got married on October 20, 1853.

## Living life in Indiana

The next year, the newlywed couple moved to Indianapolis, Indiana, and Benjamin started to practice law. His name was well known, with his grandfather being William Henry Harrison, the 9th president of the United States. Benjamin started to get involved in Republican politics, backing Abraham Lincoln in 1860.

The two lived moderately well, with Benjamin's practice not making them wealthy yet. Then the Civil War broke out in 1861, and Benjamin volunteered and served in the Civil War with distinction. Caroline stayed home and raised their two children. After the Civil War ended, Benjamin returned home to practice law. Within the next decade, he made a name for himself and became one of the best-known lawyers in the region.

His specialty was divorces. Indianapolis had become the place to go for a divorce after the Civil War, and he got wealthy quickly.

**FIRST
LADY LORE**

During the Civil War, Caroline visited hospitals and helped wounded soldiers.

Benjamin ran twice for governor of Indiana but lost both times. Then in 1881, he was elected to the U.S. Senate and served one term. Caroline and their children moved with him. However, Caroline was able to spend only some months with him in Washington, D.C., because the weather in the capital kept her away during the winter season. In 1888, he received the Republican nomination mainly because of his family name. Benjamin decided to run a front porch campaign in 1888, where people came to his home and waited for him to give speeches. Caroline proved to be a wonderful hostess to a steady stream of supporters.

## Making improvements as First Lady

Caroline Harrison became First Lady in 1889. She brought her whole family with her, which included not only her son and daughter and their families but also her father, her sister, and her niece. The White House suddenly became a crowded place.

Carline soon set out to redo the White House, but people criticized her for being too domestic, and the press frequently complained that she was engaged only in domestic chores and not more socially active. This was actually incorrect.

Caroline wanted to enlarge the White House and make it more modern. Therefore, she decided to install electricity and hired architects to expand the place. She approved a design that added two wings to the White House, making the building U-shaped. One wing contained office space; the other would have been a museum. Congress, however, refused to fund the improvements. So she had to do improvements the cheap way.

Caroline and Benjamin were afraid of electricity. They didn't trust the new invention. Therefore, every night, after they had gone to bed, a servant had to come into their bedroom and turn the light off.

Instead of expanding the White House, Carline decided to redecorate. Because she had no money for new furniture and decorations, she decided to look in the White House attics for historical art and furniture. She discovered that the attics were full of art. She took the art and redecorated the White House and sold the old moldy furniture at auctions to raise money for the White House renovations. She continued to modernize the White House and put new flooring down and finally established private bathrooms. Soon the press referred to her as "the best housekeeper the White House has ever known."

In the 19th century, the White House, like the whole capital, had a rat problem. So the attics in the White House were crawling with rats. Caroline would go up in an attic with a hired gun to shoot the rats. She would scream every time she saw a rat, and her hired gun then shot the rat.

Caroline didn't like the press very much. To eliminate contact between the press and her family, she hired a photographer to take pictures of her family, especially the grandchildren, and then handed the photos to the media. That way she was able to keep the press out of the White House. The following quote expresses how she felt about the media at the time.

"I am disgusted with newspapers and reporters. Truth is a characteristic entirely unknown to them."

## Letting her artistic side shine

Caroline was the first First Lady who was an accomplished artist and pianist. While First Lady, she put her artistic background to good use. She gave private lessons to some of the ladies in Washington, D.C. For example, she taught classes on how to paint china and even offered foreign language classes. She further designed china for the White House and started the White House china collection, which displays china from previous administrations. The pattern she designed for the White House was a combination of cornstalk and goldenrod. Today, the china exhibit in the White House has become one of the most popular tourist attractions.

## Getting involved in public causes

Caroline was a very active First Lady. She was involved in many charities, became the founding president of the Daughters of the American Revolution in 1890, and even raised money for a new medical school at Johns Hopkins University.

Johns Hopkins had just opened a hospital and wanted to start a medical school. However, they were about $100,000 short. Caroline Harrison and several other prominent women stepped up and pledged to raise the money. However, there was a catch. The women would raise the money only if Johns Hopkins would allow women to attend their medical school. The university agreed, and they raised the money quickly.

## Dying in the White House

During the winter of 1891, Caroline caught tuberculosis and never recovered from the disease. She was dying when her husband got nominated for a second term. Benjamin refused to campaign for reelection, instead opting to spend his time with his wife. His opponent, former President Grover Cleveland, who wanted his old job back, did the same out of respect for the dying First Lady. On October 25, 1892, shortly before the election, Caroline died at the age of 60 in the White House. She was the second First Lady to die in the White House. Her daughter Mary Harrison McKee stepped in to fulfill First Lady functions for the last few months of her dad's term.

REMEMBER

Caroline Harrison was better educated and did more than most First Ladies but was not treated well by the press and today is usually ignored by historians.

# Ida Saxton McKinley (1847–1907)

Ida Saxton (see Figure 11-7) was born on June 8, 1847, in Canton, Ohio. Her father, James Saxton, was a wealthy banker and very prominent in the community. Ida grew up wealthy, wearing the finest clothing, receiving the best education, and was involved in many community affairs as her social standing required. She was also quite beautiful and known as the "Belle of Canton." Ida was sent to a private school in Cleveland and later graduated from Brook Hill Seminary in Pennsylvania, a top finishing school. After graduating, she returned home and continued her involvement in community affairs. For example, she raised funds for a new Presbyterian Church in which she would later get married. She even participated in local theater and opera.

**FIGURE 11-7:**
Ida Saxton
McKinley.

Source: Library of Congress, Prints & Photographs Division,
Reproduction number LC-USZ62-73639 (b&w film copy neg.)

In 1868, Ida's sisters introduced her to William McKinley, who was a young lawyer active in Republican politics. They didn't hit it off right away, mostly because Ida belonged to a different social circle in Canton. She belonged to the rich elite and was invited constantly to functions such as masquerade parties and debutante balls. William, on the other hand, was a war veteran who was just starting his legal career and hadn't yet been accepted into Canton's top society.

## Excelling in a man's world

Later that year, Ida and her sister went on a trip to Europe to have fun and shop. After she returned, her father gave her a job at his bank, Stark County Bank. Her father didn't want to be accused of any favoritism, so he made Ida start out at the bottom as a bank teller. She had to work her way up the ladder in the bank. She did so, and soon she was a manager, handling big accounts. It was shocking back in the late 19th century to have a woman hold such a high position in a bank. However, her father, James, wanted to make sure that Ida would become a self-reliant and independent woman.

Ironically, it was Ida's job at the bank that allowed her and William to get to know each other and fall in love. William had an account at the bank that Ida worked at, and suddenly he made serval deposits a day, always waiting for a specific window to become available. After he became the prosecuting attorney for the county in early 1869, the two became engaged.

Ida and William got married on January 25, 1871, in a large wedding ceremony attended by more than 1,000 people. The newlyweds were happy. Their first child, a daughter named Katherine, was born in December of 1871.

## Living with tragedy

After Ida got pregnant again, her health problems started. First, she had phlebitis, a swelling of the veins, which caused neurological damage to one of her legs. Then, two weeks before her second child was born, her mother died, and Ida fell into a deep depression. At her mother's funeral, Ida, severely distraught, missed a step going into a carriage and struck her head. Suddenly, she started having epileptic seizures. Because seizures back then were equated with mental disease, it was kept secret. Next, her second child, a daughter called Ida, was born prematurely and died five months later in 1873. Then in 1875, three-year-old Katherine caught typhoid fever and died.

Ida was totally devastated, was never the same, and became an invalid. Being severely depressed, her immune system collapsed, and for the rest of her life, she easily caught colds and infections.

**FIRST LADY LORE**

Ida studied Buddhism and began to believe in the concept of reincarnation. She firmly believed that her daughter would be reincarnated and the two would be together again. She would stare at other children to see whether they had the lost soul of Katherine in them.

## Having a devoted husband

While Ida was suffering, her husband's political career took off. William was first elected to Congress and then became the governor of Ohio. While he was governor, Ida lived in a hotel across from the state capitol. Every morning when William went to work, he'd wave at Ida, and she'd wave back. Then exactly at 3:00 p.m., he'd come out of the state capitol and wave at her again. It was just like clockwork, and people would actually set their watches by it. The public loved it and referred to William as one of the most devoted husbands in the country.

Then in 1896, William was elected president of the United States and Ida become First Lady. Because of Ida's health, William never traveled far from her. Even during the presidential campaign, he was very attentive and even conducted a front porch campaign, where the two met supporters in front of their house so he could be close to Ida.

**TECHNICAL STUFF**

During the campaign of 1896, a 60-page biography of Ida was published as part of the campaign materials. It was the first campaign biography of a presidential candidate's wife.

# Remaining a strong First Lady

Ida was active in the White House when it came to things she enjoyed. She loved music, the theater, and especially opera. She really enjoyed it when famous actors and singers came to the White House to meet her and perform for her. She played all kinds of music, including the up-and-coming ragtime.

**REMEMBER**

William McKinley was good friends with President Hayes. They had fought together in the Civil War. For this reason, Ida got to spend a lot of time with the Hayes family in the White House and even babysat for the Hayeses' children. She was, therefore, quite familiar with the White House and its customs.

At the same time, Ida would often sit for hours in the dark because light hurt her eyes. William would loyally sit next to her. Ida kept to herself most of the time but kept herself busy. She crocheted more than 5,000 bedroom slippers that were given to people who mattered in Washington, D.C. She actually used different colors for the slippers, and each color signified what she thought of a person. The colors alerted William to what she thought of people in the capital.

**IN THEIR WORDS**

Ida was happy only when her husband was around. She used to say, "He is a dear good man, and I love him."

Ida did engage in politics at the time. As First Lady, she supported the Salvation Army and the Crittenden House, an organization that provided food and shelter to homeless women. In addition, she was quite vocal about women's rights, including the right to vote.

After William became president, the press didn't report much on her health. She was getting worse and started having fainting spells. She'd try to be a White House hostess, dressing elegantly when she was able to attend social functions, but her illnesses showed. She was too weak to shake hands, so she held bouquets of flowers to avoid shaking hands. During dinner, President McKinley would constantly watch her to check for oncoming seizures, and if she had one, he quickly put a white handkerchief over her face. After the seizure was over, he removed the handkerchief, and Ida continued with her conversation.

**FIRST LADY LORE**

In 1898, Theodore Roosevelt was with his cavalry, the Rough Riders, stuck in San Antonio, Texas. He was trying to get on a train to Florida to take a ship to Cuba to fight in the Spanish-American War. However, he wasn't given permission to board the train. After sending telegrams all over Washington to get permission to leave, he sent a telegram to the First Lady. She went to her husband on Roosevelt's behalf, and permission was quickly granted. Teddy Roosevelt thanked her and said, "Please tell Mrs. McKinley to think of the Rough Riders as her very own, and we will make her proud."

By 1900, Ida had enough of being First Lady. Her health was deteriorating, and she was afraid that William would be assassinated. The king of Italy had just been assassinated, and so had leaders in other countries. She urged William to retire. He decided otherwise and didn't even tell her about running for reelection until it had been decided.

After William was reelected in 1900, he decided to tour the United States. Ida traveled with him but got ill in California. She wasn't with him when he stopped in Buffalo, New York, later to address the Pan-American Exposition.

President McKinley gave a speech at the Pan-American Exposition in Buffalo, New York, on September 6, 1901, and shook hands with the public afterward. An anarchist by the name of Leon F. Czolgosz shot the president twice.

After the president was shot and laid there dying on the ground, he told his secretary: "My wife — be careful . . . how you tell her — oh, be careful."

Ida spent the last few days with her husband before he passed. She wasn't allowed at the memorial service because people feared for her health. However, she accompanied President McKinley's casket on the train from Washington back to Canton. She would oversee the building of a mausoleum and monument for him and visited it every day.

After William died, Ida said: "He is gone, and life to me is dark now."

After leaving the White House, Ida moved in with her sister who took care of her. Interestingly, Ida had a few good years living with her sister. Her nieces would come visit and bring their children, which brought her back to life. Even her seizures suddenly stopped after William had died. Many believe that it had been all the stress and worrying about her husband that caused them in the first place. She even started walking and gardening again. Ida McKinley died May 26, 1907, at the age of 59 in Canton, Ohio. She was buried next to her husband and their two daughters.

The National First Ladies Library, dedicated to the First Ladies of the United States, is located in First Lady Ida Saxton McKinley's house in Canton, Ohio.

# Chapter **12**

# Becoming a World Power

During the period of 1901 until 1921, we see a change in the role First Ladies performed. Suddenly, the role of First Lady became institutionalized. While the First Ladies still performed hostess functions, it became more common for them to get involved in their husband's career and even policy making.

Edith Roosevelt hired her own staff and delegated many of the traditional hostess functions. She also took a more public role in personnel decisions. Helen Taft pushed her husband into becoming president. She was quite open about it and broke several conventional First Lady norms, such as drinking, smoking, and playing cards in public. Ellen Wilson was the first one to get involved in policy making. She found an issue, had a bill drown up by Congress, and then lobbied for its passage. Edith Wilson is the most controversial of the four. She basically controlled access to her husband when he was incapacitated by a stroke, which allowed her to control policy making. To this day, historians squabble over whether she was just trying to protect her husband or actually trying to run the country.

# Edith Kermit Carow Roosevelt (1861–1948)

Edith Carow (see Figure 12-1) was born on August 6, 1861, in Norwich, Connecticut. Her parents, Charles and Gertrude Tyler Carow, were upper middle class. Her father was from a wealthy New York shipping family, but he was an alcoholic and lost a lot of money in business.

Despite this, Edith grew up comfortably in New York City. She was close to the Roosevelt family early on, because they grew up in the same neighborhood and had the same tutors, and she was Theodore "Teddy" Roosevelt's sister Corinne's best friend. She and Theodore played together and read books together. The two hung out in the same social circles and attended the same parties. They became best friends, and he even sent her letters when he toured Europe. Everybody thought they would become a couple, but they had a falling out when Theodore asked her to marry him, and she said no because her parents thought she was too young. Upset, Theodore decided it was time to leave New York.

Theodore went to Harvard in 1876 to study, and there he met Alice Hathaway Lee, who he fell in love with and married in 1880. Theodore next studied law at Columbia, hated it, and then became a politician. However, in 1884, Alice died of Bright's disease, a kidney ailment, shortly after giving birth to their daughter, Alice Lee. To make matters worse, Theodore's mother died on the same day of typhoid fever, and Theodore decided that he had to escape life and went to the Dakota Territory to live on a ranch.

## Building a life with Teddy

On a trip back East, Theodore went to a party and ran into Edith Carow again. They decided to give it another try and began to date in secret. They fell in love and were engaged in November 1885. Edith even went to Dakota to visit him on his ranch. There, she hung out with cowboys and desperados. She accepted them because they were Theodore's friends, and he loved living out West. However, he failed at ranching and lost quite a bit of money in the endeavor. So he had to move back East, and he reentered politics.

Edith and Theodore got married on December 2, 1886, in London, England, and honeymooned in Italy. Afterward, they moved to Long Island, New York, where Theodore had built a mansion called Sagamore Hill. They were happily married and had five children together, four boys and one girl, in addition to Alice from Theodore's previous marriage.

Edith ran the household, raised the children, and handled the finances while Theodore was absent politicking or going to war in 1898 when he volunteered to fight in the Spanish-American War.

Edith didn't like her husband getting into politics because she thought it didn't pay enough to support such a large family. Despite her objections, Theodore became governor of New York in 1899 and Edith, the First Lady of New York. This provided her with valuable experience on how to be a graceful hostess. However, she was not happy about him becoming the vice president in 1901.

## Taking control as First Lady

After President McKinley was assassinated in 1901 (see Chapter 11), Edith became First Lady of the United States. She moved the whole family to the White House, including the children's pets, which included not only cats and dogs but also guinea pigs, a kangaroo rat, and even a bear.

Edith proved to be an efficient First Lady, who hosted many parties and dinners and was well liked by the staff. Edith actually prepared for the role of First Lady by reading up on her predecessors and by being familiar with current events so that she could carry on intelligent conversations with her guests. Soon, Washington, D.C., considered her one of the most intelligent First Ladies ever who was also kind and graceful.

Edith further decided to bureaucratize the White House. Instead of being a hostess, she wanted to be the manager of social functions. So she hired a social secretary, Isabella Hagener, to do most of the hostess functions, such as planning and staging events. Edith also hired caterers, paid out of the president's salary, and there was no more cooking in the White House.

FIRST
LADY LORE

Edith tightly controlled the White House guest list. For example, she didn't want adulterers in the White House, and if someone was accused of adultery, she'd strike the name off the list.

**REMEMBER**

Edith was the one who had to raise the children. She was very strict and expected the children to behave. Theodore, on the other hand, played with them and let them get away with just about anything in the White House. The media loved the Roosevelt family; they wrote stories about the pranks the children played and the exotic pets that were suddenly found in the White House. The pictures of the children and pets were all over newspapers and magazines and turned out to be great press for the President and the First Lady. One of the children's favorite pranks was to hide and scare the guests in the White House and to disrupt important meetings.

To control what was printed in the media, Edith spoon-fed the media pictures of the kids and White House stories. She further included them in social events like White House marriages. The grateful press published her pictures and stories like they were their own.

Edith was also actively engaged with her husband's work. She reviewed his speeches, made corrections if necessary, and highlighted stories in the major newspapers that she thought he should read. She even handled his mail, separating important from unimportant letters and even on occasion answering them for him.

**REMEMBER**

Edith was the perfection of an invisible government. People would talk to her, and she then would talk to Theodore. She sat in on political meetings, knitting but intensively listening. After the meeting, she'd discuss the topics with her husband in private.

## Updating the White House

Edith soon figured out that the White House was too small for her family. So she went to the plans Caroline Harrison had drawn up (see Chapter 11). This time, Congress was ready to fund changes to the White House. The United States was considered a world power, and its executive mansion had to reflect this. So Congress allocated $475,000 for the endeavor. Edith was able to separate residential quarters from executive offices. Public rooms were enlarged to hold larger receptions and dinners, because with the United States being a world power, more diplomats and foreign leaders had to be invited and dined. It took a full year, all of 1902, to do this. By the time she was done, Edith added the West Wing and also a picture gallery of First Ladies, including herself. She further beefed up the security because after the McKinley assassination, her greatest fear was that someone would try to assassinate her husband.

REMEMBER

Edith loved classical music. She brought famous pianists and opera singers to the White House. At one point, she invited the whole Philadelphia Orchestra. Her husband, on the other hand, preferred Native American music and cowboy songs.

FIRST
LADY LORE

Edith started the tradition of not calling the president by his first name. He was called Mr. President. She herself addressed her husband as Mr. President in public settings.

## Enjoying a long, active life after retirement

In 1908, Theodore Roosevelt decided not to run for reelection, and he and Edith left the White House in 1909. Theodore went on hunting trips in Africa and South America. Edith mostly stayed home and ran the household. However, after Theodore went on safari for a whole year, she decided to join him in Egypt, and they rode camels together and saw the pyramids. Next, they went back to Italy where they had honeymooned.

In 1912, Edith publicly supported her husband's run for the presidency but knew he couldn't win.

IN THEIR
WORDS

Edith told him: "Put it out of your mind; you will never be president again."

Theodore started to get sick beginning in 1913. Despite this, he explored the Amazon River and volunteered for WWI in 1917. Theodore offered to create a new volunteer division and to fight in Europe. President Wilson turned him down. He died at home in 1919 at the age of 60.

REMEMBER

After her husband had died, Edith burned all their letters to maintain their privacy.

**TECHNICAL STUFF**

Edith had four sons and one daughter. All four sons fought in WWI, and her daughter served as a nurse. Her youngest son Quentin died fighting in France during WWI. Two of her other sons fought in WWII. Theodore Jr. participated in the Normandy invasion but died of a heart attack while still in France. Her son Kermit, after fighting in both WWI and WWII, died by suicide.

**REMEMBER**

Edith's son Quentin, who was killed in aerial combat in 1918 in France, is still the only presidential son to die in combat.

After Theodore died in 1919, Edith, at 58, traveled throughout Europe and Asia. Back home, she was involved in many civic activities. She worked for her church and was active in the Women's Republican Club. She even campaigned for local and national Republican candidates and against Franklin Delano Roosevelt (FDR), who was a distant cousin of her husband. In 1932, she denounced both him and the New Deal (see Chapter 14).

Finally, Edith also became an author. She contributed a chapter in a book on travel, written by her children. In her chapter, she wrote the following: "Women who marry, pass their best and happiest years in giving life and fostering it . . . and those born with the wanderfoot are sometimes irked by the weight of the always beloved shackles." This expressed her thoughts on motherhood best. While she loved being a mom, she missed out on many adventures because of it.

Edith did leave a great legacy. She and Theodore were so successful in the White House that other presidential couples tried to imitate them. When asked how they'd run the White House, Eleanor and Franklin Roosevelt said: "We would really like our White House to be like Uncle Theodore's and Aunt Edith's."

Edith Roosevelt died on September 30, 1948, at the age of 87. *Life* magazine called her "One of the strongest-minded and strongest-willed presidential wives who ever lived in the White House."

# Helen Herron Taft (1861–1943)

Helen Herron (see Figure 12-2) was born on June 2, 1861, in Cleveland, Ohio. Her father, John Herron, was deeply involved in Republican politics in Ohio, even serving in Congress, and he was the former law partner of President Rutherford Hayes. He was good friends with both Presidents Hayes and Harrison, and Helen grew up with politics.

**FIGURE 12-2:**
Helen
Herron Taft.

Source: Library of Congress, Prints & Photographs Division,
Reproduction number LC-DIG-hec-15986
(digital file from original negative)

Helen, or Nellie, as she was called throughout her life, grew up wealthy. She went to a private school for young women in Cincinnati and studied foreign languages and music. Early on, she proved to be academically adept, reading both Darwin and Goethe, and turned into a free thinker not bound by society's norms. Even though she didn't finish college, she did attend the University of Cincinnati; she educated herself and was very knowledgeable, especially in the areas of music and literature.

**IN THEIR WORDS**

At the age of 22, Nellie wrote: "I have thought that a woman should be independent and not regard matrimony as the only thing to be desired in life."

## Being a free thinker

Nellie became a teacher for two years and didn't like it. So she and several friends founded their own salon (an intellectual club), which became the meeting place in Cincinnati to discuss cultural and political affairs. She met William Howard Taft, a Yale graduate who had just begun practicing law, at a bobsledding event and invited him to join the salon. He began to regularly attend and was impressed with Nellie's intellectual abilities and became enamored with her. They started dating, and he declared his love for her. He proposed twice and got rejected twice. She eventually gave in and accepted his third proposal, and the two got married on June 19, 1886.

When asked about her salon, Nellie stated: "The purpose was to create an invitation only space for brilliant discussion of topics, intellectual and economic."

Nellie became what she was afraid of— a housewife and mother of three children. William started to move up the political ladder. Nellie at the same time began to become involved in local organizations and was responsible for the founding of what today is the Cincinnati Symphony Orchestra.

In 1890, after William had been named solicitor general for the United States, representing the government in legal actions, Nellie moved the family to Washington, D.C. She enjoyed living there and believed that she was getting closer to being First Lady.

Nellie had always wanted to be First Lady. She got to visit the White House at the age of 16, when President Hayes invited her family for a private visit, and fell in love with the place and the presidency. From then on, her life ambition was to be First Lady.

## Becoming the First Lady of the Philippines

After the United States had emerged victorious in the Spanish-American War of 1898, it won the Philippines from Spain. It became an American territory, and William Howard Taft was supposed to become its governor and transition it to civilian government. Nellie saw it as a great opportunity and convinced him to accept the position. So the family moved to Manila, the capital of the Philippines.

Nellie loved it there; William was treated like a king and she like a queen. She was involved in politics, discussing policies with her husband. They both gained valuable experience. She learned how to manage a large group of servants and host large parties, while he learned how to manage a country. While there, Nellie combated racism by American officials against the local population by inviting both Americans and Filipinos to her table and tried to help the local poor, especially women.

Nellie shook Filipino hands and danced with the locals. Many in the United States criticized her for his, preferring to segregate the Philippines. She was responsible for introducing the technology of milk sterilization in the Philippines and became the first white woman to tour the dangerous Luzon mountains.

## Moving to Washington

It all ended in 1904, when President Roosevelt made William Taft secretary of war, and they had to return to Washington, D.C. Nellie disliked the social functions in the capital, especially the weekly meetings of cabinet members' wives (which she abolished as soon as she became First Lady), and she didn't get along with First Lady Edith Roosevelt. Edith was very puritan in nature, and Nellie enjoyed a stiff drink, a cigarette, and playing cards with men (see Figure 12-3).

**FIGURE 12-3:**
Helen Taft
playing cards.

**REMEMBER**

President Roosevelt twice approached her husband and offered him a seat on the Supreme Court. That is what William Howard Taft had wanted all his life, but Nellie convinced him not to take the offer. She wanted to be First Lady.

To top it off, Nellie actually met with President Roosevelt twice to tell him that William wasn't interested in the Supreme Court but rather that he wanted to be president.

After Theodore Roosevelt decided not to run for a third term in 1908, he threw his support behind William Howard Taft. During his campaign, William wrote to Nellie daily. He easily won the election in 1908 and became President of the United States in 1909.

One of the major magazines of the time, the *Ladies Home Journal,* wrote after the election: "Had it not been for his wife, Mr. Taft would never have entered the presidential race."

# Finally becoming First Lady

In 1909, Nellie Taft finally became First Lady. She immediately broke with tradition on Inauguration Day. She became the first First Lady to accompany her husband on the parade route back to the White House after the swearing-in ceremony. Traditionally, the former president rode with the new president, but Theodore Roosevelt had already left town, so Nellie decided to hop in the car and ride with the president. Nellie said later that this was the proudest moment of her life, and this tradition of riding with the president back to the White House has lasted to this day.

Nellie set out to turn Washington, D.C., into the cultural center of the United States. She wanted to bring a symphony orchestra and opera to the capital and invited artists to the White House. Unlike Edith Roosevelt who had delegated functions in the White House to her secretary and even servants, Nellie micromanaged everything in the White House.

**FIRST
LADY LORE**

Nellie could be quite frugal at times. The presidential salary had been increased to $75,000 per year, and she took $25,000 away annually and put it into savings. By the time the Taft administration ended in 1913, she had saved $100,000.

Two months later, at the age of 47, Nellie suffered a stroke. She became partially paralyzed and unable to speak for almost one year. The White House never acknowledged that she had a stroke or seizure, calling it a nervous disorder instead. Within several months, she recovered; however, her speech was never the same. She went back to work as First Lady. In 1911, she suffered a second stroke, survived it, and went on to live a long life.

Nellie continued to discuss politics with William, even advising him at times. She sat in on important meetings justifying her presence by claiming that she was there to keep the president awake. At parties and dinners, she'd consciously remind William of names of guests and economic numbers he might have forgotten. If someone tried to talk to the president alone, she'd just appear to see what was going on. She was a strong supporter of the right to vote for women. At the same time, she didn't believe that women should run for office.

Nellie was politically active and made it acceptable for First Ladies to have an interest and be involved in politics. For example, she attended congressional hearings on dangerous workplaces for young women and sat in the front row. She toured federal workplaces to inspect working conditions and worked with cabinet members to improve these conditions. This was rare at the time.

## Creating a beautiful capital

When William was secretary of war, Nellie traveled with him to Japan. There, she saw for the first time the famous Tokyo cherry trees blossoming. They looked beautiful with their pale pink petals. She wanted to beautify the capital and the White House with cherry trees. The Japanese found out about this, and the mayor of Tokyo gifted her 3,000 cherry trees. Nellie donated them to the government to plant all over the capital. She wanted to give the people in the capital a beautiful public space to gather and listen to public concerts. For this reason today, thousands of Americans can see the famous cherry trees blossom in April in the capital.

## Writing an autobiography

President Taft wasn't unhappy to lose the 1912 elections. He retired and started to teach law at Yale University. In 1921, he finally accomplished his long-time goal of becoming Chief Justice of the United States Supreme Court. He served until 1930 when he died.

Nellie Taft became the first First Lady to attend a attend a political convention in 1912 and it was the opposition party's.

**REMEMBER**

Nellie Taft is the first First Lady to write an autobiography with a ghostwriter. It was published in 1914 and sold well.

**FIRST LADY LORE**

Nellie moved back to Washington, D.C., with William and stayed there after he died. She died on May 22, 1943, at the age of 81 and was buried at Arlington National Cemetery, only one of two First Ladies to be buried there. The other is Jacqueline Kennedy Onassis (see Chapter 15).

## MAKING THE MOST OF A SILVER ANNIVERSARY

In 1911, the Tafts celebrated their silver wedding anniversary, so Nellie decided to throw a big party. She invited almost 5,000 guests and encouraged gifts. Because it was a silver anniversary, gifts made out of silver were encouraged. Back then, no laws existed preventing Nellie from keeping the gifts, and she did keep all of them. A White House staff member later said she didn't know that that much silver existed in the world.

Nellie's three children proved to be very successful. Her daughter, Helen Taft Manning, received a doctorate from Yale University and became a history professor. Her two sons entered politics. One, Robert Taft, became a long-time U.S. Senator from Ohio; the other, Charles Phelps Taft II, became mayor of Cincinnati, Ohio.

# Ellen Louise Axson Wilson (1860–1914)

Ellen Louise Axson (see Figure 12-4) was born on May 15, 1860, in Savannah, Georgia. Her father was a Presbyterian minister. She met Woodrow Wilson when he was four years old when her father was in a meeting with Woodrow's dad, who was also a minister. They didn't see each other again for more than 20 years, when they met again in 1883.

**FIGURE 12-4:** Ellen Louise Axson Wilson.

Source: Library of Congress, Prints & Photographs Division, Reproduction number LC-USZ62-25806 (b&w film copy neg. of detail)

Woodrow Wilson had become a lawyer and visited the community to take care of some legal matters. He and Ellen actually met in church during a sermon her father was giving. The two quickly fell in love but decided to wait to get married. Ellen had to take care of her father and her siblings, while Woodrow wasn't a successful lawyer and she believed he needed a different job. Woodrow had decided to quit the law anyway and wanted to attend Johns Hopkins University to get a doctorate in political science. At the train station on his way to Baltimore, Woodrow proposed to Ellen and she said yes, to his great surprise. For the next two years, they wrote each other letters, which drew them even closer.

Ellen, who had attended Rome Female College and had excelled in the fine arts, had gone back home to take care of her father and siblings after her mother had died. After her father died by suicide in 1884, she moved to New York so that she could attend the Art Students League of New York, which was open to both sexes. She graduated in 1885, and one of her paintings won a medal at the Paris international exposition.

Woodrow, who was still studying at Johns Hopkins, wasn't happy about Ellen being so independent but accepted it, because the two had already decided to get married. She wrote him: "I was indeed meant for you — that I may do you good and not evil all the days of my life."

Ellen and Woodrow got married on June 24, 1885, in Savannah, Georgia, after he graduated from Johns Hopkins University. He subsequently accepted a teaching position at Bryn Mawr College in Pennsylvania, which Ellen wasn't happy about. The salary was low, and it was an all-female college. Ellen didn't believe that teaching only women was prestigious enough for her husband.

Three years later, Woodrow accepted a position at Wesleyan College in Connecticut, one of the most prestigious colleges in the United States. Ellen was happy. Woodrow had become an accomplished author, writing a biography of George Washington and a widely used book comparing presidential forms of government to parliamentary systems. Ellen had helped him with his books, reviewing and editing his works. She even translated books from German into English for him. She was content raising their two daughters in Connecticut but missed the South.

**FIRST
LADY LORE**

Ellen and Woodrow were proud Southerners, and when she was pregnant with her first two daughters, she traveled back to Georgia so that the girls were born in the South and could call themselves Southerners. Their third daughter was born in Connecticut, and Woodrow always complained that she didn't have a Southern accent.

## Becoming an artist and practicing for First Lady

In 1890, Woodrow became a professor at Princeton University. Here, Ellen could really focus on her artistic talents. Soon she became one of the best landscape portrait painters in the United States. She even entered her artwork in juried competitions under the pseudonym, E. A. Wilson. Her landscape portraits won awards at New York and Chicago art shows, and she started to sell her paintings.

Ellen sold quite a few of her paintings, making good money. However, she never kept a dime from her royalties but donated everything to charity.

After Woodrow Wilson became president of Princeton in 1902, Ellen suddenly assumed a public role. As the wife of a university president, she had to be a social hostess, and she oversaw university renovation and maintenance of the grounds. During this time, she redesigned the presidential grounds on campus and modernized the student hospital.

Woodrow Wilson liked the ladies. He had a long-standing affair with a widow by the name of Mary Hulbert Peck. He tried to keep the affair secret and even introduced Mary Hulbert Peck to Ellen and his daughters as just a friend. Ellen was aware of the affair, and it was very painful for her to tolerate it. However, she decided not to make a big deal out of it. Woodrow later admitted that he made a mistake and apologized to her.

Ellen wasn't openly involved in her husband's political career but helped him out behind the scenes quite a bit. For example, when she found out that William Jennings Bryan, a three-time Democratic presidential nominee, was invited to speak at Princeton in 1911, she arranged for a dinner with the Bryans so that her husband, who was now the governor of New Jersey, could settle his political differences with William. She knew Woodrow wouldn't get the democratic nomination for president without William's support. The two hit it off and became good friends, and William supported Woodrow for the presidential nomination in 1912. In addition, she worked as his informal campaign manager. She monitored news coverage and clipped out important articles for him to read.

She enjoyed small gatherings and disliked large social functions. She once said:

"I am naturally the most unambitious of women and life in the White House has no attractions for me. Quite the contrary in fact."

This might not have been true, because this First lady who supposedly couldn't care less about politics became the first First Lady to back a bill in Congress and publicly lobby for its passing, setting the stage for future First Ladies to become involved in policy making.

## Being adept at First Lady

When Ellen became First Lady, she was well prepared. She had been the wife of a university president and also had been the First Lady of New Jersey after Woodrow Wilson became governor in 1910.

Ellen was the first First Lady to get involved in policy making, by openly backing a bill in front of Congress. She even had her name attached to the bill, called the Slum Clearance Bill, or the Ellen Wilson Bill. Ellen was shocked when she came to Washington, D.C., and saw how many slum areas there were. The alleyways in between bigger streets is where most of the slums, full of shacks and poverty, were located. The people who lived there were mostly Black and new immigrants. The areas desperately needed more law enforcement and more funds to improve existing housing and build more housing. So Ellen decided to act. She took Congressmen in a White House car on tours of theses slums and arranged for a reception so that housing reformers could meet with members of Congress. She further backed the Slum Clearance Bill, which provided money to tear down and rebuild alley dwellings. The bill also provided money for more parks in these areas to beautify Washington, D.C.

As Ellen laid in the White House dying, she was asked what could be done to make her more comfortable. She responded: "I would be happier if I knew the alley bill had passed."

The Senate passed the bill the day she died, and the House of Representatives passed it a month later. However, the bill was never implemented because WWI broke out and priorities shifted. In the 1930s, the bill finally died.

Ellen's time in the White House was short. She was only in office for about one and a half years before she died of Bright's disease, an inflammatory kidney disease, which started after giving birth to her third daughter. One of the highlights of her tenure as First Lady was both of her daughters getting married in the White House and her being able to preside over the first national celebration of Mother's Day. She died on August 6, 1914, at the age of 54 in Washington, D.C., the third and last First Lady to die in the White House.

# Edith Bolling Galt Wilson (1872–1961)

Edith Bolling (see Figure 12-5) was born on October 15, 1872, in Wytheville, Virginia. Her father was a judge, William Holcombe Bolling, and he and his wife, Sallie White, had 11 children. Edith was number seven. During the Civil War, the Bolling family had lost everything, including their planation and enslaved people, and they began to live a simple life. When Edith was 15, the family finally had enough money to send her to Martha Washington College, where she studied music.

In 1893, while visiting her sister in Washington, D.C., Edith met an older businessman by the name of Norman Galt. He was a cousin of Edith's sister's husband. They got married in 1896. Norman, who was quite a bit older than Edith, died in 1908, and she took over his business, which included a jewelry store. Edith began to travel; she went to Europe and Asia and, after coming back home, became the first woman in the capital to own an electric car. She lived well, but politics didn't interest her at all.

**FIGURE 12-5:**
Edith Bolling Galt Wilson.

Source: Library of Congress, Prints & Photographs Division, Reproduction number LC-USZ62-25808 (b&w film copy neg. of cropped image)

## Meeting the President

In 1915, Edith met President Woodrow Wilson by chance. She was introduced to the president's cousin Helen Woodrow Bones, who had been helping Woodrow with hostess functions, and the two women became close friends. In March of 1915, Edith and Helen were walking on the White House grounds and ran into President Wilson. They had tea together, and for the first time in months, Woodrow was laughing and having fun. He fell in love right away.

Woodrow was enchanted with Edith and started writing her letters, and then they started dating. He proposed soon afterward, but she turned him down. Two months later, he proposed again, and this time she accepted his proposal. They became engaged, even though Woodrow's advisors believed the relationship should be kept a secret, because it had not yet been a full year since his first wife, Ellen, had died (see earlier section in this chapter). He ignored them, and they got publicly engaged in October of 1915 and married on December 18, 1915.

Woodrow's advisors were wrong. Getting married to Edith turned out to be of political benefit to him. The public loved her, and the press covered the White House in more detail again. Even Woodrow's three daughters were happy. They had feared for their dad who had sunk into a deep depression.

Edith Wilson was the first First Lady to play golf with her husband.

# Running the country

Edith became First Lady in the middle of WWI. She right away had to get to work and assume hostess functions. This proved to be difficult. Although the United States wasn't yet involved in WWI, the rest of the world was fighting each other. So she had to host diplomatic events very carefully. She found an ingenious solution. Instead of having large events to which all diplomats in the capital were invited, she held two separate events, one for the Central Powers and their sympathizers and one for the Allied Powers.

When the United States entered WWI in 1917, everything changed. The whole country was asked to make sacrifices, cut back on spending money, and live a frugal lifestyle.

Edith decided to turn the White House into a model for sacrificing. She observed meatless days just as the average American was asked to do. To save money, she got a flock of sheep so that the White House didn't have to pay someone to cut the lawn. She then auctioned off the wool from the sheep nationwide and donated the money. She further knitted sweaters for soldiers.

After WWI was over in 1918, President Wilson decided to go to Paris to become a peacemaker. He also wanted to make sure the creation of a League of Nations would be included in the talks. Edith was received like royalty in Great Britain and France and loved every minute of it. However, soon after, Woodrow started to have health problems.

The League of Nations was supposed to be an international peacekeeping organization that operated on the concept of collective security, which stated that an attack on a member state equaled an attack on all members. In theory, this concept outlawed war in the world.

After returning from Europe, Woodrow decided to tour the United States to make a case to get the U.S. Senate to pass the Treaty of Versailles, ending WWI, and to create the League of Nations. All of this was too much for his health. He collapsed in Colorado on September 26, 1919, and then suffered a stroke on October 2, 1919, in Washington, D.C. The stroke left him bedridden and able to work only sparingly. Edith and his advisors decided not to tell the public. In her memoirs, Edith claims that her husband's doctor, Francis Decrum, told her: "His resignation would have a bad effect on the country and a serious effect on our patient." Her claim to this day is disputed.

Edith became Woodrow's main advisor. She decided which issues he'd address and who he could see; this allowed her to control policy making. For this reason, some argue that she ran the country for the last year of President Wilson's presidency. She even admitted that much in the following quote.

IN THEIR
WORDS

"I, myself never made a single decision regarding the disposition of public affairs. The only decision that was mine was what was important and what was not, and the very important decision of when to present matters to my husband."

TECHNICAL
STUFF

The 19th Amendment to the Constitution, ratified on August 26, 1920, gave women the right to vote in the United States. Both Edith and Woodrow publicly supported the amendment, even though they personally didn't think that women should be involved in politics.

In 1921, after Woodrow's term had expired, the couple bought a house in Washington, D.C., and Edith took care of him until 1924 when he died. She refused a state funeral and had only a small religious service.

## Thriving as Mrs. Wilson

REMEMBER

On December 8, 1941, President Franklin Delano Roosevelt invited Edith to Congress to sit there while he called for war. She had done the same in 1917 when her husband called for war.

Edith lived 37 more years, and the rest of her life revolved around being Woodrow Wilson's wife. She chose his biographer, she wrote her own memoirs, and she collaborated to have a movie made about him. In addition, she created the Woodrow Wilson Foundation, which later helped create the United Nations, and collected his presidential papers. She also helped establish the Woodrow Wilson School of Public and International Affairs at Princeton University.

REMEMBER

The name Woodrow Wilson was dropped in 2020 from the Woodrow Wilson School of Public and International Affairs because of the president's record of racism, and the school is now called the Princeton School of Public and International Affairs.

Edith also remained active in Democratic politics and continued to run her jewelry business until 1934 when she sold it to her employees.

Edith's final act was to take part in the inauguration of President John F. Kennedy in 1961. Edith Wilson died a few months later on December 28, 1961, at the age of 89.

IN THIS CHAPTER

» Making a way for women: Florence Harding

» Advocating for the deaf and disabled: Grace Coolidge

» Giving to those less fortunate: Louise Hoover

# Chapter 13

# Changing the Roles of Women

The 1920s changed the lives of American women. They had received the right to vote in presidential elections in 1920, and due to the labor shortages of WWI, many women had entered the workforce. Overall, American women were more independent, and the life goals of getting married and having children changed. Not surprisingly, First Ladies changed, too, and became more ambitious and more involved in policy making. The first one to do so was Florence Harding, as you find out about in this chapter. In many ways, she changed the way American First Ladies performed in the White House. She was strong-willed, held her own press conferences, and felt free to express her opinions even if they differed from her husband's administration. She became more popular than her husband especially after his administration became mired in scandal after scandal. She did her best to protect him but failed in the end.

Grace Coolidge on the other hand was a more traditional First Lady. She enjoyed hosting parties and dinners and loved being around people. She was outgoing and fun, while her husband was not. At the same time, she was not very involved in politics and had no real impact on her husband's decisions.

Louise, or Lou, Hoover brought a spirt of civic mindedness to the White House. She devoted herself to public service, setting a precedent for First Ladies to champion causes of their own. She broke with tradition when it came to the role of women in society and had the most adventurous life of all of the First Ladies. Who else can say that they were in China during the Boxer Rebellion, defending herself with a gun, and loving every minute of it.

# Florence Kling Harding (1860–1924)

Florence Kling (see Figure 13-1) was born on August 15, 1860, in Marion, Ohio. Her father, Amos Kling, was a banker and the richest man in town. Her mother Louisa Bouton Kling was a homemaker taking care of Florence and her two brothers. Florence had a great childhood, and her father took a special interest in her. She was allowed to work with him in banking and soon developed people skills, especially communication skills. However, this all came to an end when she joined a roller skating group and met Henry De Wolfe, a nineteen-year-old with a drinking problem who got her pregnant. Florence's father hated him and forbade her to see him. So she ran away with him, got common-law married, and had a son, Marshall. She soon regretted her actions after Henry left her, and they got divorced in 1886.

**FIGURE 13-1:**
Florence Kling
Harding

Source: Library of Congress, Prints & Photographs Division,
Reproduction number LC-DIG-hec-30088
(digital file from original negative)

After graduating from high school in 1878, Florence had studied at the Cincinnati Conservatory to become a concert pianist. She became very good at the piano practicing for up to seven hours a day. Now being a single mother, she became a piano teacher, trying to make enough money to raise her child. However, she didn't make enough to take care of herself and her son. For this reason, she had to go back and ask her father for help. He agreed to help but only if he could raise his grandson, Marshall, by himself. She consented to his demands, and her father adopted her son. Both of them were now taken care of and Florence was able to keep close contact with her son, with her father allowing her to visit. After she got remarried, she had a room for him in her house, and he could come over and spend time with her.

While in Marion giving piano lessons, one of Florence's students was the sister of Warren G. Harding, who had become the co-owner of the local newspaper, the *Marion Star*. He made the paper successful, bought out his partners, and was soon considered Marion's most handsome and eligible bachelor. Florence's father opposed any kind of involvement with Warren. He believed that the Hardings were below them socially, and there was a rumor that some of the Hardings' ancestors had been Black. Again Florence ignored him, and he wouldn't speak to her for the next fifteen years. Florence was able to capture Warren's heart, and the two were married in Warren's house on July 8, 1891.

## Dealing with affairs

Florence was five years older than Warren and the heiress to a big fortune. Many believed that Warren married her for the money and that she, in turn, married him to restore her reputation.

**FIRST LADY LORE**

Florence didn't want to have any other children. She didn't see her son from her first marriage often and that was fine by her. She told people that she took little white pills to make sure she didn't get pregnant again.

Warren became famous for his extramarital affairs, backing up the claim that he married Florence for money. However, the couple's friends mentioned often that the two were deeply in love in the beginning and that Florence felt betrayed when Warren cheated on her repeatedly.

First, Warren had an affair with Carrie Phillips, a friend of the couple. Both Florence and Warren enjoyed hanging out with Carrie and her husband. They even vacationed together. After Florence found out about the affair, she wanted a divorce. He refused because he feared it would destroy his political career. He promised to end the affair, but he lied. It continued all the way into 1920, when he was running for president.

In mid-1920, after Warren had received the Republican nomination for president, he disclosed his affair with Carrie to Republican party officials. They suddenly became very afraid that she would talk to the press about the affair and so decided to buy her silence. In return for her silence, Carrie received an all-expense paid trip to Asia to get her out of the country, as well as an annual stipend for the reminder of her life. It was not until 2014 that hundreds of love letters between Warren and Carrie were released to the American public by the Library of Congress.

Warren had a second affair with a young lady he met while she was still in high school. Her name was Nan Britton, and she wrote a book about the affair with him after he had died and claimed that he fathered her child. DNA testing in 2015 finally confirmed her claim. In the book, she describes how Warren got her a good job in New York City and how the two would stay in hotels together, and he would check her in as his niece.

Florence was aware of the affairs, but even though they personally hurt her, she wanted to make sure that Warren became president and she First Lady. As one reporter put it: "Florence harbored a ruthless ambition to become First Lady." When her husband did poorly in early primaries in 1920 and was ready to quit the presidential race, Florence was incensed. She yelled at him that they were in this fight until hell froze over.

## Getting into politics

After they got married, Florence took over the circulation department of the news-paper, organizing its first home delivery service, and made it even more successful.

**FIRST LADY LORE**

Florence Harding was the first newspaper publisher in the State of Ohio to hire a female reporter, Jane Dixon.

Florence got bored living in a small town and running a newspaper, and so she encouraged Warren, who was a good public speaker, to get into politics. He did and was very successful at it. He was twice voted into the Ohio State Senate, and then in 1914, the people of Ohio voted him in to the U.S. Senate. Florence stood by his side, constantly watching over him, making sure that he made no mistakes. For example, Warren had to give most of his interviews at home so that she could participate and check on what he said, and, of course, she successfully kept his affairs out of the limelight. She never concealed her partnership in his political career and decisions, and he was well aware of it. He once said that his automobile is the only thing his wife didn't have a desire to run.

While Warren was succeeding in politics with Florence's help, she developed kidney problems, namely nephritis. Despite this, she went campaigning with him, sometimes shaking thousands of hands a day. Often it took 48 hours for her hands to recover. She was important to the campaign because she appealed to the new female vote, with a majority of women finally being able to vote at the presidential level in 1920. During the 1920 campaign, she traveled about 20,000 miles campaigning. She proved to be a very good campaigner, who knew how to deal with the media. Florence became the first First Lady to stage photo ops, making sure that the press was at every White House event with cameras.

This allowed her to spoon-feed the press photos of the presidential couple and even her pets. Her dog, Laddie Boy, proved to be so popular that he was used in the 1920 campaign. She even went to the Republican nomination, actively campaigning for her husband until he received the nomination.

**FIRST LADY LORE**

Florence would often consult a medium to predict her future. Shockingly, her medium predicted that her husband would become president of the United States, that he would die in office, and that she would die soon afterward. That is exactly what happened.

## Succeeding as First Lady

Warren G. Harding won the presidency easily in 1920, partly due to how Florence handled the campaign and, especially, the media for him. By now, the media included the radio and movie theaters showing news clips.

As First Lady, Florence actively supported women's rights, strongly coming out in support of women owning businesses and participating in sports. She even encouraged the appointment of female federal employees and gave speeches herself, when her husband was delayed or couldn't make an event.

**FIRST LADY LORE**

Florence Harding was the oldest First Lady up to this point. She was 61.

Florence begged her husband to support racial equality in the U.S., but he didn't accomplish much on this issue. She further vocally opposed the League of Nations and Prohibition. Soon, she was depicted in cartoons as the chief executive occupying the White House. Some of her quotes didn't help dispel this. After Warring was elected president, Florence said:

**IN THEIR WORDS**

"I know what is best for the president. I put him in the White House."

The next quote by Florence Harding depicts how she felt about women's rights. She did believe in full gender equality, stating that it was acceptable for the woman to be the breadwinner in a marriage. This was highly controversial in the 1920s.

IN THEIR
WORDS

Florence wrote in 1922:

> "If the career is the husband's, the wife can merge her own with it, if it is to be the wife's as it undoubtedly will be in an increasing proportion of cases, then the husband may, with no sacrifice of self-respect or of recognition by the community, permit himself to be the less prominent and distinguished member of the combination."

Florence proved to be a successful First Lady who was well liked by both the American public and the press. Of course, it helped that she had run a newspaper before and knew how to interact with reporters. She quickly succeeded in creating a good relationship with reporters. She remembered their names, invited them on cruises on the presidential yacht, and enjoyed giving personal interviews. The media in turn gave her good press.

One of her first acts was to open up the White House to the public, which had been closed because of Woodrow Wilson's illness (see Chapter 12). A new record for visitors was set right way with 7,000 people visiting. She greeted them and shook their hands. She gave public concerts on the White House lawn and brought back the White House Easter Egg Roll. Also she got rid of the sheep, giving the White House a more stately appearance. The American public loved her.

REMEMBER

Another passion of hers was to help veterans. Florence visited veteran's hospitals and held garden parties for veterans at the White House; if she saw a veteran walking and struggling, she'd have the presidential car stop to give the veteran a ride.

In September of 1922, Florence got really ill with nephritis. The whole country prayed for her, and mass prayers took place at movie theaters and other large places. She recovered after she was treated by Dr. Charles Mayo, the cofounder of the Mayo Clinic.

## Dying during their first term

In the summer of 1923, Florence and Warren took a trip across the United States to Alaska. The president stopped regularly to give speeches. Florence was the first First Lady to visit Alaska. That was about 15,000 miles by train. Warren hadn't been feeling well for most of the trip, and then he died suddenly in the Palace Hotel in San Francisco on August 2, 1923, at the age of 58. His death was blamed on food poisoning, and the story goes that the president and his entourage ate crab meat in Alaska and everybody got sick and recovered. Only the president didn't recover. It turned out that the president very likely didn't eat crab meat. Today, most historians believe that President Harding, who had a history of high blood pressure and heart problems, had a heart attack. Some, however, blame Florence.

Ironically, there was a coffin on board the train. It was for Florence because her health was worse, and White House staff had feared she might die on the trip. She didn't, but her husband did.

Florence stayed strong and is quoted as saying "I have to plan the funeral; I will not break down." She took her husband's coffin back by train to Washington, D.C., and millions of people lined up to pray and sing hymns for the dead president.

**FIRST
LADY LORE**

After President Harding died, some people accused Florence of poisoning him, to either protect his reputation or to punish him for his affairs. She did act a little suspicious after he died. She had him embalmed right away and allowed for no autopsy. Then after getting back to the White House, she burned a whole bunch of letters and files. It turned out that the materials she burned were very likely associated with the many scandals during the Harding administration that were about to be publicized.

**TECHNICAL
STUFF**

Following are the major scandals during the Harding administration:

>> Charles Forbes, the head of the Veterans Bureau, defrauded the government of $200 million. President Harding allowed him to flee the country. When he returned, years later, he went to jail. Charles Forbes was the first U.S. Cabinet member to be sentenced to jail.

>> Harry M. Daugherty, the attorney general, sold alcohol during Prohibition. During Prohibition, it was illegal to make or distribute alcohol.

>> Albert B. Fall, the secretary of the interior, was involved in the Teapot Dome Scandal. Teapot Dome was a federal facility where the U.S. Navy drilled for and stored oil. In 1922, Albert Fall leased the facility to two oil companies that paid him $400,000. He went to jail for his actions in 1929.

After burying her husband, Florence's health took a turn for the worse. Her kidney ailments came back, and she died on November 21, 1924, at the age of 64. She was buried next to President Warren Harding in Marion, Ohio. Florence and Warren to this day are the only President and First Lady to both die before their term was up.

# Grace Goodhue Coolidge (1879–1957)

Grace Goodhue (see Figure 13-2) was born on January 3, 1879, in Burlington, Vermont. She was the only child of Andrew Goodhue, a mechanical engineer and steamboat inspector for the Lake Champlain Transportation Company in Vermont, and Lemira B. Goodhue, a homemaker. After graduating from high school in Burlington, she attended the University of Vermont while living at home. She was a well-liked university student; she was outgoing and lively, and people enjoyed being around her.

**FIGURE 13-2:**
Grace Goodhue
Coolidge.

*Source: Library of Congress, Prints & Photographs Division, Reproduction number LC-DIG-hec-34357 (digital file from original negative)*

**FIRST LADY LORE**

Grace cofounded Pi Beta Phi, the first Greek sorority for women in the United States. After she became First Lady, the sorority was asked to present the official First Lady Portrait to her. All 1,300 sorority sisters showed up that day, and it became the largest group of women ever assembled at the White House.

Grace graduated in 1902 and was the first First Lady to graduate from a public university. Instead of getting married or staying at home, she wanted to leave the State of Vermont and start a career. Her parents reluctantly agreed, and Grace moved to Massachusetts to be trained as a teacher for the deaf at Clarke School for the Deaf in Northampton, Massachusetts.

It is here where Grace met Calvin Coolidge. He was a young attorney and lived across from her in a boarding house. One day, Grace was walking down the street, and she saw a young man in a window shaving in a room while wearing long underwear and a hat. Grace laughed out loud, and Calvin noticed her and was embarrassed. He inquired who she was so he could explain himself to her. After he got her name, he arranged for a meeting and told her that he always wore a hat while shaving so that his hair wouldn't fall into his face.

Calvin and Grace then started dating. They were the exact opposites of each other. Grace was outgoing and fun, and Calvin was very reserved and didn't talk much. Grace's mother didn't like the relationship and opposed their marriage. Grace didn't listen to her, and the two got married on October 4, 1905.

**FIRST
LADY LORE**

When they returned from their honeymoon in Montreal, Calvin gave Grace 52 pairs of socks that had to be mended. He was so cheap, he had saved socks with holes for years hoping that his future wife would mend them for him.

## Being a politician's wife

Grace and Calvin had two sons, and then Calvin entered politics. In 1907, he was elected to the Massachusetts legislature but didn't want to relocate the whole family because it cost too much. His decision worked out well for him, because he only served one term and then became the mayor of Northampton, where Grace and the kids lived. Then, in 1912, he was elected to the State Senate. Again he didn't move his family, but at least he went home on the weekends to spend time with the two boys and give Grace a break.

Grace was totally apolitical. She enjoyed raising her two sons and playing baseball with them. She notes in her autobiography that her husband never discussed politics with her. Instead, she had to rely on the local newspapers to find out about his political decisions.

When Calvin was elected governor of Massachusetts, he still refused to relocate the family because it was too expensive. He soon acquired the reputation of a cost cutter and penny pincher, which actually helped his political career. However, he had one weakness: He enjoyed buying expensive clothes and hats for his wife.

Then in 1920, Calvin became the vice presidential candidate for Warren G. Harding. Now the Coolidges had to move to Washington, D.C., and the media suddenly focused on the new Second Lady. In 1923, while President Harding was touring the U.S. and got ill, Grace and Calvin were vacationing on the family farm in Vermont, where Calvin's dad lived. In the middle of the night, a messenger arrived, waking everybody to tell them the President had died. Calvin's dad, a notary public, swore in his own son as President of the United States, and suddenly Grace was First Lady of the United States.

## Experiencing tragedy

Grace's first term as First Lady was tough and tragic. Calvin had to deal with all the scandals from the Harding administration (see earlier in this chapter), and a mourning period for the dead President had to be observed. Finally, in early 1924, the Coolidges began to host again. Grace was well prepared to function as First Lady. Afterall, she had been the First Lady of Massachusetts. It was Grace who started the tradition of inviting celebrities, such as Will Rogers and Charles Lindbergh, to official dinners, which has continued to this day.

FIRST
LADY LORE

Calvin was always afraid of financial or personal scandals during his administration because of all the scandals during the Harding administration. So, when Grace went hiking with a secret service agent in South Dakota, suddenly rumors arose about a possible relationship between the two. Even though this was totally false, Calvin was furious and fired the secret service agent.

REMEMBER

Grace Coolidge and Florence Harding never got along. Florence was quite jealous of Grace, who was a lot younger, and she wanted to replace Calvin as vice president to get rid of Grace.

The press loved Grace. She was sincere, someone who had dedicated her life to helping deaf people.

Then tragedy struck. Their younger son Calvin Jr. played tennis without wearing socks in his sneakers. He developed a blister on his toe. He didn't think much about it, but then the blister got infected. He didn't tell anyone about the blister, and the infection went into his bloodstream. The result was blood poisoning, which was diagnosed way too late, and Calvin Jr. died. This shocked the country and the world. Grace wrote a memorial poem for her son, which was published in *Good Housekeeping* in 1929 after she had left office.

## Working as a hostess and an advocate

Grace wasn't really involved in politics. However, she did make appearances and took photographs to increase female turnout in presidential elections. She also hired two secretaries to take on hosting functions and curtailed the times people could come and visit the White House.

Grace was a lifelong advocate for the deaf. She brought deaf children with disabilities and veterans with disabilities to the White House to highlight their needs to the American public. Helen Keller, who was both deaf and blind and was an advocate for the deaf, visited her frequently. Calvin knew how passionate Grace was about this cause, and when he was raising money for his presidential library, he collected about $2 million; he suddenly changed his mind and decided to give it to the Clarke School for the Deaf in Northampton, Massachusetts, where his wife started her teaching career.

**FIRST LADY LORE**

Grace Coolidge and her husband were animal lovers. While at the White House, someone sent her a raccoon for Thanksgiving dinner — yes, the raccoon was supposed to be one of the dishes. Grace was outraged and decided to raise the raccoon, which she called Rebecca, at the White House (see Figure 13-3). Grace even designed a small house for Rebecca to live in. She had many pets in the White House, but her favorite was her beloved Rebecca.

**FIGURE 13-3:**
Grace Coolidge and Rebecca the raccoon.

*Source: Library of Congress, Prints & Photographs Division, Reproduction number LC-DIG-hec-34437 (digital file from original negative)*

## Retiring and living a long life

In 1928, Calvin Coolidge decided not to run for another term. He and Grace went back home to Northampton and bought an estate called the Beeches. They enjoyed their retirement together, but then Calvin died in 1933.

Grace continued working on behalf of deaf people, and she even urged the U.S. to get involved in WWII and championed a bill, the Wagner–Rogers Bill of 1939, that would have brought Jewish children to the U.S. However, Congress refused to pass the bill. She further started writing articles for *American Magazine* in which she discussed her life and her role as First Lady. The articles provided historians with a plethora of insights into the role of First Ladies.

Grace stayed active. She rode in an airplane for the first time in 1936 on her way to tour Europe, and she spent a lot of time with her son John and her grandchildren. Grace was an avid Boston Red Sox fan. She went to the team's games, listened to them on the radio, and even though the Red Sox didn't make it, she attended the 1949 World Series between the Brooklyn Dodgers and the New York Yankees. Grace Coolidge died on July 8, 1957, at the age of 78.

The best story about Grace and Calvin is the following: Two men were talking about the couple and how different they were. The first one mentioned how Grace was a teacher for the deaf and how she taught the deaf to speak. The other man responded, "Why didn't she teach her husband?"

# Louise Henry Hoover (1874–1944)

Louise Henry (see Figure 13-4) was born on March 29, 1874, in Waterloo, Iowa. Her father, Charles D. Henry, was a banker and an outdoorsman. He really had wanted a boy, and so he raised Louise, called Lou for most of her life, as a tomboy and took her on hunting and hiking trips. She loved every minute of it. The love of the outdoors stuck with Lou for the rest of her life.

**FIGURE 13-4:**
Louise Henry
Hoover.

Source: Library of Congress, Prints & Photographs Division,
Reproduction number LC-USZ62-25811
(b&w film copy neg. of detail)LC-USZ62-21404
(b&w film copy neg.)

When Lou was ten, her dad moved the family to California, because of a job opportunity and because the weather was better suited for her mom's health issues. They ended up in Monterey, California, and Lou often went hunting and fishing with her dad. Being outdoors so much, she became interested in the various rock formations and minerals in California, and after attending a lecture on geology, she decided to become a geologist and not a teacher as she had planned. At this time, there were no degreed female geologists in the United States, but there was a program in geology at Stanford University that was open to all genders.

So Lou enrolled at Stanford University to study geology. She was the only woman in the geology program. It was there where she met Herbert Hoover, who was a senior majoring in mining engineering and was a laboratory assistant at the time. She met him when she was in his laboratory section. After Herbert graduated, he left California and became a mining engineer in Nevada and then Australia, while Lou continued her studies at Stanford. They wrote each other letters for two years, and after Herbert was offered a job in China to evaluate the conditions of that country's mines, he proposed to her in a letter, writing: "Heading to China, will you join me?" She said yes. The two were married on February 10, 1899, and then left for China.

**FIRST LADY LORE**

Lou Hoover was the first woman in the United States to receive a college degree in geology from Stanford University.

## Carrying a pistol

When she arrived in China, Lou immediately immersed herself in the Chinese culture. She learned Chinese and went with her husband on mining expeditions.

**FIRST LADY LORE**

To this day, Lou Hoover is the only First Lady to speak Mandarin.

Then in 1900, the Boxer rebellion happened. The Harmonious Fists, called by the West the "Boxers," were Chinese nationalists, who objected to foreign domination of their country and wanted to get rid of all foreigners in China. The Boxers began violent attacks against foreigners, and Lou and Herbert were trapped in the small town of Tienjin, now called Tianjin. Fearing for their lives, Westerners living there had barricaded themselves on the edge of the city. Herbert and Lou were among them, and Lou started to carry a pistol to defend herself. Often, they were under siege, and she manned the barricades fully armed. In addition, she also helped the Red Cross get supplies to people and helped out in the local hospital, dodging bullets in the process.

**IN THEIR WORDS**

Most people would consider this a horrific experience, but not Lou. She wrote to one of her friends: "You have missed the most exciting summer. You should have been here."

# Traveling the world and becoming wealthy

In 1900, the Hoovers moved to London where Herbert worked for the British mining company Bewick and Moreing and soon became a partner. Herbert, or Bert as Lou called him, was promoted several times by the company and was sent all over the world to inspect and supervise mining sites. In 1908, Herbert started his own mining consulting firm, and the family lived in London for the next seven years. Lou got to travel to Europe, Asia, and even Africa. They had two sons, and they traveled with them everywhere. For example, in 1910 alone, she and her sons traveled to France, Russia, Burma, Japan, and Korea. The Hoovers became wealthy and soon were millionaires.

**FIRST LADY LORE**

Lou Hoover translated the classic mining manual *De Re Metallica* published in 1556 in Latin into English. When it was published in 1912, it won the Mining and Metallurgical Society's gold award.

Then WWI broke out. The Hoovers were still in London, and Herbert was put in charge of helping thousands of Americans suddenly stranded in Europe. Lou helped and also assisted her husband with famine relief after the war in Europe when Herbert was in charge of the American Relief Association (ARA) to fight famine in Europe.

From 1914 to 1919, Herbert headed the Commission for the Relief of Belgium. He supervised the distribution of millions of tons of aid to Belgium and northern France. While he was busy in Europe, Lou traveled between London and their home in California. She raised money back home to feed starving Europeans, and when in London, she was involved with the Red Cross and even set up a knitting factory to help out unemployed British women.

# Getting into politics

President Wilson was impressed with Herbert Hoover's activities, so in 1917, he called him back home to become the U.S. food administrator. This position required Herbert to make sure that the United States could feed its military and the Allied troops in Europe. He was so successful that President Wilson sent him back to Europe after WWI to help starving Europeans. As the head of the American Relief Administration, Herbert provided food to 300 million people across Europe. By 1920, his job was done. It was time to move on.

When they moved back to California, they designed and built their dream house and believed they were back for good. Things changed quickly. In 1921, Herbert Hoover was appointed Secretary of Commerce, and he and Lou moved to the capital. She right way got involved in civic activities, becoming the president of the Girl Scouts of America for three years. She continued to be involved with the organization for the rest of her life.

During the 1920s, first as the wife of a cabinet member and then First Lady, Lou Hoover broke several traditional grounds. She invited pregnant women to the White House for the first time and advocated for women to continue their careers after having children. She pushed her husband to issue Civil Service Rule VII, which made it illegal to discriminate on the basis of gender, and urged women to vote and become active in politics. She even joined the League of Women Voters, an organization that provides voters with information on elections and candidates. Also, she was the first First Lady to drive herself around the capital.

**REMEMBER**

After the Harding scandals (see earlier in this chapter), Lou Hoover organized a National Women's Conference on Law Enforcement. More than 500 women from across the country attended to discuss the responsibility of women to speak out on the dangers of a dishonest and corrupt government. At the conference, she told the audience: "The women of the country are tired of seeing the law of our land ignored."

## Being charitable

In 1928, Herbert Hoover won the presidential election in a landslide. Lou Hoover was now the First Lady of the United States. She moved away from more feminist topics to more traditional ones, such as being physically active, even during pregnancy.

After the Great Depression hit in 1929, she went on the radio to urge Americans to be charitable and help out the needy (see Figure 13-5). Lou was the first First Lady to go on the radio and ask Americans to help those less fortunate. Thousands of Americans wrote her letters for help. She had to hire a secretary to answer them all. Often, she used her own money to help the needy. Whenever someone needed money badly to feed their children or provide for housing, she sent them money. Many people, after they recovered economically, sent her checks to repay their debt. She never cashed them, and Herbert found a full box of uncashed checks after she had died in 1944. Neither he nor the media had been aware of her kindness.

The job of President and First Lady was very demanding, especially after the Great Depression had hit in 1929. To get out of town, the Hoovers bought a property in the Shenandoah Mountains. Lou designed a house there, and they went as often as they could.

Lou noticed how poor and uneducated the locals were. The State of Virginia refused to help, so she and Herbert started the Hoover School, also called the President's Mountain School. They used their own money to build the school, and then the State of Virginia took over to hire and pay for teachers. Nobody ever knew about this, because the Hoovers didn't like dealing with the media. Lou, for example, didn't allow the press to cover her grandchildren or family events in the White House. They believed in privacy, and, of course, they were not career politicians but had an administrative background, so they were not used to constantly dealing with the media.

Source: Library of Congress, Prints & Photographs Division,
Reproduction number LC-DIG-hec-36310
(digital file from original negative)

**FIGURE 13-5:**
Louise Hoover on the radio.

## Dealing with staff

The Hoovers paid for their own secretaries and staff in the White House to save the country money. Both were very demanding of their employees. For example, during dinner parties, Lou relied on hand signals to communicate with the staff. Each raised finger or dropped handkerchief was a command. In addition, they always had people over. Lou enjoyed company, and the staff had to work all the time and often on short notice.

**FIRST
LADY LORE**

Lou spoke five languages, and whenever she didn't want people in the White House to know what she was saying, she talked to her husband in Chinese.

In 1928, the first African American Congressman in 28 years, Oscar De Priest, was elected from Illinois. Lou had been inviting the wives of Congressmen for tea and now faced a problem. A lot of the wives of Southern lawmakers objected to having a Black woman attend the tea. So Lou carefully sounded out the wives of Congressmen on whether they'd be willing to have tea with a Black woman. Afterward, she scheduled a special tea for Mrs. De Priest and a few select wives. After this was publicized by the media, Southern lawmaker threatened to censure Lou for having the audacity to have tea with a Black woman.

## Retiring in style

After Herbert Hoover lost reelection in 1932, Lou moved back to Palo Alto and stayed active with civic activities, such as the Girls Scouts and using her own money to fund a musical community for Palo Alto. At the same time, she still loved the outdoors. She went hiking, camping, and horseback riding until she was in her late 60s.

Herbert, however, didn't enjoy these activities much; he wanted more cultural and intellectual stimulation. So he moved to New York City, and the two lived apart for a few years. In 1940, Lou decided to join him in New York City. There, they lived in an apartment at the Waldorf Towers. On January 7, 1944, she had dinner with a friend and had just got back home. She went to her room, and when Herbert came to check on her, she laid dead on the floor. She had a heart attack and died right away. Lou Hoover was 69 years old. She was buried in Palo Alto, but her body was moved to West Branch, Iowa, where she was buried next to her husband who lived another 20 years after her death.

# 5
# Modern First Ladies

**IN THIS PART . . .**

Explore the modern era of U.S. First Ladies, starting with Eleanor Roosevelt.

Find out about Bess Truman's, Mamie Eisenhower's, and Jackie Kennedy's influence on the time they filled the role.

See how Claudia "Lady Bird" Johnson, Pat Nixon, and Betty Ford championed projects dear to their hearts.

Look at the grace and glamour of First Ladies Rosalynn Carter, Nancy Reagan, and Barbara Bush.

Understand how Hillary Clinton leveraged her time as First Lady for her own political career.

Discover how Laura Bush and Michelle Obama utilized the power of the First Lady position.

Compare and contrast the most recent First Ladies to hold the position: Melania Trump and Jill Biden.

Chapter **14**

# First Lady of the World

Eleanor Roosevelt was the most politically active First Lady in American history. She held press conferences, wrote articles for newspapers and magazines, and dedicated her whole life to help the economically and socially disadvantaged. She promoted civil rights and lobbied for equal pay for women. She argued with her husband over New Deal policies that she considered unfair to women, and won.

Eleanor further opened up the media to women, holding press conferences for only female reporters. She did her best to make sure that women got involved in politics, and by the time she left office in 1945, being involved in politics wasn't considered unladylike anymore.

Eleanor was a true humanitarian and is ranked one of the top three accomplished American First Ladies. She was the longest-serving First Lady, serving almost four terms from 1933 until 1945, when Franklin died in his fourth term. She pursued an agenda ranging from domestic social and economic issues to international concerns. She was independent, spoke her mind publicly, and sometimes was at odds with her husband and his administration. She definitely rejected the subordinate role most First Ladies had accepted to this point and set a new standard for First Ladies.

This chapter explores all these attributes and more about First Lady Eleanor Roosevelt.

# Anna Eleanor Roosevelt (1884–1962)

Anna Eleanor Roosevelt (see Figure 14-1) was born on October 11, 1884, in New York City. Her father, Elliott, was the wealthy brother of President Theodore Roosevelt. He, like his brother, was a great outdoorsman who loved to travel and hunt. Her mother, Anna, was a wealthy socialite and beauty queen, who was more interested in partying than raising her children. She used to call young Eleanor "Granny" because of the way she looked and dressed. Not surprisingly, Eleanor had self-image problems growing up. Her mother died when Eleanor was only eight years old. Her dad spoiled her as much as he could, but he was often away hunting or getting treatment for his alcoholism. He died two years later in 1894, and suddenly Eleanor and her two younger brothers were all alone. They went to live with her grandmother who was very strict.

**FIGURE 14-1:** Anna Eleanor Roosevelt.

Source: Library of Congress, Prints & Photographs Division, Reproduction number LC-DIG-ppmsca-30587 (digital file from original item)

Eleanor, who wasn't very social and was always very conscious of her looks, lived a quiet and lonely life. She rode her horses and taught herself French. Then in 1899, when she was 15, she was sent to an expensive finishing school called Allenswood Academy in England, located where Wimbledon is today. Here, she began to develop her self-esteem. The headmistress of the school, Marie Souvestre, noticed how smart she was and encouraged her to be more social and more self-confident. She took Eleanor with her on trips throughout Europe and tutored her academically.

**IN THEIR WORDS**

Eleanor once said: "I have finally learned that I have a brain."

# Marrying a Roosevelt and Living with a Dominant Mother-in-Law

Eleanor wanted to stay in London and become a teacher in the city. However, at almost 18, Eleanor had to go back to New York City to have a coming-out party, as was expected of rich girls at the time, and she was expected to go to a ton of teas, parties, and balls to hopefully find a husband. At one of these events, she met Franklin Delano Roosevelt, a young Harvard student who she was distantly related to. He was her fifth cousin, and the two had played together as kids. They started to get reconnected in 1903, wrote each other letters, and began to date. During this time, Eleanor taught immigrant children who lived in the poorest parts of town.

Franklin proposed the next year, but his mother, Sara Roosevelt, objected. Despite her objections, the couple announced their engagement in the fall of 1904. Afterward, Franklin began to study law at Columbia University, while Eleanor continued to teach. They were finally married on March 17, 1905, and her uncle President Theodore Roosevelt walked her down the aisle.

Sara Roosevelt begrudgingly agreed to have her son marry Eleanor. However, she dominated the couple's lives in their first years of marriage, sharing a home with them and even rearranging furniture in Eleanor's rooms. In addition, she forced Eleanor to quit teaching because she believed that Eleanor could bring home diseases from poor children. It wasn't until 1910 when Franklin won a New York State Senate seat that Eleanor could move away from her domineering mother-in-law. She said: "For the first time I was going to live on my own."

**FIRST LADY LORE**

Eleanor Roosevelt is the only First Lady who didn't have to change her last name after she was married. She already had the same last name as her husband.

# Moving in Social Circles

In 1910, when the Democratic Party approached Franklin Roosevelt and asked him to run for the New York State Senate, he had great name recognition, sharing a last name with the recent two-term president Theodore Roosevelt, plus he had the money to pay for his own campaign. Franklin narrowly won the seat, and the whole family moved to Albany, the capital of New York.

In the New York State Senate, Franklin turned out to be a crusader, pushing for social and economic reforms. He refused to submit to party pressure, acting more like an Independent than a Democrat. Before he won reelection in 1912, he started to support Woodrow Wilson, another Democratic reformer, which turned out to be a good political move when Wilson gave him a job after becoming president in 1913.

President Wilson rewarded Franklin for his loyalty by naming him assistant secretary of the Navy. He held this position for the next seven years. Eleanor moved the whole family to Washington, D.C., and became active in the capital's social circles, hosting parties and dinners. After the U.S. entered WWI in 1917, she started to volunteer for the Red Cross. In 1918, the Democratic Party asked Franklin to run for governor of New York, but he declined. However, in 1920, the Democrats needed a young, energetic vice presidential candidate to balance their fairly bland candidate for the presidency, James Cox. They picked Franklin Roosevelt. He and Eleanor campaigned their heart out, but the Democratic ticket lost badly to the Republican candidate, Warren G. Harding.

REMEMBER

Eleanor Roosevelt owed a lot to Louis Howe, an old newspaperman and campaign manager for Franklin. Running Franklin's campaign in 1920, he had a chance to observe Eleanor on the campaign trail and discovered how useful she could be for Franklin's future campaigns. After Franklin got polio, Eleanor had to step in and be not only a supportive spouse but also an active spouse to keep his political chances alive. Howe encouraged Eleanor to take speaking lessons to lower her high pitch and taught her how to get comfortable speaking in front of large crowds. After Franklin got elected president in 1932, Howe promised Eleanor that she was next. He promised to make her president in ten years. Howe never got around to keeping his promise, though, because he died in 1936.

# Getting Active in Politics in the 1920s

Between 1906 and 1916, Eleanor had six children, with five surviving into adulthood. During this time, she showed no interest in politics and felt unqualified to even debate and discuss it. She lived for her family and children. She wasn't even interested in women's suffrage and stated that she didn't know the difference between federal and state politics. Two events changed all of this. First, there was the American entrance into WWI in 1917; and second, there was her husband's infidelity, which she discovered in 1918.

Eleanor had lived in Washington, D.C., since 1913, finally getting some distance from her domineering mother-in-law. She had observed how other politicians' wives worked for charities and were involved in helping the less fortunate. When WWI broke out, she decided that she had to be one of them. There was a shortage of male workers, and women had to take their place. She began to work for the Red Cross, helped set up canteens for servicemen, and visited wounded soldiers in hospitals. To her great surprise, she enjoyed every minute of it.

In 1918, she opened one of Franklin's letters by mistake and found out about his affair with her social secretary, Lucy Mercer. She offered Franklin a divorce. He considered it, but his mother said no and even threatened that if he got divorced, she'd cut him off, and he would suddenly be poor. So Franklin stayed married. He apologized to Eleanor and promised not to see Lucy again (which turned out be a lie), and she forgave him. The two stayed married, but their marriage became more of a political arrangement. They stayed together for the sake of politics, both hoping to climb the political ladder of the country. They learned to live separately and were never together for more than six months for most of the 1920s.

REMEMBER

Eleanor burned the love letters she and Franklin had written to each other when she found out about his relationship with Lucy Mercer. Franklin, on the other hand, continued his relationship with Lucy, and she was the one who was by his side when he died, not Eleanor.

Eleanor threw herself into her work. She learned how to type and do shorthand. She attended conferences, such as the International Congress for Women Workers, and joined the League of Women Voters, for whom she put together monthly reports on what was happening in Congress.

Eleanor became a Democratic Party operative. She edited national Democratic party publications, sat on the board of labor unions, and served on the Democratic Platform Committee in 1926. At the same time, she taught civics and history at a girls school in New York City. By the time Franklin was the presidential nominee for the Democratic Party, Eleanor was a political force of her own. During the 1932 campaign, newspapers ran stories not only about Franklin but also on Eleanor's political career. The philosophy Eleanor had decided to live by can be summed up by the following quote:

IN THEIR
WORDS

"The future is literally in our hands to mold as we like, . . . but we cannot wait until tomorrow."

In 1925, the Roosevelts built a second home far away from Franklin's domineering mom. It was a fairly nice cottage with a pool, and that is where Eleanor hung out and relaxed. The property was along the Val-Kill Creek, and Eleanor called it just Val-Kill. Here, they met friends and political cronies. Val-Kill became Eleanor's main house and office after 1937. She invited a lot of famous people, including Winston Churchill and John Steinbeck.

# Becoming First Lady of New York

In 1921, Franklin was afflicted with polio, which partially paralyzed him for the rest of his life. He needed a cane and leg braces to walk. Eleanor stood by him and helped as much as she could, handling his day-to-day medical care. She encouraged him to continue in politics after his mom told him to retiree, live well, and enjoy his money. When asked whether his disease had affected Franklin's mental state, Eleanor replied:

"Yes, anyone who has gone through great suffering is bound to have a greater sympathy and understanding of the problems of mankind."

When the governor of New York, Al Smith, received the Democratic presidential nomination in 1928, he gave up the governorship of New York State. Smith asked his friend Franklin Roosevelt to run for the position. Franklin was reluctant, but Eleanor convinced him to become a candidate. Eleanor drove him to campaign appearances and even picked up voters and drove them to the polls. Whenever Franklin was unable to give a scheduled speech, she'd step in and give a speech on his behalf. Soon, she noticed she was really good at it and started giving her own speeches. Franklin won the governorship, and the Roosevelts were back in public life.

When it comes to politics, Eleanor once said, "Women must learn to play the game as men do."

After being reelected as governor of New York, Roosevelt became a viable candidate for the 1932 Democratic presidential nomination. Not only was he a great speaker who was well known to the electorate, but, as governor of New York, he also could deliver the largest state in the United States at the time.

Eleanor was excited about the prospect of being First Lady. As soon as Franklin announced that he was running for president in 1932, she started writing biographical profiles for him and helped him with his campaign appearances and his speeches. Franklin later admitted that he rarely gave a speech that Eleanor hadn't read in advance and commented on.

# Being an Activist First Lady

For the first 100 days of her husband's administration, Eleanor (see Figure 14-2) was trying to find the role she wanted to play in the White House. She offered to take an official administrative or advisory role in her husband's administration but was rejected. After receiving reports on the miserable conditions in the country she started her fact-finding tours of the country in the summer of 1933.

**FIGURE 14-2:**
First Lady Anna
Eleanor
Roosevelt.

Source: Library of Congress, Prints & Photographs Division,
Reproduction number LC-DIG-hec-37027
(digital file from original negative)

In 1933 alone, she traveled 38,000 miles. After seeing the misery many Americans faced, she became active in trying to improve the livelihood of poor Americans. She had to stop teaching in New York City when she became First Lady and so had more time to focus on all her other activities.

**IN THEIR
WORDS**

After becoming First Lady, Eleanor said, "There may be ways in which I can be useful."

Soon Eleanor became the liberal in the White House so Franklin could appeal to more conservative voters, especially Southern Democrats without whose support Franklin couldn't win reelection. By 1941, after her husband had won an unprecedented third term, she was considered one of the most powerful people in Washington, D.C., and was called a Cabinet member without portfolio and a part of Franklin's kitchen cabinet.

## Advocating for women's rights

In her speeches, Eleanor advocated for women's rights and equal pay for women. One of her major success stories was to kill legislation called the Economy Act. It would have cut the federal payroll by 25 percent, and whenever a husband and wife were both employed by the federal government, the wife would have lost her job and not the husband. Eleanor lobbied her husband and his Cabinet hard, and the Act was withdrawn.

Also, during the Roosevelt administration, the first woman in U.S. history was appointed to serve in a presidential Cabinet. Frances Perkins served as secretary of labor throughout Roosevelt's administration. In addition, the first two women were appointed ministers (the position is compatible to today's ambassador) to head the U.S. diplomatic teams in Denmark and Norway.

Eleanor wasn't a radical feminist, meaning that she believed in slowly empowering women until they held positions in society that they could use to start a political career. She said: "The presidency will never go to a woman, until women have first established themselves in prominent business and government positions."

**REMEMBER**

To show the world that women were able to fly planes as well as men, Eleanor flew with her good friend Amelia Earhart. Her husband, however, opposed her getting a pilot's license herself.

## Advocating for civil rights

Eleanor became active in Franklin's New Deal programs. She championed the National Youth Administration, which funded part-time jobs for high school and college students, and she insisted on having noted Black educator Mary McLeod Bethune head the program.

In 1939, Eleanor resigned out of protest from the Daughters of the American Revolution. The organization, to which every First Lady automatically belonged, didn't allow Marian Anderson, a famous Black opera singer, to perform in Constitution Hall, owned by the organization. Eleanor believed that was unacceptable and invited her to the White House instead to perform for the King and Queen of England. Eleanor also quietly worked behind the scenes promoting an outdoor concert for Marian at the Lincoln Memorial to a crowd of 75,000 with a national radio audience.

She then wrote a column titled "My Day," which was widely published in the United States, explaining her decision to the American public.

Eleanor further made sure to lobby on behalf of African Americans. She invited prominent African Americans to the White House, and Roosevelt's administration consulted with the National Association for the Advancement of Colored People (NAACP) on policies impacting them. During WWII, Eleanor supported the Tuskegee airmen, a group of African American military pilots and airmen, even flying with them.

REMEMBER

Many people hated Eleanor Roosevelt, including Southern Democrats who were segregationist and conservative Republicans who didn't like the New Deal. J. Edgar Hoover, the head of the FBI, was asked to find incriminating information on her to silence her and collected over 3,000 files on Eleanor.

Eleanor refused to have secret service protection in the White House, or when she traveled, even after retirement. Though the Ku Klux Klan had put a bounty on her head in the 1950s, Eleanor refused protection instead often carrying a Smith & Wesson .22 pistol. The secret service had told her that she could travel by herself only if she carried and learned how to shoot a pistol. So she did. From 1933 until 1962, she traveled without protection because she felt that was the only way to get close to the average American.

## Working the media

Eleanor Roosevelt was very active in both newspapers and magazines and also the radio. By 1936, she was a syndicated columnist. She offered her ideas on policies in her syndicated newspaper column "My Day" six days a week from 1936 until her death in 1962. She also wrote an advice column for *Woman's Home Companion* and later *McCall's* magazine titled "If You Ask Me." In 1937, she published her autobiography *This Is My Story*, which became a bestseller. Throughout her life, Eleanor wrote 8,000 newspaper columns and more than 500 articles, gave 75 speeches annually, and wrote 150 letters each day without any secretarial help. Being a syndicated columnist and writing a bestselling book generated a nice income for Eleanor. Being already very wealthy, she didn't take the money but donated all of her income to charitable organizations such as the Red Cross.

FIRST
LADY LORE

Even though Eleanor was independently wealthy, she was frugal when it came to clothing. Instead of spending thousands of dollars on dresses as other First Ladies had done, she often bought inexpensive dresses for about $10.

In 1933, Eleanor held her first press conference, hosting 35 female journalists. She wanted to make sure that female journalists were able to get firsthand information to write stories, which in turn forced the male-dominated field to hire more female journalists. Overall, Eleanor held 348 press conferences throughout her career, and most of them were closed to men.

Also in 1933, Eleanor started to be on the radio. She actually had her own show on the radio before Franklin began to use radio for his famous fireside chats.

**FIRST LADY LORE**

Lorena Hickok was the leading female political journalist at the time. She was the only woman who could get front-page newspaper coverage. In the 1932 presidential campaign, she was assigned to cover Eleanor and fell in love with her. For decades, historians didn't know whether the love was just emotional or if it became physical. Hick, as Eleanor called her, taught Eleanor how to deal with the press and define her own message. As soon as Eleanor became First Lady, Hick resigned her day job and moved into the White House. She lived there for years, working for both Eleanor and Franklin and later the Democratic National Committee. She even had Sunday dinner with them and traveled with the First Lady. It was said that Eleanor wouldn't make a major career decision without Hick. Today, there are 3,000 letters between Eleanor and Hick, confirming the love between the two and that physical relations did happen.

After the 1940 election, Eleanor took the unpaid federal position of Assistant Director of the Office of Civil Defense (OCD). This made her the first First Lady to have a federal position within her husband's administration. Her choice turned out to be controversial when she appointed friends to positions within the agency.

## Supporting the troops

In 1941, after the Japanese had attacked Pearl Harbor, Eleanor addressed the nation before her husband did. In the radio address a few hours after the attack, she attempted to reassure the American people that they were safe and the country was prepared to defend itself.

In addition, as early as 1942, Eleanor traveled to both Europe and the Pacific to support American troops and increase their morale. She went to London and helped out with the local Red Cross, and then in 1943, she toured to see American troops in the Pacific. She actually flew in an uninsulated aircraft, and her eardrums shattered. Despite being deaf in one ear afterward, she continued her trip to visit American troops.

# The Story Isn't Over: Moving on After the White House

In 1945, President Franklin Roosevelt was exhausted when he returned home from the Yalta Conference, which ironed out the details of the end of WWII. He went to Warm Springs, Georgia, for a brief vacation. While sitting for an official presidential portrait, he suddenly complained of headaches. Two hours later, on April 12, 1945, Franklin Delano Roosevelt died of a cerebral hemorrhage. Eleanor wasn't with him at the time, but his mistress, Lucy Mercer, was.

REMEMBER

Throughout his presidency, Franklin and Lucy had seen each other in the White House whenever Eleanor traveled. Even though Franklin had promised Eleanor to end the affair, it continued for the rest of Franklin's life. Lucy was with him when he died and was quickly escorted away by Secret Service agents when Eleanor arrived.

President Truman offered Eleanor to stay longer in the White House, but she left within a week. When she arrived in New York City, she is quoted as saying, "The story is over." This was far from true. After a small funeral service for President Franklin Roosevelt, held in Hyde Park, New York, she was offered to run for Senate or governor or become a college president. She turned down all of these offers and moved back to Val-Kill.

President Truman then appointed her to the first American delegation to the United Nations (U.N.), which had just been established in 1945. Here, she chaired the Human Rights Commission from 1946 until 1953 and was in charge of the Drafting Committee of the Universal Declaration on Human Rights (see Figure 14-3). After 300 meetings and more than 3,000 hours of debate, she got the U.N. to pass the Universal Declaration of Human Rights in 1948. Without her efforts, there would have never been the Universal Declaration on Human Rights. She continued to work at the U.N. until she was almost 70 years old.

Eleanor stayed active in Democratic politics. She worked tirelessly for the Democratic nominee for president in 1952 and 1956, Adlai Stevenson, and then supported John F. Kennedy in 1960. During the Kennedy administration, she served on the board that developed the Peace Corps and then chaired the Presidents Commission on the Status of Women. She died on November 7, 1962, at the age of 78, of tuberculosis.

Eleanor's funeral was attended by three living presidents: Harry Truman, Dwight Eisenhower, and John F. Kennedy. President Kennedy ordered all U.S. flags lowered to half-staff worldwide. In 1963, Eleanor Roosevelt had a 5-cent stamp issued with her image in her honor. Eleanor was the second First Lady, after Martha Washington, to be depicted on a stamp.

**FIGURE 14-3:**
Eleanor Roosevelt
and The Universal
Declaration of
Human Rights.

Source: Library of Congress, Prints & Photographs
Division, Reproduction number LC-USZ62-
107008 (b&w film copy neg.)

Chapter **15**

# Three Cold War First Ladies

This chapter looks at the three First Ladies during the early Cold War years. The first, Elizabeth Truman, who everyone called Bess, was a small-town girl from Missouri, who loved her secluded rural lifestyle and never changed. The second, Mamie Eisenhower was a devoted wife, mother, and grandmother and appealed to traditional women. She was popular, and her image was on campaign buttons and even a piggy bank in the 1952 and 1956 campaigns. She became the country's "mother" and "grandmother," and when asked how she wanted to be remembered, she said: "Just as a good friend." The third, Jacqueline Kennedy, referred to as just Jackie, became a bridge between traditional First Ladies and the modern area. She was only 31 when she became First Lady. She was beautiful and rich and started her own fashion trend. She was covered on TV, and with 90 percent of all Americans owning a TV, America suddenly had a new star.

# Elizabeth Virginia Wallace Truman (1885–1982)

Bess Truman was born Elizabeth Virginia Wallace (see Figure 15-1) on February 13, 1885, to Margaret and David Wallace in Independence, Missouri. Her dad owned a flour business that had made him wealthy, and she grew up comfortably, loving athletics, especially tennis and riding horses.

**FIGURE 15-1:**
Elizabeth Virginia
Wallace Truman.

In 1903, disaster struck. Bess's father died by suicide after his business failed. Bess was deeply affected but decided to never talk about it again. And she didn't. Her daughter, Margaret, believed that it was this event that made Bess so private and was the main reason why she did not want to talk to the press. Bess believed that her dad's death was nobody's business and shouldn't be talked about at all. Her family, her mother and three younger brothers, had to move in with her grandparents. She was 19, and her grandfather decided to enroll her in a finishing school where she learned social graces and domestic tasks and where she was able to finish her education.

## Finding early romance

Bess and Harry Truman first met when they were children. They met at Sunday school when he was six and she was five. Harry developed a crush on Bess right there at the tender age of six and wouldn't change his mind or his feelings for her for the rest of his life. However, his family was poor, and he even had to work in a drugstore as a young boy to help make ends meet. After he graduated high school in 1901, his family had no money to send him to college, so he had to work on the family farm.

Harry was short and nearsighted and loved to play piano and read. Bess was an athlete who rode horses and played whatever sport was in season. They went to school together, became close friends, and then started dating around 1910.

After Bess left for finishing school, Harry moved to Grandview, Missouri, where he worked on the family farm. He met Bess by accident again. He was visiting his aunt in Independence and found out that she had borrowed a cake plate from Bess's mom. So he volunteered to return it, and that is how he met Bess again. He started writing letters to her and visited often. In 1913, he included a marriage proposal in one of his letters. He wrote: "If I bought you a ring, would you wear it on your left hand?"

Bess felt that she was too young to get married and turned him down. Harry was very persistent, and she finally told him in 1917 that she was ready. This time, Harry said no, because his national guard unit was about to be deployed with the U.S. entering WWI. He promised her he would ask again when he returned from the war. He kept his promise, and when he returned from fighting in France, he asked Bess again to marry him. The two got married on June 28, 1919. Both were in their mid-30s, which was considered late for a marriage back then.

Harry opened his men's store the same year, and Beth helped him, keeping inventory and being responsible for advertising.

In 1922, Harry's political career began, and in 1924, the couple's only child, Margaret, was born. Harry's political career suddenly took off. By 1934, he was a U.S. Senator from Missouri.

## Getting into politics

**TECHNICAL STUFF**

In 1924, Harry Truman approached the Pendergast family, the dominant Democratic political family in Missouri, about running for public office. They liked Truman, so they ran him for judge of the eastern part of Jackson County, Missouri, even though he had no background in law. Because the Pendergasts controlled state politics at the time, Harry won the position. Harry excelled as a judge. He actually reduced the county's debt by 60 percent while he was in charge of the infrastructure budget. In 1934, the Pendergast family approached Harry and asked him to run for the U.S. Senate. He accepted and ran a spirited campaign, pledging to support President Roosevelt's New Deal programs. His campaign and his reputation for being an honest man helped him win a position in the Senate.

In 1944, everybody expected Franklin Roosevelt to run for a fourth term. The country was at war, and a change in leadership might have undermined the war effort. The big question was who would be Roosevelt's running mate. The current vice president, Henry Wallace, was a liberal who supported union rights and civil rights, which made him unacceptable to Southern Democrats. So Roosevelt went searching for someone else. He found Harry Truman, who had supported Roosevelt's foreign and domestic policies from the beginning.

Harry really didn't want the job, but he didn't dare turn down his president. So he became the vice presidential nominee for the Democratic Party. He campaigned vigorously for the ticket and became the vice president of the United States in January 1945.

## Being a strong First Lady behind the scenes

Bess was shocked when she suddenly became First Lady, after President Roosevelt had died in office on April 12, 1945. After Harry was elected to the Senate, Bess had moved to Washington, D.C. Harry hired her as his secretary to help with mail. It was the first time that Bess had left Independence, Missouri. She soon found out that she didn't fit in well with the other wives of Congressmen and stopped attending their meetings. She just wanted to be alone with her husband and daughter. When she became First Lady, nobody knew much about her, and that is exactly how it stayed for the next seven years. Bess believed that publicity was undignified and unbecoming of a lady.

Bess Truman had a tough act to follow. With Eleanor Roosevelt being the most activist First Lady in the history of the country, Bess decided she wouldn't even try to top her. When asked about becoming First Lady, Bess said:

**IN THEIR WORDS**

"I was very apprehensive. The country was used to Eleanor Roosevelt. I couldn't possibly be anything like her. I wasn't going down into any coal mines."

At first, Bess agreed to have Eleanor Roosevelt introduce her to reporters. Bess had only one press conference where the questions had to be submitted in writing and she then answered with one or two words. She hated the whole event and never had another press conference after she found out that other former First Ladies didn't meet with the press. So she decided not to either. She canceled her press conferences and never scheduled another one. She told the public:

"You don't need to know me. I am only the president's wife and the mother of his daughter."

When asked, why she didn't want to address the public, Bess said:

"I am not the one who was elected. . . . I have nothing to say to the people."

Bess remained a 19th-century woman, believing a woman shouldn't be publicly involved in politics, and she stayed behind her husband's shadow. She rarely issued statements, and if she did, it was because she had to and it was for nonpolitical causes, such as appealing for financial support for the Girls Scouts or the March of Dimes.

Privately, it was a different story. With Bess not interested in being publicly involved with politics, people assumed that she wasn't well informed and didn't know much about ongoing issues. They were completely wrong. Bess was closely involved with Harry's work. She edited his reports and speeches and discussed policy options with him. President Truman once said: "I never make a report or deliver a speech without her editing it." He discussed not only the Korean War with her but also the dropping of the atomic bomb and the Marshall Plan. As he said: "Her judgment has always been good." In addition, Bess was the only one who could control her husband's temper, which often got him into trouble.

Bess did the absolute minimum to fulfill her social obligations as First Lady but clearly didn't enjoy it. She answered her correspondence and entertained at the White House but infrequently and in simple ways. She handled the White House bookkeeping and supervised the daily menu. In private, she was funny, and the White House staff loved her. The Trumans were the closest family to be in the White House. They were happy and laughed a lot. She was one of the most beloved First Ladies when the White House staff was asked.

When the Trumans moved into the White House, it was falling apart. Ceilings had dropped, plaster was trickling down from the walls, and parts of the building were considered a fire trap. The Army Corps of Engineers wanted to tear the whole building down, but Bess and Harry said no. Instead, they moved out, into a house across the street, and remodeled the White House. When the White House reopened, the public loved it.

## Retiring to Independence

In 1953, Bess and Harry moved back to Independence, Missouri, after Harry had decided not to run for reelection. Bess was happy. She arranged for her daughter's wedding in 1956 and enjoyed reading and watching sports. In 1957, the couple dedicated the Harry S. Truman Presidential Library in Independence, and Bess's last public appearance was in 1976 when she joined President Ford in a ceremony celebrating the expansion of the Harry S. Truman Library. Bess Truman died on October 18, 1982, in her beloved Independence, Missouri, at the age of 97, and was buried next to her husband on the grounds of the Harry S. Truman Presidential Library.

**TECHNICAL STUFF**

Harry and Bess Truman were the last presidential couple not to have Secret Service protection after retirement. The city of Independence provided one retired police officer who stood guard on the back porch of their house. After John F. Kennedy was assassinated in 1963, Secret Service protection was provided to former presidents and their wives.

# Mamie Doud Eisenhower (1896–1979)

Mamie Doud (see Figure 15-2) was born on November 14, 1896, in Boone, Iowa. She was one of four daughters of John Sheldon Doud, who had become wealthy with a meatpacking business, and Elivera Mathilda Carlson, a homemaker. At the age of eight, Mamie's family moved to Colorado, and she attended public schools in Denver. After she graduated high school, she attended Miss Woollcott's private finishing school where she learned social graces and foreign languages. Her parents were preparing her to marry someone from the upper class.

**FIGURE 15-2:**
Mamie Doud Eisenhower.

Source: Library of Congress, Prints & Photographs Division, Reproduction number LC-USZ62-25814 (b&w film copy neg. of detail)LC-USZ62-6241 (b&w film copy neg. of detail)

**FIRST LADY LORE**

Mamie Doud Eisenhower was the last First Lady born in the 19th century.

The Douds were wealthy, and when one of Mamie's sisters developed rheumatic fever, they bought a vacation home in San Antonio, Texas. Mamie spent the winters there to get away from the Colorado snow, and in San Antonio, Mamie met a second lieutenant by the name of Dwight Eisenhower, who everybody called Ike. Both were immediately attracted to each other. She later said that she found him just about the handsomest male she had ever seen. They began to date, even though her father was worried about Mamie marrying a military man. He was afraid that the pay was too low and that the constant traveling would get to Mamie after a while. On Valentine's Day 1916, Ike proposed marriage. They were married on July 1, 1916, in Denver at her family's home and then moved to San Antonio where Ike was stationed at Fort Sam Houston.

## Being a military wife

At first, it was tough for Mamie to live on a budget. Her dad had told her not to expect any kind of monetary support from him, and she had to learn how to cook. On September 24, 1917, her son Doud Dwight Eisenhower was born; however, the young boy died of scarlet fever in 1921. The Eisenhowers were devastated. A second son John Sheldon Doud Eisenhower was born in 1922, and he, like his dad, went on to have a distinguished military and diplomatic career.

**FIRST LADY LORE**

Mamie's grandson married Julie Nixon, the daughter of her husband's vice president Richard Nixon.

Being a military officer had its perks and downfalls. Mamie had to move frequently, from Panama to the Philippines to France and, of course, throughout the United States. Mamie estimated that she moved 27 times in 37 years while her husband was in the military. Wherever they were posted, she'd turn their home into a place where they could entertain fellow officers. Soon she had hosting down to a science, and their home was called Club Eisenhower. This would come in quite handy when she became First Lady.

While Ike was moving up in the military ranks, Mamie stayed at home raising their son. After the Japanese attack on Pearl Harbor, Ike was called to Washington, D.C., to head up the Army's War Plans Division. Mamie got an apartment for the family and lived there throughout WWII, while her husband became the supreme commander of the Allied Forces in Europe. The two would see each other only for 12 days in the next three years.

During the war, Mamie was part of the American Women's Volunteer Service aiding the war effort and she provided support for wives of officers at the front.

During WWII, Ike allegedly had an affair with his Irish driver and secretary Kay Summersby. She wrote a book detailing their affair, which was later turned into a made-for-TV movie. Most historians today believe that the affair never happened, but Mamie was very hurt by the allegations.

After WWII was over, Ike came home and was appointed the president of Columbia University for two years. Then he was called back to Europe to supervise the creation of NATO, and in 1951, President Truman appointed him the Supreme Allied Commander of NATO. At this time, high-level officials within the Republican Party began to recruit him to run for president. Mamie had thought that the two could retire in peace. Ike had even bought a farm near Gettysburg, Pennsylvania, for them to retire on. However, his country called upon him one more time.

## Appealing to the average American

Mamie became a tremendous hit during the 1952 campaign. She actually shook about 700 hands a day. She appealed to the average American housewife. (Keep in mind that in the 1950s, most women were still housewives.) She bought clothes off the rack, not from fine clothing stores, and gave brief interviews mostly on nonpolitical topics. When it was found out that Mamie's favorite color was pink, everybody suddenly wanted to buy pink items. Every woman tried to copy her look, and she set off a rage for bangs. Mamie pink and the Mamie bangs were the trend of the 1950s.

Mamie's gown for the presidential inaugural contained 2,000 pink rhinestones.

Mamie proved to be a gracious hostess. She dressed well, and her dinner parties at the White House were elegant. The only time she talked publicly was to tell the nation that her husband was fine and recovering well after having a heart attack in 1955. For a period, she answered his correspondence for him and reassured the public that he was ready for a second term. Otherwise, Mamie handled the food and the entertainment for the White House, took care of her family, and stayed out of politics.

Mamie was a strong supporter of desegregation. She was an honorary member of the National Council of Negro Women, and she was responsible for integrating the Easter Egg Roll on the White House lawn. She also publicly supported her husband sending troops to Little Rock to desegregate the school system in Arkansas.

Mamie was the last First Lady not to have a pet cause to push for. She became the spokesperson for the American Heart Association, but that was about it. Talking to Rosalyn Carter in 1977, she said: "I stayed busy all the time and loved being in the White House, but I was never expected to do all the things you have to do."

**FIRST
LADY LORE**

Mamie and Bess Truman were close friends, even though their husbands disliked each other. Bess actually taught a Spanish class in the White House that Mamie attended.

Americans wrote Mamie by the tens of thousands. She wasn't just a First Lady; she had become a first mother and grandmother to the nation. She answered each letter and wrote thoughtful responses. Then she signed the letters with, "Bless you, Mamie E." Future First Lady Pat Nixon was so impressed, she told Mamie, "People are marveling that you have personally signed so much mail, and they are filled with admiration and appreciation."

By 1956, Mamie had started to really enjoy being First Lady. She encouraged her husband to run for a second term, and he won in a landslide. By the time her term as First Lady was up in 1961, Mamie Eisenhower hadn't given one press conference or influenced and contributed to her husband's domestic and foreign policy. She truly stayed out of his business. However, she became a celebrity for many American women who loved her, and her way of clothing and hairstyle became the fashion trend in the 1950s for the more mature female crowd. She was so popular that her birthday celebration was televised live in 1956.

**FIRST
LADY LORE**

The media went after Mamie very unfairly, claiming that she had an alcohol problem. Occasionally, Mamie would stagger and stumble while walking, and the media claimed she was drunk. In reality, Mamie Eisenhower was afflicted with an inner ear disorder, Meniere's Disease, which caused her symptoms.

After their term was over, the Eisenhowers went to their ranch in Gettysburg, Pennsylvania, and enjoyed life until Ike died in 1969. Mamie continued to live on the farm until she died on November 1, 1979, of a stroke just short of her 83rd birthday.

# Jacqueline Lee Bouvier Kennedy (1929–1994)

Jacqueline Lee Bouvier (see Figure 15-3), or Jackie, as she was called, was born on July 28, 1929, in Southampton on Long Island, New York. Her father, John Vernon Bouvier II, was a wealthy stockbroker, and her mother was a socialite in New York's wealthy circles. Her dad drank too much, and her mother cheated too much, and so they filed for divorce in 1936. Jackie grew up living with both parents. In the summers, she spent time with her dad and grandpa on his East Hampton estate, and in the winter, she lived with her mom in a large Manhattan apartment. It was her grandpa who got her interested in reading and poetry. Often, they'd memorize and recite poems together.

**FIGURE 15-3:**
Jacqueline Lee
Bouvier Kennedy.

*Source: Library of Congress, Prints & Photographs Division,
Reproduction number LC-USZ62-21796
(b&w film copy neg.)LC-USZ62-25815
(b&w film copy neg. of detail)*

In 1942, Jackie's mother remarried a wealthy lawyer who lived on two large estates, one in Rhode Island and one in Northern Virginia. Jackie spent her time living in Virginia, close to the capital, and Rhode Island. She attended the finest private schools and loved to read, dance, and write stories and poems. Her great passion was horseback riding, and she soon became an excellent equestrienne. After graduating high school, Jackie attended Vassar College to study art history for two years. Then she went to France to study at the Sorbonne in Paris, and finally she attended George Washington University in Washington, D.C., from which she graduated with a bachelor of arts degree in French literature.

**FIRST
LADY LORE**

In 1951, Jackie won a contest sponsored by *Vogue* magazine. She had to submit a personal profile, a magazine layout on high fashion, and an essay on three "People I Wish I Had Known." She picked Russian Ballet choreographer Serge Diaghilev, the French poet Charles-Pierre Baudelaire, and English playwright Oscar Wilde. The big prize was a one-year job with *Vogue*, spending six months in Paris and six months in New York. However, she didn't take the position but instead took a job at the *Washington Times-Herald* as an inquiring camera girl (see Figure 15-4). With this job, she not only took pictures but also interviewed people. Among her interviews were Second Lady Pat Nixon, future president Richard Nixon, and a Congressman from Massachusetts, John F. Kennedy.

**FIGURE 15-4:**
Jacqueline Lee Bouvier as a photographer.

Source: Library of Congress, Prints & Photographs Division, Reproduction number
LC-USZ62-132830 (b&w film copy neg.)

# Joining forces with JFK

In 1951, Washington newsman Charles Bartlett and his wife were playing matchmaker for Jackie and John F. Kennedy (JFK), who everybody called Jack. They invited both for dinner to meet. The two dated for a little bit, but nothing much came from it. They became friends, talking on the phone and sending each other postcards when they traveled.

By 1953, after Jack had become a U.S. Senator representing Massachusetts, they'd have the occasional date, going out for lunches and watching movies. Later that year, Jackie traveled to London to report on the coronation of Queen Elizabeth II, and she brought Jack a few rare books as a present. He met her at the airport when she returned, and they were engaged within 24 hours. The engagement was announced in June 1953, and the two got married September 12, 1953, on Jackie's family's Rhode Island estate. It was a huge affair, with 600 people attending the wedding and 1,700 at the reception.

**REMEMBER**

Jackie wasn't very political in the beginning. She introduced her husband to an appreciation of the fine arts and dining and occasionally translated documents on the French war in Indochina from French into English.

The first three years of marriage were tough for the couple. Jack had a painful back injury dating back to his service in WWII, which made it almost impossible for him to walk. He had several surgeries, and one almost killed him. During his recovery, Jackie read to him, and they played cards and board games.

While recovering, Jack wrote a book in which he discussed U.S. politicians who risked their political careers to support unpopular issues. Jackie helped him with his research and helped edit the work. The book *Profiles in Courage* was a major hit in 1957 and won the Pulitzer prize.

Jackie also had her own health issues. She suffered two miscarriages in 1955 and 1956. While she was facing health issues, Jack repeatedly cheated on her, but then in 1957, their daughter, Caroline, was born. This saved the marriage and brought the two closer one more time. In 1960, while her husband was campaigning for the presidency, Jackie gave birth to their second child, John Kennedy Jr., which further cemented the marriage.

## Becoming a First Lady everyone admired

Jackie showed no interest in politics but decided to actively campaign for her husband in 1960. Her husband's campaign advisors didn't believe that she'd be an asset during the campaign. Boy, were they wrong! The public soon fell in love with her. She was witty and intelligent. She held her own press conferences, hosted fundraising events, and even met with voters. She was able to reach out to new immigrants because she was fluent in Spanish, Italian, and French. Jackie even taped campaign commercials in Spanish to appeal to Hispanic voters in states such as Texas. She held so many campaign appearances in other languages on a regular basis, that her husband once said: "I assure you my wife speaks English."

As First Lady, Jackie became famous for hosting elegant parties and dressing well. Every fashion magazine reported on her, and the Jackie look became a worldwide sensation. Soon she was the most admired woman in the world.

During the year that Jackie became First Lady, the most popular show on Broadway was the musical *Camelot* about the castle and its legendary king, King Arthur. The name Camelot was applied to the Kennedy White House, because of the atmosphere and ongoing festivities in the White House (Camelot). The president and Jacqueline hosted one festive party after another for foreign dignitaries, movie stars, great scientists, and talented artists. In addition, the First Lady recreated the White House's historical past by collecting antique pieces and merging them with modern settings. Soon the media called it the Kennedy Style.

Jacqueline was a popular First Lady. She was attractive, charming, rich, fashionable, had a good-looking husband, and had two children roaming through the White House. The media loved all of this. It made for great stories without focusing on politics as usual.

The media had a field day with Jackie. *The New York Times* called her fanatically chic and stated that she captured the fashion vote. Ninety percent of all Americans owned a television set by the early 1960s, and soon television dominated the media. Candidates' wives became active on TV and began to campaign for their husbands.

## Turning celebrity

Jackie enjoyed nice clothing. She spent up to $30,000 on dresses annually and decided that the world needed to be shown that the U.S. could produce high fashion as found in France and Italy. She contacted famous American designer Oleg Cassini and asked him to create fashionable clothing for Jack and herself. She told him: "I want Jack and myself to dress as if Jack were president of France." So she became the Godmother of the American high fashion industry.

In 1961, two TV networks produced documentaries on Jackie, turning her into a massive celebrity. The documentaries not only discussed her upbringing but also focused on how she popularized the pillbox hat, bouffant hairstyles, and the name Jaqueline for baby girls.

## Restoring the White House

Jackie's most enduring legacy is the restoration of the White House. She decided that it was time to turn the White House into a showcase for American art and history. She wanted it to be equivalent to the great executive buildings in Europe. She set up the White House Historical Association and began to raise funds for her project. She established a fine arts committee and tried to have wealthy donors pay for the restoration project. She was able to collect over a million in donations. Next, she hired curators, historians, and art experts to bring out the historical significance of the building. She was instrumental in rebuilding whole bedroom sets from the Monroe and the Lincoln administrations. In addition, she added a nursery and private dining room, with its own adjoining kitchen to the White House.

Jackie's efforts to restore the White House paid off. In 1962, she hosted a one-hour TV special in which she showed off the newly remodeled White House and gave viewers a tour. The special was televised in 106 countries and watched by almost 60 million people in the U.S. alone. The White House had become a national and international sensation. Jackie later won an Honorary Emmy Award for her show.

**FIRST LADY LORE**

A young woman by the name of Barbara Bush watched the special and sent Jackie a letter in which she expressed her admiration for her. Barbara Bush, of course, became First Lady in 1989.

Jackie further had Air Force One repainted with the design still used today, and she changed seating arrangements in the White House to round tables to encourage group conversation during White House dinners.

## Going international

Jackie traveled widely with her husband and made friends with many foreign leaders, including French President Charles de Gaulle and Indian leader Jawaharlal Nehru. In addition, Jackie was the first First Lady to go on vacation out of the country by herself. She went to Europe and India, riding elephants and going yachting with Europe's rich. This made her even more popular.

## Living through an assassination

The year 1963 turned out to be a horrible year for Jackie. First, she lost a son, Patrick, when he was two days old, and then she decided to accompany her husband on a campaign trip to Texas. Coming back from one of her solo vacations, Jackie had agreed to travel to Texas with her husband in November of 1963 to help him campaign for the upcoming 1964 presidential election. Jack was gearing up for his reelection campaign, and Texas was thought to be a crucial state.

By now, President Kennedy had become unpopular in parts of the country. Many Southerners didn't like his attempts to improve relations with the Soviet Union and his push for civil rights. At first, he wanted to travel by himself, but Texas governor John Connally told him: "You have to bring Mrs. Kennedy, because she is so popular; you'll have much bigger crowds." So he did. Jackie stole the show right away in Houston talking with Hispanic voters in Spanish.

On November 22, 1963, the couple visited Dallas, Texas. The route of the motorcade was lined with thousands of well-wishers, and it was a beautiful sunny day. The president ordered the bulletproof roof removed so that he and Jackie could enjoy the great weather. Jackie was waving to people when suddenly a bullet struck the president. Jackie shouted, "He's been shot!" and then a second bullet hit him in the head, and he slumped against her. They were rushed to the hospital where Jackie had to watch while the doctors tried to save her husband. However, President Kennedy died half an hour later. Jackie, still wearing the blood-soaked dress, had to stand next to Vice President Johnson as he was sworn in as president (see Figure 15-5). She refused to take off her blood-spattered pink suit she had worn while seated next to her husband. She stated:

> "I want them to see what they have done to Jack."

Back in Washington, D.C., Jackie made all the funeral arrangements herself, using Abraham Lincoln's funeral as a guide. She became a symbol of strength for the nation. She met with foreign dignitaries, thanked the American public on national television for their sympathy, and lit the eternal flame on her husband's grave at Arlington National Cemetery. In an interview a few days later for *Life* magazine, she said:

**IN THEIR WORDS**

"There will be great presidents again, but there will never be another Camelot."

Jackie had no place to go, but President Johnson let her stay until she found a place. When she left the White House, she left a card in the Lincoln bedroom, which she had recreated and shared with her husband. It read: "In this room lived John Fitzgerald Kennedy with his wife Jacqueline, during the two years, 10 months, and two days he was president of the United States."

## Marrying a billionaire

Not surprisingly, Jackie and her children stayed in the news after she left the White House. She oversaw the construction of the John F. Kennedy Library in Boston and campaigned for her brother-in-law Robert Kennedy when he ran for president in 1968. Again tragedy struck when he was also assassinated. Jackie now believed that there were people out there trying to kill off the Kennedys. To escape all of this, in 1969, at the age of 40, she married Greek billionaire Aristotle Socrates Onassis, who was quite a bit older than she was. The American public was incensed that she married someone who was not an American and began to turn away from her.

Jackie said that she loved him because he was able to get rid of the constant reminder of the Kennedy legacy. She said, "Aristotle Onassis saved me at a moment when my life was engulfed with shadow."

After Aristotle Onassis died in 1975, Jackie moved back to New York City and became a consulting editor for Viking Books and then Doubleday Books three years later. Her daughter, Caroline, became an attorney and had three children. Her son, John Jr., passed the New York Bar and launched his own political magazine called *George.* He died in 1999 in an airplane crash near Martha's Vineyard in Massachusetts.

Jackie died of cancer (lymphoma) on May 19, 1994, at the age of 64 and was buried next to John F. Kennedy in Arlington National Cemetery.

# Chapter 16

# Becoming Politically Active

The three First Ladies discussed in this chapter all set precedents by being politically active and not just staying in the White House hosting parties. With their political and social activities, they set a new standard that every First Lady since had to follow.

First was Claudia "Lady Bird" Johnson. She had been active in Washington, D.C., politics since the mid-1930s and was well prepared for becoming First Lady overnight after John F. Kennedy's assassination. After she became First Lady, she said:

**IN THEIR WORDS**

"I realized that I had a pulpit and I could use it, and I could use it for good."

This would become the new standard for First Ladies.

Pat Nixon came next. She truly was a working-class First Lady, growing up in poverty and providing for her brothers after her parents had died. Pat Nixon could be one of the most charming people a person would ever meet, but only in a small group. As soon as she had to face a large crowd, she became uncomfortable, stiffened up, and appeared to be distant. The media soon gave her the nickname Plastic Pat.

Betty Ford was the most candid First Lady in her political views. She discussed moral issues like abortion and supported the equal rights amendment openly. Often, she'd conflict with her husband and the Republican Party on issues, and that was okay with her. When she was asked questions, she responded to the public and talked openly with the American people. People loved her candor, but not necessarily her political views.

# Claudia Alta Taylor Johnson (1912–2007)

Claudia Alta Taylor (see Figure 16-1) was born on December 22, 1912, in Karnack, a small town in East Texas. Her father was Thomas Taylor who was a storekeeper and farmer. Her mom, Minnie, died when Claudia was only five. Claudia grew up wealthy, and the family was able to afford several servants. The story goes that one of the servants gave Claudia the nickname "Lady Bird," saying she was as pretty as a ladybird, or ladybug. She was known by this name all her life. However, Lady Bird herself gave the real story of how she got her nickname after she had retired from being First Lady.

During an interview, Lady Bird confessed that she used to have two little African American playmates and that they called her Lady Bird because they didn't like the name Claudia. However, back then, it was considered inappropriate in the South for white children to play with Black children, and so the story had to be changed.

Lady Bird attended local public schools and excelled in just about every topic. However, she was very shy and reclusive. She even sabotaged her chances at being Valedictorian, so she would not have to give a speech in public. After high school, she attended a private junior college for women, St. Mary's Episcopal College for Women, in Dallas, until she transferred to the University of Texas at Austin in 1930. There, she studied history and journalism and graduated in 1934 with two degrees. Being independently wealthy due to her father, Lady Bird wanted to leave Texas to become a journalist in New York or Washington, D.C., or a teacher in Alaska or Hawaii.

As a student at the University of Texas, Lady Bird had her own car and an unlimited expense account at Neiman Marcus, but she was very cheap. She wore her aunt's old clothing and bought items secondhand. For the rest of her life, Lady Bird was both very rich and very frugal.

## Marrying Johnson and moving to D.C.

A college friend introduced Lady Bird to Lyndon B. Johnson. They went on a date, and during the date, he proposed to her. Her friends told her to wait, but Lady Bird wanted to consult her father. Her father took one look at Lyndon and said, "This time you brought home a man," and not only gave his approval but encouraged her to marry Lyndon.

On the day of their wedding, Lyndon forgot Lady Bird's wedding ring, so he ran to a Sears store right before the ceremony to pick up a ring for $2.50.

They got married on November 17, 1934, less three months after they first met, and moved to a small apartment in Washington, D.C, where Lyndon worked for Democratic Congressman Richard Kleberg as his secretary. Lady Bird wasn't used to living in such a large city, and it took time for her to adjust.

After a brief career as a schoolteacher, Lyndon Johnson used his father's political connections to get appointed secretary to Democratic Congressman Richard Kleberg in 1931. The Democratic incumbent of Lyndon's home district in Central Texas suddenly died in 1937. Lyndon ran for the open seat in the special election held to fill the position and won.

After Lyndon decided to run for the House of Representatives, Lady Bird found out that the race cost about $10,000. She called her father, who still liked Lyndon quite a bit, and asked for an advance on her inheritance. He wired her the money the next day, and Johnson was able to successfully launch a campaign for the seat.

**TECHNICAL STUFF**

In 1941, one of the Texas senators died in office. Lyndon decided to run for the vacant seat. Even President Roosevelt endorsed him, saying that Lyndon was a good old friend. Lyndon almost pulled off a victory. In the end, he lost the race by just 1,311 votes out of more than 600,000 cast. He ran again for the Senate in 1948, now a war hero. The election was even closer than the 1941 election, but the result was in Lyndon's favor this time — he won by 87 votes out of 900,000 cast. His political enemies made fun of the closeness of the election and called him "Land-slide Lyndon."

Lady Bird enjoyed Washington, D.C. She was active with the other congressional wives and very soon knew just about everybody who mattered in the capital. This would prove to be very beneficial when she abruptly became First Lady a couple of decades later.

## Getting familiar with politics

Lyndon Johnson was still serving in the House when the United States entered WWII. He became the first Congressman to volunteer for the military. He served in Australia and New Guinea, where the Japanese almost shot down his plane in 1942. The plane Lyndon was on, suddenly experienced mechanical problems but was able to return and land safely, despite heavy Japanese fire.

Lyndon received the Silver Star for bravery and returned home a hero. While he was off fighting in WWII, Lady Bird ran his congressional office on his behalf. She did a great job, and most people never knew that her husband was gone until after he returned.

Managing her husband's office changed her life. Lady Bird learned about policy issues and how to play the game of politics in Washington, D.C. She further answered letters of constituents, escorted them through the halls of Congress, and showed them the sites in Washington, D.C. By the time Lyndon returned home, Lady Bird had gained a lot of self-confidence and was ready to participate in policy making.

**REMEMBER**

In the Senate, Lyndon Johnson soon became one of the leaders. He worked hard, and then he suddenly had a heart attack in 1955. He had to stop his three-pack-a-day cigarette habit, and it took him five weeks to recover in the hospital. Lady Bird spent the whole time with him, sleeping in the room next to his.

## MAKING A MEDIA EMPIRE

In 1943, Lady Bird inherited a chunk of land and money from her mother's and uncle's estates. She decided to buy unprofitable Austin radio station KTBC for $15,500. She turned it into a profitable business, hiring new staff and managing it herself. Whenever she was back in Texas, she helped out at the station, even mopping floors and cleaning windows. After the radio station suddenly became profitable, Lady Bird decided to buy a TV station in 1952. She got a license for the first TV station in the Austin area and became a millionaire. She was the only First Lady to become a millionaire before her husband became president. After her husband passed, Lady Bird became a full-time businesswoman and resumed her role of running her media empire with great success.

## Helping a presidential campaign

In 1960, John F. Kennedy picked Lyndon Johnson to be his vice president. Kennedy was from Massachusetts and needed a moderate Southerner on the ticket to be able to carry the South. Lyndon fit the bill. He was more experienced than Kennedy and as Senate majority leader had great connections in Congress. After Kennedy won the election, Lyndon became one of the most powerful and influential vice presidents to date. However, it was not only Lyndon but also Lady Bird who had a role to play.

Lady Bird campaigned tirelessly for her husband and John F. Kennedy. She was charming and popular. Democratic leaders referred to her as their secret weapon. During the campaign, she traveled through Texas and held tea parties for thousands of women. She took pride in herself that she shook hands with everyone who attended one of her tea parties. Robert Kennedy later said: "Mrs. Johnson won Texas for us." If Kennedy would have lost Texas, he would have lost the election to Richard Nixon.

## Advocating for her husband and her causes

Lady Bird became First Lady after the assassination of President Kennedy. She had a tough act to follow — Jaqueline Kennedy was one of the most beloved First Ladies ever — and her husband, Lyndon Johnson, assumed the presidency under tragic circumstances. Therefore, she dreaded becoming First Lady. She told a friend: "I feel as if I am suddenly on stage for a part I never rehearsed." In reality, Lady Bird was well prepared for the job. She networked with congressional wives for decades and had often filled in for Jaqueline Kennedy when Jaqueline was with child or just didn't want to show up for events. During her tenure as First Lady,

Lady Bird was a loving wife who helped her husband cope with the stress of the Vietnam War and a changing American society.

After a required period of mourning, entertaining in the White House started in early 1964. Lady Bird preferred small receptions so she could get to know people. She proved to be a good hostess and entertainer. She went back to her Texas roots and had barbecues and hoedowns, which were very popular with foreign dignitaries. Over her tenure as First Lady, she entertained more than 200,000 people in the White House.

During the 1964 election, Lady Bird campaigned for her husband across the South, becoming the first First Lady to campaign on her own. President Johnson once said: "Voters would have happily elected her over me." She backed her husband's push for civil rights and voting rights legislation and wanted to embark on her own whistle stop campaign, traveling through eight Southern states by train. Because of President Johnson's support for civil rights, his advisors had decided it would be too dangerous for him to travel to the South. So Lady Bird decided to go in his place. At first, her husband's advisors refused, but, after a while, they begrudgingly agreed. She toured the Deep South by train, referred to as the "Lady Bird Special." Whenever protesters showed up to demonstrate against her husband's civil rights push, she'd say: "This is a country of many viewpoints. I respect your right to express your own. Now is my turn to express mine."

During her tenure in the White House, Lady Bird gave 164 speeches and made 700 public appearances. She ran the White House like the chairwoman of a large corporation, employing at times 20 or more people in the White House herself. When she left office in 1969, she was considered an outstanding First Lady, and Gallup ranked her third in their list of First Lady rankings, right after Eleanor Roosevelt and Abigail Adams.

## Pushing for the Head Start Program

Studies had shown that five- and six-year-old children who came from a poor background when they started public school were behind their richer counterparts. They were both less prepared to get an education and intellectually behind. In February of 1965, President Johnson announced the Head Start Program, designed to remedy this situation. Lady Bird had met with the original planning committee and then became the public voice for the program. She arranged for a reception where her husband announced the program and afterwards called for Head Start volunteers; 200,000 Americans signed up to volunteer.

The program sent less-prepared students to the Head Start preschool programs. The program taught learning skills to low-income children, giving them a head start in life.

The Head Start Program is still going strong and was last reauthorized in 2007. At that point, over 22 million children had participated in it since its inception.

## Beautifying the country

During her time as First Lady, Lady Bird toured poorer parts of the country to find out about the horrible living conditions many Americans faced. She noticed the ugliness of not just how people lived but also of parts of the country, especially if they were located next to highways. Lady Bird believed that there was a link between natural beauty and quality of life. For her, crime and juvenile delinquency were more likely to occur if people faced ugly surroundings.

For this reason, she suggested the idea of highway beautification to her husband, who then proposed it as the Highway Beautification Act in 1965, also called Lady Bird's Bill. The bill was designed to improve the beauty of America next to highways. Lady Bird had been especially disgusted by billboards and junkyards. So the bill provided states with money to get rid of them and plant trees and flowers instead. Congress at first opposed the bill, but President Johnson pushed hard for it, and it finally passed. He said:

**IN THEIR WORDS**

"You know, I love that woman and she wants that highway bill. By God, we're going to get it for her."

Lady Bird further supported federal monies for urban renewal and also for the expansion of mass transit in Washington, D.C., and the preservation of historic buildings.

By the time her term as First Lady ended, Lady Bird had become a political activist and a consummate politician. She set the tradition of First Ladies having political pet causes and actively pursuing them. From then on, every First Lady was expected to have a cause and/or project they'd pursue during their term.

# Going back to Texas

Lady Bird was happy when Lyndon Johnson decided not to run for reelection. His health had been declining, and she was worried about him. As early as 1964, Lady Bird had written in her diary that it would be time to leave the White House after her husband's second term ended in 1969. In March of 1968, Lyndon announced that he had reconsidered and wouldn't run for another term.

The Johnsons retired to their ranch in the Hill Country in Texas, close to where Lyndon had been born. In 1970, Lady Bird published her memoirs *A White House Diary*, revealing behind-the-scenes details of the Johnson presidency. The book was more than 800 pages long, and it was just a small part of her actual notes.

Lady Bird was also actively involved in the planning of her husband's presidential library. She picked the place, the University of Texas at Austin, and went with architects over the smallest details for the buildings.

President Johnson died after suffering a third and fatal heart attack in 1973. Lady Bird wasn't with him when he passed. She was in Austin, visiting the Lyndon Johnson Presidential Library, which had been recently dedicated. By the time she got to him, he was already dead.

After Lyndon's death, Lady Bird continued to work for nature and conservation programs. She was very much interested in wildflower preservation and established the Lady Bird Johnson Wildflower Center in Austin, Texas, which has become a popular tourist attraction today.

Lady Bird was further put on the board of the Regents for the University of Texas. She stayed physically active until her late 80s, swimming daily, until she became partially blind in the 1990s and suffered a stroke in 2002. Lady Bird Johnson died on July 11, 2007, in Austin, Texas, at the age of 94. Both Lady Bird and her husband are buried near Stonewall, Texas, in the family cemetery.

Lady Bird's great legacy is in regard to the American environment. She was the first First Lady to work for environmental protection and public conservation. Many consider her to be one of the founders of the American environmental movement.

# Thelma Catherine Ryan Nixon (1912–1993)

Thelma Catherine Ryan (see Figure 16-2) was born on March 16, 1912, in Ely, Nevada, where her father worked as a miner. Her dad, William, and mother, Kate, nicknamed her Pat, because the family was Irish and she was born the day before St. Patrick's day. She went by that name for the rest of her life. Soon after Pat was born, the family moved to California and operated a small farm. Early on in her life, Pat worked on the farm, picking tomatoes and peppers. She even helped her dad drive the family wagon, pulled by horses, to the local market to sell their products. After her mom died when she was 13, Pat became the woman of the house and took care of her father and two brothers.

**FIRST LADY LORE**

Pat's mother was an immigrant from Germany. This makes Pat the first First Lady to have an immigrant for a parent.

**FIGURE 16-2:**
Thelma Catherine
Ryan Nixon.

*Source: Library of Congress, Prints & Photographs Division, Reproduction number LC-USZ62-35648 (b&w film copy neg.)*

When Pat was 17, her dad suddenly died, and she continued to take care of her brothers. She took a bunch of part-time jobs to keep the family going. She managed to attend Fullerton Junior College and then moved to New York to work as an X-ray technician and stenographer while taking classes at Columbia University.

**FIRST
LADY LORE**

Pat wanted to visit her relatives in New York but didn't have the money to travel. So she drove an elderly couple in their car to New York City. When she got there, her aunt, a nun, got her a job at Seton Hospital. She stayed in New York until her brothers had made enough money for her to come back home and study in Southern California.

In 1934, Pat moved back to Southern California and began to take classes at the University of Southern California. Despite working several jobs, including being a dental assistant and an actress for walk-on scenes, she was an excellent student, graduating cum laude in 1937 with a degree in business. To be on the safe side, she also received her teaching certificate and acquired secretarial skills.

After graduating, Pat started to teach at Whittier High School. She taught typing, cheerleading, and theater for the school. Pat always loved the theater, so in 1938, she tried out for a part in the Whittier Community Theatre. There, she met another inspiring actor, a young lawyer by the name of Richard Nixon.

# Building a life with Nixon

Richard liked Pat right away and asked her to go out on a date with him. She told him no because she was so busy. So he said: "You shouldn't say that because someday I'm going to marry you." Later, she agreed to a date with him, and on that first date, he asked her to marry him. She said no and told her friends: "I thought he was nuts or something."

For the next two years, Richard courted Pat, sending her flowers and candy and even poems, but Pat wasn't ready yet. She was dating other men and even tried to fix him up with one of her friends. Finally, in 1940, his persistence paid off, and she finally said yes. The two were married on June 16, 1940, in Riverside, California. After honeymooning in Mexico, they lived in Whittier where Richard practiced law and Pat still taught school.

Then in 1941, the attack on Pearl Harbor happened, and the U.S. entered WWII. Both Pat and her husband took jobs with the Office of Price Administration (OPA), a government agency that helped oversee rationing programs, and moved to Washington, D.C. Richard then enlisted in the Navy and spent most of the next three years in the South Pacific. Pat moved back to California to work for OPA in San Francisco. Richard retired from the military in 1946, with the rank of lieutenant commander.

After WWII ended and Richard had just returned home, the California Republican Party approached him and asked him to run for Congress. Pat and he decided it would be a good career move, and she helped him at his campaign headquarters and traveled with him when he made campaign appearances. Pat helped as much as she could, even though she was 9 months pregnant. Only six hours after she delivered the baby, she went back to help her husband with his campaign, working on his speeches from her hospital bed.

Richard Nixon won the seat in 1946, and the family — with daughter Tricia — moved to the capital. Pat helped out in Richard's congressional office with great skill without ever being paid for it, but was mostly at home taking care of two small children.

**TECHNICAL STUFF**

The California Republican Party asked Richard Nixon to run for the 12th district's congressional seat, held by longtime Democratic Congressman Jerry Voorhis. Richard had no issues on which to attack Voorhis, so he researched Voorhis's past and found that he had been a socialist, believing in powerful unions and government-owned industries. Richard accused Voorhis of still being a socialist and of being soft on Communism. The Cold War, the period after the end of WWII when the relationship between the Unites States and the Soviet Union was characterized by suspicion and animosity, was just starting, and with Americans feeling scared and belligerent about Communism, the accusation was enough to help Richard Nixon win the seat.

Then Richard's political career took off. He was reelected in 1948 and then went on to win a Senate seat in 1950, and by 1952, he was the vice presidential nominee on the Republican ticket with Dwight D. Eisenhower.

## Becoming Second Lady

After being selected as Eisenhower's vice presidential nominee, Richard was accused of financial improprieties. *The New York Post* reported that Richard had set up a fund to help out fellow Republicans and that many wealthy Californians had donated money to it. Although this wasn't illegal, Eisenhower was running on an anti-corruption platform and so it looked bad. Many in the Republican Party called for Richard's resignation as the vice presidential nominee.

In September 1952, Richard Nixon went live on national television and gave his famous Checkers Speech. Pat stood right behind him and supported him. The story goes that he believed that his political career was over and didn't want to give the speech at all. He was ready to quit, but Pat convinced him to keep on going, even though she started to harbor doubt about his political career. He actually had to promise her that he wouldn't run again for office after his vice presidential term was up in 1961. Of course, he broke that promise several times in the next decade.

In his speech, Richard disclosed all his financial assets and told the U.S. public that he was innocent of any wrongdoing. He further revealed that he had received a puppy, by the name of Checkers, as a gift. He told the public that his children loved the dog and that he'd rather resign as Eisenhower's vice presidential nominee than return the little puppy and hurt his children. He said: "The kids, like all kids, loved the dog, and I just want to say this, right now, that regardless of what they say about it, we are going to keep it."

When he left the studio, Richard thought his career was over. But letters expressing support for him poured in, and his career was saved.

Pat enjoyed being Second Lady. She always had wanted to see the world, and as the wife of a vice president, she got to travel, visiting not only Europe but also Africa, Asia, and even the Soviet Union.

By 1960, Pat was ready to become First Lady. She was very disappointed when her husband lost a close election to John F. Kennedy. The couple moved back to California, and Pat urged Richard not to run for governor of the state in 1962. He had to run against a very popular Democratic incumbent Edmund G. Brown and lost. It looked like her dream of becoming First Lady was over.

Richard, however, didn't retire from politics but remained active in the Republican Party. He campaigned and raised funds for Congressmen in the 1966 election, and by 1968, he was the leading Republican presidential candidate. Pat helped him with his speeches and did research on campaign topics. His wins were her wins; his defeats her defeats. This time he narrowly won the presidency, and Pat was finally First Lady of the United States.

## Being active and popular

As First Lady, Pat focused especially on retired military and physically challenged people. She invited them to the White House for private tours. Soon she noticed the challenges this group faced, and so she had ramps built in the White House to make the building accessible for people in wheelchairs, created audio tours for the blind, and established tours in sign language for the deaf. Her work soon went nationwide, and she became an advocate for the disabled. She further supported volunteerism and charity work.

In addition, Pat got to travel even more as First Lady. She became the first American First Lady to visit Communist China and the Soviet Union.

Pat was a pretty good hostess in the White House, but she felt most useful traveling as First Lady. She loved exploring the world and wanted to make a difference in people's lives. In 1970, a major earthquake hit Peru. More than 50,000 people died, and the U.S. wanted to send help and show its support for the Peruvian people. However, Peru had a revolutionary leftist government. The government opposed President Nixon's policies in Latin America and was very anti-American. So President Nixon decided to send his wife instead of going himself. She went and won over the Peruvian people and even the government. The government officially thanked the U.S. for sending Pat Nixon, and relations between the two countries improved.

Pat further traveled to South Vietnam to visit troops and became the first First Lady to travel to combat zones.

**FIRST LADY LORE**

In 1972, Pat accompanied her husband to China. While the president met with the Chinese leadership, Pat was allowed to travel the country, and the media followed her while she toured China. At one of the gala dinners, Pat, who was a heavy smoker, pointed to a pack of Chinese cigarettes that was decorated with Pandas. She said: "Aren't they cute? I love them." Chines Premier Zhou Enlai, upon hearing this, told her "I'll give you some." So he gave the Nixons two pandas as a gift. This is how the National Zoo in Washington, D.C., got its first two pandas.

Pat Nixon is the most widely traveled First Lady in the history of the U.S. She visited 83 different countries. Hillary Clinton ranks second having visited 82 different countries.

# Being left out

In his memoirs, Richard Nixon admitted that his wife was left out of all decision making. He never asked her for her opinions. Pat even said: "He never tries anything out on me." In 1952, she found out that her husband had accepted the vice presidential position on television, and in 1968, he didn't consult her before he decided to run for the presidency again. He didn't even inform her that he had decided to resign in 1974. She had to hear it from his secretary.

President Nixon didn't discuss politics much with his wife. When Watergate happened, Pat was taken off guard. She received most of her information from the media. She had no knowledge of the break-in, but she knew that her husband had been taping what was going on in the White House. She urged him to destroy the tapes right away because, at this point, they hadn't been subpoenaed and were considered private property. If he had listened to his wife and had destroyed the tapes, legally, he could have served out his full term. He didn't listen to her and subsequently lost his job.

Not being involved in any decision making, Pat turned her attention to traveling as First Lady, becoming a goodwill ambassador for the United States. In addition, she continued to restore the White House. She wanted to get authentic antiques to the White House, because Jackie Kennedy had acquired copies of antiques if the original ones couldn't be found or were just too expensive. Pat, on the other hand, approached wealthy Americans for donations to the White House, and many responded and donated antiques or loaned them to the White House.

By 1972, when her husband got reelected in a landslide, Pat had become more comfortable with the media and discussed her own political opinions. She even went as far as publicly stating that she hoped that her husband would appoint a woman to the Supreme Court. So in 1971, when two Supreme Court openings occurred, she lobbied her husband hard to appoint a woman to one of them. When he didn't, she was so upset that she didn't talk to him for weeks.

# Retiring disgraced

President Nixon addressed the nation on August 8, 1974, to announce his resignation. In his speech, he told the country that he no longer had the support he needed to continue the fight. He never admitted any guilt or error in the Watergate affair, and he continued to claim that he was innocent. The new president, Gerald

Ford, gave Richard Nixon an unconditional pardon on September 8, 1974, making him safe from any prosecution.

So Pat went back to California in 1974. She enjoyed reading books and gardening. Then her husband got really sick. She took care of him when he nearly died of phlebitis, an inflammation of the veins, and had to spend 23 days in the hospital. In 1976, she suffered a stroke that left her partially paralyzed. For quite some time, she slurred her speech and couldn't move her left side; however, she was able to recover fully.

In 1980, the Nixons moved to New York City and later bought an estate in New Jersey to be closer to their children and grandchildren. Pat Nixon died on June 22, 1993, at the age of 81, after battling emphysema and then lung cancer. Her husband died the following year. Both are buried at the Richard Nixon Library in Yorba Linda, California.

# Elizabeth Ann Bloomer Ford (1918–2011)

Elizabeth Ann Bloomer (see Figure 16-3) was born on April 8, 1918, in Chicago, Illinois. She moved to Grand Rapids, Michigan, when she was a young child. Her father, William Bloomer, was a sales representative who was gone quite a bit. Betty, as Elizabeth was called, suffered a lot with an absent father and swore never to marry a man who'd be gone for long times like her dad was. Her mother, Hortense Bloomer, was very domineering. Betty had to wear white gloves when shopping, and her mother put a sign on her that read, "Please do not feed this child," because Betty had a tendency to eat too much in her youth.

## Perfecting her stage presence

When she was eight, Betty began to study dance and excelled at it. She was so good that when she was a teenager, she herself became a teacher of dance. For this reason, Betty got comfortable being on stage and in front of an audience. This would come in handy later in life.

After graduating from high school in Grand Rapids, Betty decided to move to New York City to pursue a career in dance. Her recently widowed mother objected. She didn't want her young daughter to live by herself in such a large and dangerous city. So the two compromised, and Betty attended Bennington College in Vermont for two summers, where she studied dance with Martha Graham, one of the best-known modern dancers.

**FIGURE 16-3:**
Elizabeth Ann
Bloomer Ford.

Source: Library of Congress, Prints & Photographs Division,
Reproduction number LC-USZC4-2019
(color film copy transparency)LC-USZ62-51913
(b&w film copy neg. of cropped image)

In 1939, Betty finally moved to New York City and took more dance classes, and Martha Graham hired her for her concert troupe. Betty enjoyed the big city and even modeled to support her career. However, she never made first rank, and so she moved back to Grand Rapids where she established her own dance troupe. In 1942, she married William G. Warren, a furniture dealer. The marriage was a disaster, and they got divorced five years later. Betty said: "My friends were getting married, and I thought I had to get married, too."

After her divorce, Betty took a job as the fashion coordinator at a Grand Rapids department store and taught dance on the side. Some mutual friends set her up with Gerald Ford, a young lawyer and WWII veteran, who also had played football for the University of Michigan. They started dating, and Gerald proposed a few months later. She accepted, without knowing that he was planning a career in politics and had decided to run for Congress.

## Marrying a man like her father

The wedding had to be delayed because Gerald Ford had decided to run for Congress. His district was very conservative, and his advisors didn't believe that a man who married a divorcée could win the Republican primary. So they waited until after Gerald Ford won the primary and then got married. The two married on

October 18, 1948, shortly before the general election. Betty didn't know much about politics and didn't believe that Gerald, more commonly called Jerry, could win. To her great surprise, he won not only the Republican nomination but also the seat in Congress.

Jerry went on to serve in Congress for the next 25 years representing the fifth district in Michigan. By 1965, he had become the minority leader in the House of Representatives. As minority leader, he accepted up to 200 invitations a year to campaign and raise money for other Republican candidates. So Betty was alone often. She basically became a single mom. Even though they had moved to Virginia, Betty had married a man who, like her father, was absent a lot, and she had to raise four children mostly by herself.

By then, Betty had developed several health problems, including arthritis and a very painful pinched nerve, and was in constant pain. In addition, she experienced a minor breakdown that forced her to a see a psychiatrist. To combat her pain, she was prescribed a wide range of painkillers and also tranquilizers and sedatives to control her mental state. Soon, she became dependent on them. Her drinking habit made the situation even worse.

The Fords had planned to retire in 1976, after the Republican Party didn't win control of the House of Representatives in 1972 as Jerry had hoped. However, things turned out differently.

**TECHNICAL STUFF**

Gerald Ford never wanted to be president. He actually turned down the vice presidency when President Nixon asked him to be his running mate in 1968. Jerry's great desire was to become Speaker of the House of Representatives. In 1973, President Nixon's vice president, Spiro Agnew, resigned because he had been involved in a bribery scandal. Nixon needed a replacement quickly. He considered Ronald Reagan, the governor of California, but opted for Gerald Ford. He had good ties to Congress, was well liked and respected by his peers, and could easily win confirmation.

The Senate ratified Jerry by a vote of 92 to 3. The House followed suit and approved Jerry by a vote of 387 to 35. Gerald Ford became the vice president of the United States on December 6, 1973. Just a few months later, after President Nixon had resigned, Gerald Ford suddenly found himself president of the United States.

## Talking to the American people

Betty Ford and her family were liked by the media. They seemed like every other American family. They had three college-aged sons and a daughter in high school. Betty was an instant hit with the American public. She was able to communicate well and had a tendency to speak her mind. She conveyed a personal warmth, sincerity, and openness and, by 1975, became one of the most admired women in the country. She enjoyed hosting large dinners and being on stage.

She promised the American public that she'd be authentic and speak her mind. She didn't lie. She said:

> "I promise to do the best I can, and if they don't like it, they can kick me out, but they can't make me somebody I'm not."

## Battling cancer

Several weeks after her husband took office, Betty found out she had breast cancer. She had a radical mastectomy, and one of her breasts was removed. Subsequently, Betty had to endure several rounds of radiation and chemotherapy. She openly discussed the disease and surgery with the American public, which shocked the country. Up to this point, breast cancer had been a disease nobody talked about and wasn't even mentioned in obituaries as the cause of death. Thousands of women thanked her, and many more went to their doctors for checkups. One of them was the Second Lady, Margaretta "Happy" Rockefeller, whose exam led to the discovery of breast cancer. She also had to have a mastectomy and afterward lived a long life. Betty brought the disease into the open and initiated a national conversation about the disease. She transformed how women looked at the disease and made them go for annual check-ups. She saved countless lives in turn.

## Being controversial

Betty was back to work shortly after her treatment and gave hundreds of interviews in which she openly spoke her mind, even if it went against her husband's and the Republican party's policies. She soon became the most public First Lady in U.S. history. For example, she not only publicly supported the equal rights amendment that would have prohibited discrimination based on gender, but she also actually lobbied for it nationwide. To make contacting local and state lawmakers easier, she had a second phone lined installed in her office, from which she could lobby. To top it off, she applauded the legalization of abortion, which her husband and most in the Republican Party opposed. The White House issued a statement: "The President has long since ceased to be perturbed or surprised by his wife's remarks."

Her husband valued her opinions and even admitted that she had been very influential when it came to the pardoning of former president Richard Nixon. Betty encouraged her husband to pardon Richard Nixon for the good of the country so that the country could finally heal. Controversial back then, today most historians and political observers consider the pardon to have been the right move.

# Retiring early and doing more good

Betty was disappointed when her husband lost the presidential election of 1976. She had campaigned intensely on his behalf and was hoping to the last minute that he could pull out a victory.

President Ford lost his voice campaigning right before election day, and Betty had to give the concession speech and had to read the note sent to President-elect Carter congratulating him.

The couple then retired to Palm Springs, California. By 1978, Betty's problems with alcohol and drugs worsened. The Ford family staged an intervention and checked her into the Long Beach Naval Hospital Alcohol and Drug Rehabilitation Service to detoxify herself. She was very public about her struggles, and again the American public rallied to her side. Instead of keeping quiet, she openly discussed her struggles in her memoir *A Glad Awakening*.

Thousands of people wrote to her pleading for help, and so in 1982, she founded the Betty Ford Center for Drug and Alcohol Rehabilitation, attached to the Eisenhower Medical Center, outside of Palm Springs, California. It was an inpatient clinic for drug and alcohol dependency. She was its chairperson until 2005 and also its major fundraiser. Every year, she held an alumni event for people who had successfully overcome their dependency problems, and while she talked to people and celebrated with them, former President Ford cooked hot dogs for everybody.

In 1999, the Fords were awarded the Congressional Gold Medal. At the event, President Clinton said in his speech:

> "Perhaps no First Lady in our history, with the possible exception of Eleanor Roosevelt, has touched so many of us in a personal way . . . because you showed us it was not wrong for a good person and a strong person to be imperfect and ask for help. You gave us a gift and we thank you."

Betty Ford died of old age on July 8, 2011, at the age of 93.

# Chapter **17**

# Ending a Cold War

This chapter covers three First Ladies who carried on the tradition of being politically and socially active during their tenure. Rosalynn Carter was a contributor not only to her husband's campaigns but also to his policies. She truly became his right-hand woman. She traveled alone on her husband's behalf around the world and even sat in on Cabinet meetings. As she once said: "Jimmy and I were always partners."

Rosalynn Carter today is considered the most successful postpresidency former First Lady. She is also listed as one of the top ten First Ladies in American history.

Nancy Reagan was glamorous, outspoken, and influential behind the scenes. She and Ronald Reagan had a remarkable partnership in their strong marriage. This soon became a working partnership in politics, too. She always made sure that the people around him had his best interests in mind. She was the first First Lady to become the unofficial personnel chief in the White House.

Barbara Bush had a tough act to follow. She was family oriented and preferred to be around the average person. In 1989, *Time* magazine called her a down-to-earth First Lady and a breath of fresh air. In the same article, *Time* also coined her nickname "The Silver Fox," referring to her gray hair. Today, she is still admired by many.

# Eleanor Rosalynn Smith Carter (1927–)

Eleanor Rosalynn Smith (see Figure 17-1), who went by just Rosalynn, was born in Plains, Georgia, on August 18, 1927. Plains was a small town of about 600 people and full of dirt roads. She was the oldest of the four children of Wilburn Edgar and Frances Allethea Smith. Her father was a farmer and mechanic who died when Rosalynn was only 13. She, therefore, had to help her mother, who was a seamstress, with housework and taking care of her younger siblings, while working a job at a local beauty parlor. Despite all of this, she turned out to be an excellent student in high school.

**FIGURE 17-1:**
Eleanor Rosalynn
Smith Carter.

Source: Library of Congress, Prints & Photographs Division,
Reproduction number LC-USZCN4-117
(color film copy neg.)LC-USZC2-14 (color film copy slide)
LC-USZ62-62546 (b&w film copy neg.)

Rosalynn's best friend was Ruth Carter, the younger sister of Jimmy Carter. So she knew Jimmy, but the two didn't socialize much in high school. After graduating from high school, where she was class valedictorian, Rosalynn attended Georgia Southwestern Junior College, and Jimmy joined the U.S. Naval Academy. They began to date when she was a freshman in college. They dated for about six months mostly through letter writing and then Jimmy proposed marriage, but she turned him down because she wanted to finish college first. When he asked again later, she accepted, and the two got married on July 7, 1946.

# Relishing travel but returning home

Rosalynn was happy to leave her small Southern town. Being a Navy wife, she was able to travel all over the country. Her three sons were born in three different states, Virginia, Hawaii, and Connecticut. She also lived in California and New York. Even though she was mostly a mother at this time raising her sons by herself, she enjoyed her independence. Rosalynn loved being away from her small town and was heartbroken when Jimmy told her in 1953 that it was time to move back to Plains, Georgia, to run his late father's business. In her autobiography *First Lady from Plains,* she wrote: "I argued, I cried, I even screamed at him." This was the only time she and her husband had a serious disagreement in their marriage.

**TECHNICAL STUFF**

In 1953, Jimmy Carter's father was diagnosed with and died from cancer. Jimmy returned home to take over the family business. He proved to be an excellent businessman, and he turned the small company into a large peanut warehouse business. By the time Jimmy Carter became president, he was a millionaire.

# Changing gears to politics

By 1953, they were back living in Plains. Jimmy had taken over his father's business and Rosalynn was the business's bookkeeper. She was ecstatic when Jimmy decided to get involved in politics. For her, it was a way out of small-town living. She became his partner in politics, helping him campaign and even campaigned by herself for him. Later, during his presidential campaign in 1976, she traveled by herself to 41 states to give speeches on Jimmy's behalf.

**FIRST LADY LORE**

Rosalynn had a big fear of public speaking. Talking to a large crowd made her physically ill. So Jimmy told her not to read or memorize a prepared script but to talk to people freely about items she enjoyed and was interested in. She tried this approach, just using a few notecards, and suddenly started enjoying talking to people.

Jimmy Carter's political career started in 1960, when he won a seat on a local school board in Plains, Georgia. Two years later, he was elected to the Georgia State senate. By 1966, Jimmy thought that he was ready for the governorship. He entered the race and finished a disappointing third. Jimmy didn't take the loss lightly; he went into a major depression and thought that his political career was over. His sister encouraged him to find religion, and the Carters became born-again, turning themselves into Evangelical Christians. Encouraged, Jimmy ran for governor again in 1970 and won this time.

For Rosalynn, becoming First Lady of Georgia proved to be very beneficial. She started gaining confidence and traveled the state to find issues she was interested in. She found them quickly, and they were mental health, education, and care for the aged.

# Running for president

As early as 1972, Jimmy Carter wanted to be president. He established a campaign committee and had a detailed strategy drawn up. In early 1975, Jimmy announced his candidacy. He was a virtual unknown, and nobody gave him much of a chance. However, Jimmy was a candidate who supported integration and civil rights but also was a Southerner. His appeal was that he ran as an outsider because of corruption and Watergate. The Carters were also Christian fundamentalists, which helped them mobilize the Christian right in the 1976 election.

Jimmy campaigned hard and kept discussion of his position vague on various issues while calling for a return to morality and an end to corruption in the federal government. His platform resonated with a public that had recently dealt with Vietnam and Watergate.

**FIRST LADY LORE**

In 1976, Rosalynn campaigned hard for her husband. Jimmy needed Florida badly to win the election. So she and her friend Edna Langford drove to small towns all over Florida and looked for radio and/or TV station stations. They'd stop as soon as they found it, introduce themselves, and ask whether they'd like an interview. Rosalynn even brought her own sheet of questions the interviewer could use.

# Loving it as First Lady

Rosalynn was a newcomer in Washington, D.C. She had no connections and no support system in the capital. She did have limited experience being the First Lady of Georgia but wasn't really interested in playing the traditional role of hostess in the White House. She wrote in her memoirs:

**IN THEIR WORDS**

"Once presidents' wives had been confined to official hostess and private help-meet, but . . . Nowadays the public expectation is just the opposite, and there is a general presumption that the projects of a First Lady will be substantive, highly publicized, and closely scrutinized. I am thankful for the change."

Rosalynn loved being First Lady. She threw herself into her role and right away became politically active. She pushed for the passage of the Equal Rights Amendment (ERA) and became a proponent for the rights of the mentally ill. In 1977, she began to work as the Honorary Chairperson of the President's Commission on Mental Health, which worked on the treatment and rights of mentally ill health patients. In 1978, she became a major lobbyist and even testified in front of Congress, for the Mental Health Systems Act, which ended the unnecessary institutionalization of mentally ill people and provided federal grants to community health centers. In other words, the bill demanded that mental illness had to be treated like any other disease. The bill was finally passed by Congress in 1980.

## Being an official U.S. representative

Rosalynn traveled to Latin America and the Caribbean in 1977 on behalf of the president. While previous First Ladies had traveled abroad themselves, they had never gone in an official policy capacity representing the U.S. government. Rosalynn had prepared for the trip by getting briefings from the State Department and had even learned Spanish. She met with foreign leaders discussing policies and local concerns. When she came back, she fully briefed the Senate Foreign Relations Committee on the trip.

That had never happened before, and she was widely criticized by the media and some of the foreign leaders she had met. They weren't sure whether she had the power to negotiate or even speak for her husband, and the press didn't like the fact that someone discussed official U.S. foreign policy with foreign leaders, who hadn't been elected by the people. Her subsequent trips were less official; for example, she traveled to Thailand in 1979 to inspect refugee camps.

However, Rosalynn played an active role in the 1978 Camp David Accords, which ended up being the crowning moment of the Carter administration's foreign policy. President Carter met with Israeli Prime Minister Menachem Begin and Egyptian President Anwar Sadat in Camp David, Maryland. He had also invited their wives to provide a more congenial atmosphere at the meeting. Rosalynn's job was not only to entertain the wives but also to take notes at the meetings. After 21 days, an agreement was reached, thereby ending the state of war between Israel and Egypt, and Rosalynn had almost 200 pages of notes. To this day, her notes provide the most accurate reporting of the historic accords. And Sadat and Begin won the Nobel Peace Prize for negotiating the accord.

## Being an assistant president

Rosalynn attended Cabinet meetings, not as a participant but as an observer gathering insight into her husband' administration. She held weekly working lunches with her husband where the two discussed policy, even foreign policy events such as developments in the Middle East. She studied up on proposals in front of Congress and actively lobbied Congresspeople on her pet issues. Rosalynn soon was called the assistant president.

Rosalynn further institutionalized the role of First Lady when she established her own workspace in the East Wing of the White House, which today is called the Office of the First Lady. In addition, Congress passed the Public Law 95–750 in 1978, allocating funds for the first time not just for the upkeep of the White House but also for assistance and services to First Ladies in connection with the president's duties. In other words, First Ladies today have their own budget in the White House.

Jimmy Carter even called her: "A very equal partner and a perfect extension of myself."

Rosalynn was not just disappointed when her husband lost reelection in 1980, but she was actually very bitter about the loss. She blamed the press for poor coverage of her husband's policies and feared having to move back to Plains, Georgia. Rosalynn wrote in her memoirs: "Everybody pretended like they weren't bitter, but I sure was."

## Being active in retirement

After leaving office, both Rosalynn and Jimmy Carter stayed active. They founded the Carter Center at Emory University to study democracy and human rights. Rosalynn Carter became a vocal advocate of human rights throughout the world and, together with Jimmy, has traveled extensively, monitoring elections in many countries. So far, the two have monitored elections in 37 countries.

Further, Rosalynn continued her work on behalf of the mentally ill and cofounded Every Child by Two, a program that provides for early childhood immunization. Rosalynn and Jimmy also participate in Habitat for Humanity, where they don't just raise money but actually help build low-income housing with their own hands.

In 1999, President Clinton awarded Jimmy and Rosalynn Carter the Presidential Medal of Freedom for their humanitarian service, and in 2002 Jimmy received the Nobel Peace Prize for bringing peace to the Middle East while president. Today, Rosalynn Carter is one of the most respected individuals not only in the United States but in the world.

Rosalynn truly loved being First Lady and being involved in politics. In her autobiography, she wrote: "I would be out there campaigning right now if Jimmy would run again. I miss the world of politics."

# Nancy Davis Reagan (1921–2016)

Nancy Reagan (see Figure 17-2) was born Anne Frances Robbins in New York City, New York, on July 6, 1921. Her mother, Edith Luckett, an actress, nicknamed her Nancy, and it stuck. Her mother was separated from her husband and divorced him when Nancy was two, so Nancy rarely saw her father, Kenneth Robbins, an automobile dealer from New Jersey. Her mother, being an actress, toured the country frequently and left young Nancy behind with an aunt in Maryland until

Nancy was eight. Edith tried to see her daughter as often as possible, and whenever she was in New York City doing a show on Broadway, young Nancy was invited to attend.

**FIGURE 17-2:**
Nancy Davis
Reagan.

Source: Library of Congress, Prints & Photographs Division,
Reproduction number LC-DIG-ds-00126 (digital file from original item)LC-USZ62-91452 (b&w film copy neg.)

**FIRST LADY LORE**

One play required Nancy's mother to die on stage. Nancy wasn't told about this and sat in the audience watching the character her mom played die. She began crying, and her mother had to wave to her from the stage to let her know she was okay.

## Catching the acting bug

As a child, Nancy enjoyed dressing up and pretending to be an actress like her mom. Her mother finally got remarried to a man named Loyal Davis, a wealthy neurosurgeon and head of the Department for Surgery at Northwestern University near Chicago. He adopted Nancy and became the father she never had before. She now went by Nancy Davis.

Nancy enjoyed fine clothing, expensive dinners, and hanging out with the wealthy in Chicago. She attended a private school and then went off to Smith College in Massachusetts to study drama. During WWII, she and her mother volunteered as nurses' aides, and in the mid-1940s, Nancy moved to New York City to star in a small role in a play on Broadway.

The play ran for six months, and Nancy stayed in New York for the whole time. She socialized with her mother's friends, including Clark Gable. Soon she was invited to do a screen test in California, which had been arranged by another one of her mother's friends, Spencer Tracy. She did well and subsequently moved to California to star in 11 movies.

## Meeting Ronald Reagan

Nancy met Ronald Reagan in 1949. She had contacted him because her name appeared by mistake on a list of Communist sympathizers in Hollywood. Ronald, as president of the Screen Actors Guild, took care of the problem for Nancy and fell in love with her. The romance developed slowly because Ronald had been recently divorced from actress Jane Wyman and wanted to take his time. They were finally married on March 4, 1952.

At their wedding, the best man for Ronald Reagan was famous actor William Holden.

After the wedding, their daughter Patti was born, and Nancy became a doting mother. By the late 1950s, Nancy's and Ronald's movie careers were coming to an end. Ronald turned to television. He hosted a half-hour television show and traveled around the country giving speeches on behalf of General Electric. In his speeches, Ronald tackled many political issues. After campaigning and voting for Republicans Eisenhower and Nixon, Ronald officially changed his party affiliation from Democrat to Republican in 1962.

Ronald Reagan's big political break occurred in 1964. The Republican nominee for president, Barry Goldwater, was doing poorly in the polls and having problems raising money. Ronald gave an impassioned speech on Goldwater's behalf, blasting big government and praising individual initiative. The televised speech raised hundreds of thousands of dollars for Goldwater and turned Ronald into a national conservative icon.

For this reason, in 1966, a group of businesspeople asked Ronald Reagan to run for governor of California. He accepted and beat the incumbent Pat Brown by almost a million votes.

## Taking on the governorship

Nancy had never been interested in politics. However, she traveled with her husband to campaign appearances and slowly learned how to become a politician's wife. At first, she hated the capital in Sacramento. The governor's mansion hadn't been updated in years, there were no good stores to shop at (she was used to shopping in Beverly Hills), and it was hot during the summertime. She also despised the major newspaper in the city, the *Sacramento Bee*, because it constantly criticized her husband.

At first, Nancy treated the staff like servants, which garnered many complaints, but after a while, she figured out how to treat the staff properly and the complaints stopped. This lesson proved to be very helpful when she became First Lady of the United States.

As soon as she became First Lady of California, Nancy and her husband decided to build a new governor's mansion, while they lived in a rented house, instead of renovating the old governor's mansion. Because the new governor's mansion was not finished on time, the Reagans never had a chance to live in it.

Next, Nancy looked for a cause to be identified with. She visited wounded veterans coming home from Vietnam and became interested in substance abuse issues. She also wrote a syndicated newspaper column and donated all her revenue to the National League of Families of American Prisoners and Missing in Action in Southeast Asia.

In 1975, Ronald Reagan announced his candidacy for the Republican presidential nomination. President Ford had been in office for just a year, and the conservative wing of the Republican Party backed Ronald Reagan.

After losing out on the Republican nomination by a narrow margin in 1976, Ronald ran for the Republican nomination again in 1980. He was now the clear front-runner for the nomination. He faced incumbent president Jimmy Carter in the general election and focused on Carter's weaknesses and called for a restoration of U.S. power, major rearmament, and, especially, a smaller government with less regulation and a major tax cut. He won the election in a landslide.

## Becoming First Lady

Nancy Reagan was First Lady for eight years. Historians have divided her tenure as First Lady into three phases, which I discuss further in the following sections:

» Phase one began right in 1981. During it, Nancy was mostly interested in hosting glamorous parties. She got the finest dresses and the most expensive dinnerware collection for the White House she could find.

» In phase two, Nancy turned toward social causes. Her most famous one was the war against drugs. Here, she came up with the Just Say No campaign.

>> Phase three occurred during Nancy's second term as First Lady. Her husband had health problems by now, and his administration was involved in the Iran-Contra scandal. She suddenly became fiercely protective of him and saw her job as making sure that her husband could get well and serve out his second term.

## Acting like a queen

After becoming First Lady in 1981, Nancy staged expensive and elegant parties in the White House. She loved entertaining and was embarrassed about how run down the White House had become. She wanted a complete renovation of the building and new furniture, new upholstery, and new drapes and curtains. She also realized right away that there was no full set of China for a large state dinner and so a new one had to be bought. Congress had allocated only $50,000, and she budgeted $900,000. Instead of asking Congress for more money, she asked private donors to put up the money. They did, and of course it helped that they received a 50 percent tax deduction on their donations.

Nancy's social spending spiraled out of control, and the press criticized her for overspending while the country was in a recession and her husband was cutting the federal budget. Many in the media just ignored the fact that her spending money came mostly from private donations and didn't cost the taxpayer any money. For example, the $200,000 she spent on new White House China turned out to be a private gift. So she was criticized because she was able to renovate the White House using mostly private money.

Nancy Reagan had a tough first year. By 1982, she had become the administration's number-one public relations problem. Many Americans looked upon her as Queen Nancy, and the press only fostered this image. So the White House decided that a remake was in order. In 1982, Nancy announced that she would donate designer clothes she had received as gifts to museums, and she started to focus on serious issues. She even cracked jokes about herself, saying that she would never wear a crown because it would mess up her hair. Within a few months, her public approval ratings increased.

## Campaigning for Just Say No

Nancy's First Lady cause was the war against substance abuse. She became the spokesperson for the "Just Say No" campaign, which encouraged people to resist drugs. Nancy believed that the whole campaign should be a private rather than public effort. She even took her crusade against drugs to the international level, inviting first ladies from around the world to a First Ladies Conference in 1985 and hosting the second international drug conference at the United Nations in the same year. When people criticized her efforts, she said:

"If it saves one child's life, it's worth it."

## Protecting her husband

On March 30, 1981, President Reagan delivered a speech at a hotel in Washington. He was shot by a crazed assassin, John Hinckley, while waiting outside the hotel. Doctors found that the bullet had hit the president's left lung and lodged itself just an inch from his heart. On his way to the operating table, the president cracked several jokes, including telling his wife, "Honey, I forgot to duck," which turned him into a hero with most U.S. citizens. He returned to work only 12 days later, having achieved almost mythical status.

After the assassination attempt, Nancy feared constantly for Ronald's life. So she consulted famous astrologer Joan Quigley to help with his schedule to keep him safe. Joan later claimed to have chosen times and days for press conferences, State of the Union addresses, and even flights on Air Force One.

## Advising a president

By the time President Reagan's second term started, Nancy had become an indispensable advisor to him. Not only had she prepared him for his 1984 presidential debates with Democratic challenger Walter Mondale, but she also had urged him to get the Soviet Union under its new leader Gorbachev to the negotiating table. She believed that Gorbachev was ready to negotiate and that her husband had a chance to end the Cold War. After President Reagan's colon cancer surgery, she even stood in for him and received foreign dignitaries at the White House.

President Reagan gave a talk after his surgery in which he discussed how important First Ladies had been in the history of the country. About his wife, he said the following:

"Nancy is my everything. When I look back on these days, Nancy, I'll remember your radiance, and your strength, your support, and for taking part in the business of the nation, I say to myself, but also on behalf of the nation, thank you partner. Thanks for everything."

Afterward, the *New York Times* coined the term *associate presidency* for the role Nancy Reagan played in the Reagan administration. The American public wasn't too concerned about her role because the previous two First Ladies, Rosalynn Carter and Betty Ford, already had been closely involved in their husband's administration, and this was considered the new normal.

## Becoming an informal chief of staff

Nancy had always been closely involved in her husband's campaigns. During the 1976 failed and 1980 successful presidential campaigns, she helped hire and fire political consultants. During Ronald's second term, she engineered the firing of the chief of staff Donald Regan after the Iran-Contra Affair. While her husband was recovering from prostate cancer, his Chief of Staff Donald Regan wanted him to hold a news conference to discuss the Iran-Contra Affair. Nancy said no and suggested instead a scripted apology. Ronald Reagan followed Nancy's advice, gave a widely applauded scripted address to the country in which he apologized for the Iran-Contra Affair and regained his popularity. She saved not just his presidency but also his legacy in American history. Donald Regan was subsequently fired.

**TECHNICAL STUFF**

President Reagan's policy successes came to an abrupt halt in late 1986, as he spent the remainder of his term dealing with the Iran-Contra scandal. A story broke in Lebanon in November 1986, revealing that the Reagan administration had been selling weapons to Iran in exchange for freeing U.S. hostages in Lebanon. The exchange was illegal, and it embarrassed the Reagan administration. The profits from the illegal arms sales were then used to fund the Contras in Nicaragua, which was also illegal. Congress had repeatedly refused President Reagan's requests to give aid to the Contras — so-called freedom fighters trying to overthrow the Nicaraguan government. Congress instead passed a bill making military aid to the Contras illegal. In the end, Congress issued a 690-page report stating that Ronald Reagan was unaware of the illegal doings of some of his staff, though it criticized his management style.

## Facing health issues

Beginning in 1985, health problems hit the Reagans. Ronald was diagnosed with colon cancer in 1985 and prostate cancer in 1987, and Nancy was diagnosed with breast cancer and had to have a mastectomy. Like Betty Ford, she went public and discussed the disease and surgery. Worried about her husband, Nancy became involved and tried to protect not only his legacy but also his health. She wanted him to work less and have a more relaxed schedule. She was happy when his term was over by 1989.

Right away, Nancy went to friends to raise money for the Reagan library, which opened in 1991 and is still considered the most beautiful of all the presidential libraries. Her husband appreciated all she did for him and said:

**IN THEIR WORDS**

"Put simply, my life really began when I met Nancy and it has been rich and full ever since."

She also established the Nancy Reagan Foundation to continue to fight drug abuse and in the early 2000s became an advocate for stem cell research, lobbying the Bush White House.

In November 1994, Ronald Reagan announced that he had Alzheimer's disease. His public appearances decreased, and Nancy attended the 1996 Republican National Convention on his behalf. By 1999, the disease had progressed to a point where Nancy decided to live in semi-isolation away from the public's eye. The ten years her husband was fighting the disease were, according to her, the longest goodbye. She won the American public over in these years she cared for him and established the Ronald and Nancy Reagan Research Institute, which is a part of the National Alzheimer's Association.

Ronald Reagan died on June 5, 2004, at the age of 93. Nancy was never the same afterward and died March 6, 2016, of congestive heart failure. She was 94. As one of Ronald Reagan's long-term advisors said: "Without Nancy there would have been no Governor Reagan and no President Reagan."

# Barbara Pierce Bush (1925–2018)

Barbara Pierce (see Figure 17-3) was born on June 8, 1925, to parents Marvin and Pauline Pierce. Her father was a magazine publisher and her grandfather an Ohio State Supreme Court justice. In addition, the Pierce family was related to former president Franklin Pierce.

Barbara grew up happy in the town of Rye, close to New York City, and went to an exclusive private boarding school in South Carolina. She met George H. W. Bush during a 1941 Christmas vacation at the Greenwich, Connecticut, country club when she was 16. He was only 17 at the time, but it was love at first sight, and they were secretly engaged 18 months later. However, they waited to get married because George joined the Navy in 1942 and became a pilot and flew bombing missions in the Pacific during WWII. While waiting for him to return, Barbara attended Smith College but never completed her degree. During his deployment, they wrote each other letters, which brought them even closer. After he got his first leave, the two got married on January 6, 1945.

REMEMBER

While serving his country, George became one of the youngest and most distinguished pilots of WWII. He flew more than 50 bombing missions against Japan. In 1944, his plane was shot down by the Japanese. He survived hours in the Pacific Ocean before a U.S. submarine rescued him. He then spent several weeks on the submarine, and everybody back home thought he was dead. Barbara wasn't told about this because her family didn't want to worry her.

Source: Library of Congress, Prints & Photographs Division,
Reproduction number LC-USZ62-98303 (b&w film copy neg.)
LC-USZC4-1701 (color film copy transparency)

**FIGURE 17-3:**
Barbara Pierce
Bush.

## Making family priority #1

After WWII had ended, George went to Yale University and, after graduating in 1948, took his wife and young son George W. to Texas to work in the oil industry. In Texas, the two had five more children. Sadly, daughter Robin died at age three of leukemia, and Barbara said: "Because of Robin, I love every living human more."

**FIRST
LADY LORE**

Barbara was devastated by Robin's death; it very profoundly affected her. She went through a period of depression, and that is when her hair turned white.

Family meant everything for Barbara. She devoted her entire life to family and her husband. George was often an absent father because of work, first in the oil industry and then in politics. Barbara's focus was on her family and constantly establishing new homes. From 1945 until 1989 when she became First Lady, Barbara had moved 28 times.

**IN THEIR
WORDS**

Barbara said of this time: "This was a period for me, of long days and short years, of diapers, runny noses and earaches."

George was very successful in the 1950s and 1960s, and he became very wealthy. He turned to politics in the late 1960s.

Like his father, George was a moderate Republican. In 1962, he became the chairman of the Republican Party in Harris County (Houston), Texas. A couple of years later, he thought he was ready to run for office. His father had been a senator, so he figured he should be one, too. He ran against incumbent Democrat Ralph Yarborough in 1964 and lost. However, he gained the attention of the Republican Party by receiving a record number of votes for a Republican in Texas. Former vice president Richard Nixon took George under his wing, and in 1966, George H. W. Bush became the first Republican to represent Houston in the House of Representatives.

Next came a whole slew of political offices, which moved the Bushes around the country and around the globe.

Barbara enjoyed some of her husband's positions. She loved living in New York City while George was the U.S. Ambassador to the United Nations. She had a suite at the Waldorf tower and entertained a lot. After President Ford offered George the job of U.S. Envoy to China, Barbara was ecstatic. She loved China; it was exciting, vibrant, and unexplored. She toured the country and even learned some Chinese. She was very unhappy to leave after one year. Back in Washington, D.C., where George had become the head of the CIA, she felt alone — all her kids had left, and George couldn't discuss issues with her like he had done in previous positions. She went into a deep depression for almost a year.

## Becoming Second and then First Lady

In 1980, George H. W. Bush ran for the Republican presidential nomination. He was the only real challenger to Ronald Reagan. He ran as a moderate, pointing out his differences with the more conservative Reagan. When Reagan won the nomination, he selected George to be his running mate. George had to promise to support Reagan's policies, even if he disagreed with them. He did, and Barbara was happy to become Second Lady.

Barbara Bush tried very hard to be friends with Nancy Reagan and her husband. However, the Reagans weren't really interested. They preferred to be social in their own little circle and excluded the Bushes from personal events. There seemed to be some friction between her and Nancy. So the Bushes were rarely invited to the White House unless it was for formal occasions.

Then in 1988, George won the presidency, and it was Barbara's turn to be First Lady. She stayed out of politics until her husband's term had ended. She believed that one of the reasons for her popularity was that she wasn't openly political. She told Raisa Gorbachev that her appeal was that she was old, white-headed, and large and that she stayed out of her husband's affairs but was tough and combative and stood up for herself. At the same time, she admitted that she did have some influence over her husband, stating:

"You have to have influence. When you are married for 47 years, if you don't have any influence, then I really think you are in deep trouble."

In 1988, her husband's campaign advisors told her to lose weight and dye her hair so that she would have a more youthful appearance for the American public. She told them: "We can do anything, but you can't make me lose weight or dye my hair."

Barbara Bush was one of the most beloved first ladies of the 20th century. She was called everybody's grandmother, and she was friendly, witty, and just like everybody else. She was the center of a large family, with five children and twice as many grandchildren.

## Fighting illiteracy

Barbara had always been interested in reading and writing because one of her sons had been dyslexic. According to studies, parents who can't read can't read books to their children, and the children won't reap the educational benefits of being read to. Experts have stated that reading to children is the most important thing parents can do to prepare them for school, and there are links between poverty, crime, and reading and writing abilities.

Early on, Barbara focused on involving the whole family on learning how to read and write, and this became her cause as First Lady. She had actually identified literacy as her First Lady cause as early as 1980 just in case her husband would win the presidency. He did not, but eight years later he would, and she was now able to focus on it.

Barbara used to say: "The home is the child's first school, the parent is the child's first teacher, and reading is the child's first subject."

Barbara raised funds for literacy programs and supported teachers training. She took it even a step further during her time as First Lady. She became the host of a ten-part radio show called *Mrs. Bush's Story Time*, where she read stories and promoted the idea of family reading. She also wrote a bestselling book *Millie's Book as dictated to Barbara Bush*, a collection of photographs and supposed musings of the family dog. The book became a bestseller, and she earned $800,000 in royalties, which she donated to her Barbara Bush Foundation for Family Literacy that she had established in 1989.

Barbara further raised money for the United Negro College Fund, the Morehouse College School of Medicine, and for many hospitals such as Sloan-Kettering in New York City, where her daughter Robin had been treated for leukemia.

## Winning over a hostile crowd

In June of 1990, Barbara was asked to be a commencement speaker at Wellesley College, a traditional, very elite college for women. She was supposed to be the substitute speaker for Alice Walker, an African American author and activist, who had been the students' choice but had to cancel. One hundred and fifty graduates objected, stating that she was an inappropriate speaker because she owed her successes to her husband and had never graduated from college.

Instead of canceling the speech or being upset with the students, she said she respected the students' views. She showed up and brought Raisa Gorbachev, the wife of the Soviet president, who was a university professor, along. Both women — university professor and college dropout — gave speeches, and Barbara made the following comment at the end of her speech: "Somewhere out in this audience may even be someone who will one day follow in my footsteps and preside over the White House as the president's spouse." She then paused and added: "I wish him well." This won over the audience and turned the event into a public relations coup for Barbara.

FIRST LADY LORE

Barbara Bush's speech at Wellesley in 1990 is still a classic today. It is listed as the #45 speech in American Rhetoric's Top 100 Speeches of the 20th Century.

## Capturing popularity

By 1992, Barbara was more popular than her husband, and she went out and tirelessly campaigned for him. He was aware of her popularity and answered questions during the campaign, starting with: "Well, Barbara and I think . . ."

IN THEIR WORDS

When asked why she had become so popular, Barbara said: "My mail tells me a lot of fat, white-haired, wrinkled ladies are tickled pink. I think it makes them feel better about themselves. I mean, look at me — if I can be a success, so can they."

After the election of 1992, she couldn't believe her husband lost. She believed that he had done a superb job, but at the same time, she was also ready to go back to Texas to retire.

# Creating a legacy

Barbara continued to be active in retirement. She served as hostess for many events at the George H. W. Bush Presidential Library at Texas A&M University and gave speeches on behalf of her favorite causes. Barbara even admitted that she was pro-choice and supported gay rights, positions that would have conflicted with her husband's and the Republican Party's stances.

Soon she became one of the most popular First Ladies ever. She published her memoirs *Barbara Bush: A Memoir* in 1994, which became a massive bestseller. In 2001, she became the Second First Lady, after Abigail Adams, to see her son, George W. Bush, become president.

REMEMBER

Barbara created a Bush dynasty in the U.S. Her oldest son George W. became governor of Texas in 1994 and a two-term president from 2001 to 2009. Her other son Jeb became governor of Florida in 1998, served two terms, and then had an unsuccessful run for the Republican presidential nomination in 2016. Her grandson George P. Bush is currently the Land Commissioner of Texas and is running for the position of Texas Attorney General in 2022.

Barbara loved spending time with her children and 14 grandchildren in her summer house in Kennebunk Port, Maine, and she selectively campaigned for her sons. After her son Jeb lost the Republican presidential nomination to Donald Trump in 2016, she refused to back the Republican ticket and wrote in her son's name as a write-in candidate. After the election, her husband even admitted to voting for Democrat Hillary Clinton.

By 2018, Barbara's health was declining. She was suffering from congestive heart failure and COPD (chronic obstructive pulmonary disease). Barbara died on April 17, 2018, at the age of 92. Her funeral was attended by fellow First Ladies Melania Trump, Michelle Obama, Laura Bush, and Hillary Clinton. Her husband, President George H. W. Bush, only survived her by seven months. He died on November 30, 2018, at the age of 94. Both are buried at the George H. W. Bush Presidential Library in College Station, Texas.

IN THEIR
WORDS

When asked about her legacy, Barbara said: "I'd like to be known as someone who really cared about people and worked very, very hard to make America more literate."

Today, Barbara Bush has become an American classic. She is still popular for her common-sense approach to running the White House and for being down to earth and being able to connect with the average American.

# Chapter **18**

# Almost Becoming President

Hillary Clinton is one of the most, if not the most, controversial First Ladies in American history. She was the most socially active First Lady since Eleanor Roosevelt, working tirelessly for women's rights globally. Instead of simply playing second fiddle to her husband, she was determined to build her own career and become just as influential as the president was. Her pet issues were women's rights, education, and children — all issues she started feeling strongly about while a teenager. Chairing the Arkansas State Commission on Education allowed her to improve education in Arkansas. Later, she built a career as one of the leading attorneys in the United States. In both 1988 and 1991, she was named one of the top 100 attorneys in the U.S. by the *National Law Review*.

Hillary turned her First Ladyship into the start of her own political career, separate from her husband's. With this, she redefined the role of American presidential spouses in U.S. politics. For more about Hillary's career as First Lady and in politics, read on.

# Hillary Rodham Clinton (1947–)

Hillary Rodham (see Figure 18-1) was born on October 26, 1947, in the Chicago suburb of Park Ridge. She was the oldest of three children born to Hugh and Dorothy Rodham. Her father owned a fabric store, and her mother was a homemaker. She was active in sports, enjoying swimming and tennis, and she participated in ballet and the Girl Scouts.

**FIGURE 18-1:**
Hillary Rodham Clinton.

Source: Library of Congress, Prints & Photographs Division, Reproduction number LC-DIG-ds-00125 (digital file from original item)LC-USZ62-139377 (b&w film copy neg.) LC-USZ62-107702 (b&w film copy neg.)

Hillary's parents insisted that she join a Methodist church group, which she did. The pastor of this group, Don Jones, made an impression on her. While her father was a staunch Republican and her neighborhood was 99.5 percent white and middle class, he was a progressive and not only instilled an independent political streak in her but also provided her with a social conscience. For example, her church group served as babysitters for working parents in the area and raised money for poor children in Chicago.

**FIRST LADY LORE**

When Hillary was four years old, she was bullied by a little girl named Suzy. She came back home crying, and her mom told her, "This house is no place for cowards. You go back out there and you knock that girl off her pins." That is exactly what Hillary did the next day, and when she came home, her mom asked how it went. Hillary said, "Now I can play with the boys."

Hillary's mother also imprinted the idea of never getting divorced. Her mother's parents had divorced and then abandoned her. So divorce was out of the question for both her mom and also Hillary. Later on, when her husband, Bill Clinton, asked for a divorce in 1989 after falling in love with someone else, Hillary said no and told him to end the affair. He did.

Hillary excelled in high school, debating political opponents as part of a mock election and becoming class vice president. When she graduated in 1965, her classmates voted her as the girl most likely to succeed. After high school, she attended Wellesley College in Massachusetts. She became more interested in social justice issues after the assassination of Dr. Martin Luther King Jr., whom she had personally met with her church group. The assassination of Dr. King Jr. changed her political views and turned her into a progressive liberal by 1968.

Hillary graduated from Wellesley in 1969, with honors and a degree in political science. In a letter of recommendation to law school, one of her professors wrote: "She has the intellectual ability, personality, and character to make a remarkable contribution to American society." Not surprisingly, Hillary was selected to be the college's first student commencement speaker. Instead of coming up with a traditional commencement speech, she asked her classmates what she should speak about. This is how it was decided that she would address social justice issues such as the war in Vietnam, the political assassinations of Dr. Marin Luther King Jr., and Robert Kennedy in her speech. Her speech went well and was even discussed in *Life* magazine, which was her first media exposure.

## Meeting Bill Clinton

After graduating from Wellesley, Hillary went to Yale Law School, where she was active in the campus civil rights organization and published a well-known paper on the rights of children. She worked with poorer youth in New Haven, Connecticut, and later, in 1973, joined the Children's Defense Fund (CDF) as an attorney and board chairperson.

**FIRST
LADY LORE**

Hillary actively pursued women's rights on campus at Yale. Because of her efforts, every female bathroom at Yale was equipped with tampon dispensers.

Hillary met Bill Clinton at Yale University in 1970, and the two got closer when they discovered that both were backing George McGovern, the Democratic candidate for president in 1972. That summer, they both went to Texas to work for the McGovern presidential campaign. Hillary was attracted to Bill fairly quickly, liking his physique and his Southern charm, while Bill liked her assertiveness.

REMEMBER

The story of how Bill and Hillary met is a classic one. They were both in the library and kept catching one another's eye and finally she walked up to him and said that if they were going to keep looking at one another they might as well meet.

After graduating from Yale University in 1973, Hillary started to work for the Children's Defense Fund, and Bill went back to Arkansas to teach law at the University of Arkansas. Soon afterward, Hillary was called to Washington, D.C., to become a legal assistant for the congressional committee that was discussing whether to impeach President Nixon. Nixon chose to resign in August 1974, before Congress had a chance to impeach him. Hillary now had to make a choice: Stay in Washington, D.C., and work on her career or join Bill in Arkansas. She chose Arkansas and Bill.

FIRST LADY LORE

When Hillary left for Arkansas in 1974, her friends told her that she was crazy for leaving her promising career behind in Washington, D.C. She told them, "Bill Clinton is going to be president someday, and I'm going to marry him." One of her friends asked whether Bill was aware of this. Hillary just said, "Not yet."

They got married on October 11, 1975, in Fayetteville, Arkansas. Like Bill, Hillary took a teaching position at the University of Arkansas School of Law, while heading the legal aid clinic on campus. The two were totally different professors; he gave everybody good grades, had fun in the classroom, and didn't take things seriously. She was well prepared and tough. Their law school dean openly said that if he had to make a choice of who to keep on the faculty, Bill or Hillary, he'd pick Hillary.

## Starting a career and getting into politics

After three years of teaching, Hillary decided to join the most prestigious law firm in Arkansas, Rose Law Firm, located in Little Rock, Arkansas, and became its first female full partner. Then Bill was elected governor in 1978, after having lost a Congressional race in 1974 and having become Attorney General of Arkansas in 1976, making Hillary the First Lady of Arkansas. She continued to work her job full time and soon was the breadwinner for the family. Being governor of Arkansas didn't pay well, and she had to make up for this.

REMEMBER

During Bill's first term as governor, Hillary became a liability. She had refused to take his last name, which upset many traditional voters in Arkansas. In addition, she wore no makeup, dressed in jeans and cheap clothing, and often looked like a hippie. She wasn't the Southern lady the people of Arkansas had expected. After Bill lost reelection in 1980, she changed. She suddenly started to play the role of a Southern lady, wore expensive clothing, had her hair done, and even held teas for other ladies. Also, she added Bill's last name and started going by Hillary Rodham Clinton. This helped Bill win the office back in 1982, and he held it for the next ten years.

By this time, they had a daughter, Chelsea Victoria, born in 1980, and Hillary became active as First Lady of Arkansas, while still keeping her full-time job as a lawyer. She became the chairperson of the Arkansas Education Standards Committee, an unpaid position. In this function, she traveled throughout the state, held meetings, met with teachers and parents, and then recommended improvements to the Arkansas educational structures. Because of her work, new standards were implemented, including teacher testing and smaller classrooms. Arkansas education did improve measurably because of her efforts.

Throughout her husband's years as governor, Hillary worked for children. She started a home instruction program for preschool youth and served on the board of the state's children's hospital.

## Moving up to First Lady

In 1992, Bill Clinton decided to run for president with Hillary's full support. He believed the incumbent president George H. W. Bush was vulnerable because he had neglected domestic politics, instead focusing purely on foreign policy. He was right. However, during his campaign, Bill had to overcome personal attacks involving a long-lasting relationship he had with an Arkansas state employee and nightclub singer, Gennifer Flowers. Bill and Hillary appeared on the TV show *60 Minutes* to defend their marriage and ask the media and the public to respect their privacy. The strategy worked. Bill's affair didn't become an issue in the 1992 campaign.

**IN THEIR WORDS**

During the interview with *60 Minutes,* Hillary said: "I'm sitting here because I love him and respect him, and I honor what he's been through and what we've been through together." Then she went on to tell voters that if they didn't like what they represented and if they were still skeptical, "Heck, don't vote for him."

Her outspokenness made her a campaign issue. She often said, "If you vote for him, you get me." When asked by the press if the role of First Lady would constitute a conflict between being a lawyer and a First Lady, she told them, "I suppose I could have stayed home and baked cookies and had teas, but what I decided to do was pursue my profession, which I entered before my husband was in public life." Millions of traditional housewives felt slighted, and the press had a field day with the comment.

Afterward, she had to change her tone a little to stop offending too many voters. She participated in a cookie bake-off with First Lady Barbara Bush and allowed her daughter to appear publicly and in magazines to highlight her motherly side. She also wore more feminine clothing and smiled more. It worked, and her image improved.

Hillary once famously said: "I am surprised at the way people seem to perceive me, and sometimes I read stories and hear things about me, and I go Ugh. I wouldn't like her either."

# Becoming co-president

After Bill Clinton won the 1992 presidential election, the press was excited and called Hillary "first partner" and even "presidential super spouse." She had graduated from college, worked her whole adult life, even while being First Lady of Arkansas for more than a decade, raised a child, and was now an example of a woman with power and influence. They expected her to be become a co-president, and she did.

Hillary was a very active First Lady. She participated in meetings on Cabinet choices and even made her own recommendations for presidential Cabinet members. She took an office a few feet from the oval office to always be close to her husband and be aware of all political ongoings. Right away, he put her in charge of changing healthcare in the United States.

## Failing with healthcare

One of Bill's major campaign promises was to reform the healthcare system in the United States. To fulfill this promise, he appointed Hillary as the leader of a task force in 1993. This task force, called the Presidential Task Force on National Healthcare Reform, had the job of coming up with a way to restructure the U.S. healthcare system. No First Lady had ever been given such an important assignment.

The task force's plan, called the Health Security Act, or more popularly known as Hillarycare, was more than 240,000 words long and contained provisions that would obligate businesses to provide medical insurance for all their employees. It would have fused the free market with federal regulations. In other words, universal healthcare would be assured. Opponents, insurance companies, other businesses, and Republicans criticized the plan as too complicated and charged that it gave the federal government too much control over medical care. The opponents launched a successful public relations effort to get the public on their side. With the public opposed to it, the task force's plan was never even submitted to Congress, and the Democratic Party lost control over the House of Representatives and the Senate in the 1994 elections.

One of the problems Hillarycare faced Hillary had created herself. She alienated the members of the congressional committee by showing no deference to them, by coming across as a know-it-all, and by insisting that the task force meetings be secret. Soon members of Congress and the American public began to oppose her way of running the task force and then later the act overall.

## Dealing with scandal — Part I

In 1993, a financial dealing the Clintons had in Arkansas became an issue for the Clinton presidency. The Clintons were involved in a land-development deal in Arkansas in 1978, called the Whitewater Development Corporation. When the deal went sour, the Clintons lost a chunk of money, as did their business partners. Later, these partners, James and Susan McDougal, opened a small savings and loan. The savings and loan went under in 1989; it was later bailed out by the federal government. President Clinton was accused of using his position as governor of Arkansas to help out his former business partners.

A federal investigation, headed by independent counsel Kenneth Starr, filed no charges against the Clintons. But the Clintons' former business partners, the McDougals, and the governor of Arkansas, Jim Guy Tucker, were convicted of wrongdoing. During the investigation, Hillary was subpoenaed in front of a grand jury, becoming the first First Lady to testify in front of a grand jury.

The press further discovered that Hillary was involved in financial dealings where she turned $1,000 into $100,000 in a few months, trading in future commodities in 1979. No wrongdoing was discovered, but many perceived her not only as ambitious but also as greedy. Hillary perceived all of this as an attack by especially conservative men who felt threatened by a strong woman. She said: "It's not me personally they hate; it's the changes I represent."

In 1994, Paula Jones, a former secretary for the state of Arkansas, accused President Clinton of sexual harassment. The case was at first dismissed, but Paula appealed it. Rather than go to court, the Clintons paid her $850,000 to drop the case.

Things calmed down by 1995, and Hillary started writing a weekly newspaper column dealing with more traditional issues, such as student test scores and mammograms. She also published her first bestseller in 1996 titled *It Takes a Village: And Other Lessons Children Teach Us*.

## Hating her second four years

Bill Clinton's second term was plagued with scandal, and he almost got himself removed from office. Hillary tried to be away from Washington, D.C., as much as possible. She traveled around the world, becoming the First Lady who traveled the second most in the history of the U.S., after Pat Nixon. She talked about issues dear to her heart, such as education, schooling, and healthcare. She defended her husband during the 1998 impeachment proceedings but kept her own feelings about Bill's affairs private. Publicly, she defended him, saying it was a right-wing conspiracy bent on destroying him. However, when he admitted that he had lied to her and the American public, she was furious because he had misled her.

## Dealing with scandal — Part II

During the Paula Jones case, lawyers became aware of a rumor that President Clinton was having an affair with one of his interns, 24-year-old Monica Lewinsky. In early 1998, President Clinton denied the affair under oath. Evidence later contradicted his testimony. Ms. Lewinsky admitted to the affair and stated that Bill told her to lie in front of a grand jury, a criminal offense. In August 1998, President Clinton appeared in front of a grand jury and admitted the affair, contradicting his earlier testimony. A few days later, the president apologized for the affair and admitted to the U.S. public that he had lied.

The Lewinsky Affair almost destroyed their marriage and alienated Chelsea from her father. When she found out that Bill had lied to her, Hillary threw things at him. She decided at this time that it was her turn to start a political career. However, her husband had to survive impeachment hearings for that to be possible. Nobody would vote for the wife of a president who had been impeached and removed from office. So she supported him in public and was affectionate, while privately starting to focus on her political future.

**TECHNICAL STUFF**

In December 1998, the House of Representatives voted to impeach President Clinton on two charges: obstruction of justice and perjury (lying under oath). The Senate, however, failed to muster the two-thirds majority vote needed to convict and remove President Clinton. So his presidency was saved, and he served out his term.

## Owning her own political career

When Bill Clinton's presidency ended, Hillary was 53 and ready to start her own political career. After the long-term Democratic Senator from New York, Patrick Moynihan, announced his retirement, she decided on becoming a U.S. Senator. She and her husband were very popular in New York State, and she knew she would easily win the election. So she became the first First Lady to run for office. She did her homework and studied the state and met with voters. She moved to New York in late 1999 and established residency. Hillary and Bill also decided that they would never get divorced but instead cohabit and still help each other. In February 2000, she announced that she would run for the open Senate seat in New York. She easily won the election and became the state's first female senator and the first First Lady to win a seat in the U.S. Senate. (See Figure 18-2). She got easily reelected in 2006.

As senator, Hillary continued to work on issues she had centered on as First Lady. She focused on universal healthcare and prevention and a cure for HIV/AIDS. After the attacks on the United States on September 11, 2001, she voted yes to allow for the U.S. to invade Afghanistan and later Iraq but then changed her mind after military intelligence showed that there were no weapons of mass destruction to be found in Iraq. Her vote authorizing force against Iraq cost her progressive support in 2008 when she ran for the Democratic nomination for president.

## Running for president — Part I

In January 2007, Hillary Clinton announced that she was running for the Democratic nomination for president. It proved to be a close race against her major challenger Barack Obama, the junior Senator from Illinois, but in the end, Hillary lost, even though she had won the popular primary vote. She then hoped to be Obama's vice presidential pick, but he picked Joe Biden instead. Hillary conceded with grace and, in a rousing speech, threw her support behind Barack Obama.

## Serving as secretary of state

New President Obama appreciated Hillary's grace and support and appointed her his secretary of state in 2009. Hillary's agenda was to push for female rights, empower women, and establish gender equality globally. In addition, she tried to strengthen ties with U.S. allies. On top of her list was Pakistan. She traveled to

Pakistan in 2009 and held town hall meetings with ordinary Pakistani citizens and gave several interviews to the Pakistani media. She was also behind sanctions on Iran in 2010, which finally brought the country to the bargaining table.

REMEMBER

On May 1, 2011, she was with President Obama as they watched via satellite how Navy seals raided Osama bin Laden's compound and killed the terrorist leader.

On September 11, 2012, a mob affiliated with an Al Qaeda faction attacked the American consulate in Benghazi, Libya. Four Americans, including U.S. Ambassador Christopher Stevens, were killed. The Obama administration didn't call it a terrorist attack right away and didn't react to it forcefully. Congress and many in the American public blamed the president and his secretary of state. Congress opened up a two-year inquiry and published an 800-page report two years later. Hillary took responsibility for the attack. While she wasn't faulted for the attack on the consulate, the investigation discovered that she had used her private email server during her four years as secretary of state. This would come back to haunt her in the 2016 presidential campaign.

## Running for president — Part II

After President Obama won reelection in 2012, Hillary stated that she wouldn't be interested in a second term as secretary of state and resigned in 2013.

After leaving office, Hillary wrote another volume of her memoirs *Hard Choices* and went on a countrywide book tour. Many speculated that she was getting ready for a second run for president in 2016. They were right.

By 2016, Hillary had the Obama electoral machine behind her and had already established a Hillary grassroots operation. After a spirited race against Vermont Senator Bernie Sanders, she became the first female Democratic presidential nominee in the summer of 2016.

### Being careless

In March of 2015, it was revealed that Hillary Clinton has used personal email accounts on a nongovernment-maintained server instead of using a server maintained by the government when conducting official business as secretary of state. This violated State Department protocols and federal laws. This became a major issue in the 2016 campaign and contributed to her eventual defeat. Classified information was sent, even though Hillary claimed that no classified information was on her sever. An FBI probe was initiated and found that 2,100 emails were classified. On July 5, 2016, the FBI concluded its investigation. The director of the FBI stated that even though there was no evidence that Hillary intended to violate the law, she was extremely careless.

## Getting rich

After leaving political office in 2013, Hillary and her daughter joined the board of the Clinton Foundation set up by her husband in 1997. The Clinton Foundation accepted donations from foreign governments, many authoritarian and major human rights violators, as well as from foreign private citizens who had links to their governments. Hillary resigned from the board of the Clinton Foundation in 2015 when she got ready for her second presidential run. By 2016, the Clinton Foundation collected almost $2 billion in donations to spend on humanitarian projects globally.

In addition, Hillary hit the speaking circuit, making up to $225,000 per speech. From 2014 until 2015, she made more than $11 million from her speeches. In addition, she had received an $8 million advance for her autobiography.

# Losing in 2016 and moving on

Hillary Clinton came very close to being the first female U.S. president. She carried the popular vote by about 2 percent but lost out in the Electoral College. To her great dismay, she lost several traditional Democratic states, which she had assumed were in her safe column. Her husband had warned her and told her to focus on Pennsylvania, Michigan, and Wisconsin, instead of trying to win Arizona and Georgia as her advisors had suggested. She didn't listen to Bill and lost all three states and the general election.

After losing the election, Hillary published her third memoir in 2017 titled *What Happened* about the 2016 election. Her book sold 500,000 copies by year's end. In October 2019, she announced that she was writing a book with her daughter, Chelsea, titled *The Book of Gutsy Women: Favorite Stories of Courage and Resilience,* and in 2021, Hillary announced that she was co-writing a fictional book titled *State of Terror,* which would be published in the fall of 2021.

On January 2, 2020, Hillary Clinton became the new chancellor at Queen's University Belfast, one of the major research institutions in Great Britain. The position is ceremonial, and Hillary will have to be present only at graduations and act as an advocate for the university abroad.

Finally, Hillary launched a political action organization called Onward Together, which has become a major fundraiser for progressive causes. She received a lot of support for running again in 2020 but decided to sit out the election.

Today, Hillary Clinton is still the best-known female politician in the world. In terms of her political career and her actions, she created a new path for future First Ladies to follow. Similar to her great idol, Eleanor Roosevelt, she has changed the way we perceive First Ladies forever (see Figure 18-3).

**FIGURE 18-3:**
Eleanor Roosevelt
passing the baton
to Hillary Clinton.

Source: Library of Congress, Prints & Photographs Division, Reproduction number
LC-DIG-ppmsca-68660 (digital file from original)

# Chapter 19

# Using the Power of the Position

Laura Bush was a noncontroversial First Lady. Unlike her predecessor Hillary Clinton, she chose topics that all of America could unite behind. She was similar to her mother-in-law, Barbara Bush. The two even had similar interests. Both cared about literacy and childhood education. Even while her husband's approval ratings dipped, Laura was able to remain popular until her tenure ended in January 2009. People who disliked her husband and his policies still supported her because of her humanitarian concerns. She was involved in many good causes and was nonpartisan. For example, she praised Hillary Clinton for running for president in 2008 because she was opening new possibilities for women.

As the first African American First Lady, Michelle Obama devoted herself to positive social change with a focus on childhood obesity. She was well educated, having a Princeton and Harvard education, and was truly her husband's partner even though she entered politics reluctantly. She wanted to change the plight of Black and poor people in the United States and believed this could be done through community outreach. She branded herself mom-in-chief and openly talked about balancing family with life in the White House. She wanted to increase the well-being of the nation through fitness-focused initiatives and better eating habits and later worked with Laura Bush to improve the lives of women, especially in Africa.

This chapter delves deeper into the lives of these two women and their time as First Lady.

# Laura Welch Bush (1946–)

Laura Welch was born on November 4, 1946, in Midland, Texas (see Figure 19-1). She was the only child of Harold Welch and Jenna Hawkins Welch. Her father owned a construction business while her mom was a homemaker, who read frequently to young Laura, instilling in her a love for books. Laura had a nice middle-class upbringing, living the American dream. She loved school and early on decided to become a teacher. When she was young, she even arranged her dolls in a line so that they resembled students and she could teach them. In high school, she also studied ballet and joined the Girl Scouts.

**FIGURE 19-1:**
Laura Welch
Bush.

Source: Library of Congress, Prints & Photographs Division,
Reproduction number LC-DIG-ppbd-00372 (original digital file)

**FIRST
LADY LORE**

Laura and George W. Bush attended the same middle school, but they never met. She wore glasses, was studious, and loved to read; he didn't care that much about education and wanted to be a baseball player.

Laura's happy childhood came to an abrupt end when she was 17. She was involved in a car accident that killed one of her friends. Laura was driving her parents' car near Midland and ran a stop sign. She hit another car and killed her classmate and friend. She was never cited, but she would always blame herself for this.

After high school, Laura attended Southern Methodist University (SMU) and graduated in 1968 with a degree in education. She taught reading to grade school children in both Dallas and Houston.

REMEMBER

Laura moved to Houston to teach in a minority school. She credits the two years she taught at John F. Kennedy Elementary School with opening her eyes to economic inequalities in life. She decided to focus on education, especially literacy, to help minority students.

In Houston, she almost met George again. They lived in the same apartment complex but never encountered each other. Laura was home at night, studying and preparing lectures for the next day, while George was out partying.

In 1971, Laura moved to Austin, where she pursued a library degree at the University of Texas at Austin. She graduated in 1973 with a master's degree in library science and became the librarian for a local public school, first in Houston and then in Austin.

FIRST
LADY LORE

Laura Bush is one of five First Ladies with a graduate degree. The others are Pat Nixon, Hillary Rodham Clinton, Michelle Obama, and Jill Biden.

## Meeting and marrying George

In 1977, a friend of Laura's invited her to go to Midland for a barbecue. Here, mutual friends introduced her to George W. Bush, who owned an oil business at the time. He immediately knew she was "the one," and the two started dating. Only three months later, on November 5, 1977, they got married in Midland, Texas.

FIRST
LADY LORE

Laura agreed to marry George only after he promised that she'd never have to make a political speech in her life. Obviously, things turned out differently.

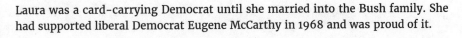

Laura was a card-carrying Democrat until she married into the Bush family. She had supported liberal Democrat Eugene McCarthy in 1968 and was proud of it.

REMEMBER

Only one month after her marriage, Laura gave her first political speech when George decided to run for Congress. He lost and then decided to focus on his oil business.

Laura gave birth in 1981 to twin daughters, Jenna and Barbara, named after their two grandmothers. At this time, Laura quit teaching and became a homemaker.

George was a heavy drinker when he was younger. So Laura told him, "It's either me or Jim Beam." For this reason, when he turned 40, George gave up drinking and also took God into his heart, after having had long discussions with family friend, the Reverend Billy Graham.

## Moving to Washington, D.C.

In 1987, Laura and her family moved to the capital because George was working on his father's, George H. W. Bush's, presidential campaign. After George H. W. Bush was elected president, Laura and the family moved back to Texas, where her husband had become a managing general partner of the Texas Rangers baseball team. His association with the team and his famous last name made George W. Bush a household name in Texas.

In 1994, George told Laura that he wanted to run for governor of Texas. She wasn't happy about that. She didn't believe that he could defeat popular incumbent Democratic Governor Ann Richards. To her surprise, her husband won the election and soon became known nationwide. He was easily reelected in 1998 and became the front-runner for the Republican presidential nomination in 2000.

While First Lady of Texas, Laura was active. She held luncheons for prominent Texas writers and organized the Texas Book Festival — an annual celebration of books and authors that became a major fundraiser for public libraries in Texas. In 1998, she started the Early Childhood Development Initiative to prepare children to read before they start school. She especially believed that literacy was the key to success later in life and once said:

**IN THEIR
WORDS**

> "George and I wanted to teach our children what our parents taught us — that reading is entertaining and important and fun."

Laura became very popular in Texas across party lines, and in the six years her husband was the governor of Texas, no criticism of her was heard from either side.

By 2000, Laura was very supportive of her husband's run for the presidency, and she had become an expert public speaker and campaigner. In 2000, she gave a keynote address at the Republican National Convention, and then she traveled thousands of miles, giving interviews and campaigning for her husband.

## Championing the First Lady role

Laura Bush had an easy time adapting to the job of First Lady. She had visited the White House many times when her in-laws lived there and was close to Barbara Bush, a popular former First Lady (see Chapter 17). As First Lady, Laura continued her interests in education and literacy. In 2001, she started the National Book Fair together with the Library of Congress, which she based on her successful Texas example. About 200,000 people still attend the National Book Fair annually. In addition, Laura started the Laura Bush Foundation for America's Libraries, which has given away millions of dollars to U.S. libraries.

Then the terrorists attacks of September 11, 2001, happened. Afterward, Laura encouraged people to stay calm and tell their children that they were safe. *The New York Post* referred to Laura as the "First Mom," comforting and reassuring a whole nation. She visited people injured in the 9-11 attacks and consoled those who lost loved ones.

**IN THEIR WORDS**

After September 11, 2001, Laura said: "I think we just have to make sure we tell our children that we love them and that America is a strong country, and we will get through this."

In November 2001, Laura became the first First Lady to take over the president's weekly radio address. In her speech, she denounced the oppression of women and children in Afghanistan under the Taliban regime. In the next few months, she gave five more speeches, urging help for Afghan women. She brought up equal rights for women while boosting morale in the fight against terrorism. In other words, she combined feminism with patriotism, and both sides, liberal and conservative, loved it.

**FIRST LADY LORE**

When Laura went to Austin to visit her daughter Jenna in college, a couple of Middle Eastern women approached her in a department store and thanked her for her efforts on their behalf. That is when she realized she could make a difference using the power a First Lady possesses.

## Fighting disease and campaigning for women's rights

As First Lady, Laura Bush traveled the world to battle diseases, such as AIDS and malaria, and championed women's rights, especially in Third World countries. She promoted education and the advancement of women in Asia and Africa, especially Afghanistan. As First Lady, Laura visited 75 countries, but they weren't ceremonial tours. She focused on real issues such as AIDS spreading rapidly in Africa. Using her husband's program, the President's Emergency Plan for AIDS Relief (PEPFAR), Laura became the voice for battling AIDS in Africa. She further became the honorary ambassador for UNESCO's literacy decade.

**TECHNICAL STUFF**

In 2003, President Bush started PEPFAR. It is the single largest global response to any disease, having spent $85 billion by 2021 to combat AIDS globally. The program now provides for the testing of 50 million people annually and has saved over 20 million people mostly in Africa.

## Pushing for change and making a difference

Beginning in 2002, Laura began pushing for the No Child Left Behind (NCLB) Act. The NCLB Act was signed into law in 2002, creating standards-based education and providing more federal funding to improve and assess test scores for public school students. Again, the legislation was bipartisan and apolitical in nature and enjoyed wide support at the time.

Laura supported her husband's decision to seek a second term. She campaigned quite a bit in 2004 for his reelection and campaigned solo in key states. She rose above politics and didn't attack her husband's opponent. Her approval ratings were 80 percent by 2006. Her husband's were half of that.

REMEMBER

After Hurricane Katrina hit in 2005, Laura established the America's Libraries Gulf Coast Library Recovery Initiative Grant to rebuild libraries destroyed by the storm.

## Fighting oppression in Burma

On October 10, 2007, Laura Bush published an opinion piece in *The Wall Street Journal* titled "Stop the Terror in Burma." The piece dealt with the human rights violations of the Burmese military dictatorship. Days later, *The New York Times* called her the administration's leading voice on Burma. In August 2008, Laura went to Thailand to visit the Mae La refugee camp, where thousands of Burmese refugees were housed in deplorable conditions, to draw more attention to the issue. She visited a clinic dealing with 35,000 refugees and called for Burmese opposition leader and Nobel Prize winner Aung San Suu Kye to be released from prison.

# Retiring but staying active

After Laura Bush's tenure as First Lady ended in 2009, she stayed active and occasionally waded into politics. In 2010, she published her memoirs *Spoken from the Heart*, for which she had received a $1.6 million advance. In the book and on the *Larry King Show*, she, for the first time, expressed support for same-sex marriage and abortion. She admitted to staying out of her husband's politics and policy making most of the time. She said: "We talk about issues, but I'm not his advisor; I'm his wife. . . . I find that it's really best not to give your spouse a lot of advice. I don't want a lot of advice from him."

After leaving the White House, Laura and George moved to Dallas but spent a lot of time on their ranch in Crawford, Texas. Laura got involved in the planning of the Bush Library and Bush Institute. Both were established at her alma mater, Southern Methodist University.

In 2013, Laura and then–First Lady Michelle Obama met in Africa for a conference on women's issues and education and then joined again in 2014 for a conference on Africa sponsored by the White House and the Bush Institute.

TECHNICAL
STUFF

After retiring, President George W. Bush founded the George W. Bush Institute in 2009, which includes Women's Initiative programs that work with First Ladies around the world to improve the lives of women and children globally. The institute is a public policy center located in Dallas, Texas, with the goal of advancing freedom in the United States and globally, by increasing economic growth, educational opportunities, women's rights, and global health.

The George W. Bush Presidential Center, which contains the Presidential Library and Museum, was opened in 2013 and is located on the campus of Southern Methodist University in Dallas, Texas. It's the second largest presidential library in the United States and will be the future burial place for President George W. Bush and his wife, Laura.

IN THEIR
WORDS

When asked whether she had any regrets after being First Lady for eight years, Laura said: "Maybe if I have a regret, it's just that I didn't do more."

# Michelle LaVaughn Robinson Obama (1964–)

Michelle LaVaughn Robinson is the younger of two children of Fraser and Marian Robinson (see Figure 19-2). She was born in Chicago, which was still heavily segregated at the time, on January 17, 1964. When she was little, the family was able to move into a more diverse neighborhood with better schools. Together with her brother, Craig, Michelle grew up in a tight-knit family. They went on family vacations, played board games, and socialized with the large extended family they had in Chicago. Both children described a family-centered childhood with their dad at the heart of the family.

Michelle's dad was a precinct captain, getting people out to vote, and a community organizer. He worked for the city as a pump operator at a water plant. Michelle's mom was a homemaker and stay-at-home mom. Both parents were heavily into education, Michelle's mom started reading to the children and doing math with them at an early age. Michelle and her brother, therefore, excelled at school, skipping second and third grade, respectively and both attended Princeton University.

Michelle had to undertake a 90-minute trip each day just to make it to her high school, Whitney Young High School. There she was told by a counselor that she was not Ivy League material. Boy did she show her counselor when she was admitted to Princeton University.

Michelle majored in sociology and immediately became involved in community service. She was responsible for Princeton setting up a daycare center for the university staff's children and starting a reading program for children of the campus's manual laborers.

## Meeting of the minds

Michelle graduated cum laude in 1985 and then entered Harvard Law School and graduated with a J.D. in 1988. Next, she joined the Chicago law firm of Sidley & Austin, where she specialized in telecommunications law. While there, she was assigned to mentor her future husband, Barack, who was an intern from Harvard Law School at the time.

Barack was immediately infatuated with her, but Michelle didn't reciprocate his feelings. She finally agreed to a date with him, after he took her out for ice cream after a company picnic. He was especially surprised how stable her family life had been, with his having been all over the place. After they were engaged in 1991, he took her on a trip to Africa to meet his late father's relatives.

Three years after they first met, the two got married on October 3, 1992. They were married at Chicago's Trinity United Church of Christ by the Reverend Jeremiah A. Wright. Michelle quit her job at the law firm, and the couple decided to live in Chicago to pursue community service. Michelle took a job as assistant for Chicago Mayor Richard Daley and then became assistant commissioner of planning and development for the city. Then she moved on to work as executive director of the Chicago branch of Public Allies, a part of President Clinton's AmeriCorps project. In this capacity, she placed young Americans in nonprofit business organizations. In 1996, she became associate dean of students and director of the University of Chicago's Community Service Center, where she placed students into internships.

In 2002, Michelle moved on to become the University of Chicago Medical Center's executive director of community affairs. In 2005, she was promoted to vice president of external affairs and community relations. When her husband became the Democratic candidate for president, Michelle stepped down and joined him on the campaign trail.

**FIRST LADY LORE**

Barack was afraid to talk to Michelle about entering the realm of politics, so he approached her brother, Craig, and the two discussed it. Craig then talked to Michelle and her mother and convinced them it was the right thing to do.

## Balancing politics and family life

After graduating from Harvard and getting married, Barack Obama decided to get into politics. He directed the Illinois Project Vote, which registered Chicago's Black population, and helped Bill Clinton win the state in the 1992 election. After joining a prestigious civil rights law firm and teaching part time at the University of Chicago, Barack's chance to enter politics came in 1995. He decided to run for an open State Senate seat in Illinois and easily won the overwhelmingly Democratic district in 1996. Michelle got her first taste of politics. She collected signatures for her husband and arranged for fundraisers.

After having her first child, a daughter, the marital dynamic changed. Michelle was working a well-paying but very demanding job, while Barack was away being a state senator. She now struggled to maintain a work-life balance with a politician husband who was absent much of the time. She soon resented him being a politician and was early on opposed to him running for the U.S. Senate.

While working a high-paying and very demanding job, Michelle had two children: Malia Ann, born in 1998, and Natasha (Sasha), born in 2001. They would be the first young children to live in the White House since Amy Carter.

In 2004, when the Republican Senator Peter Fitzgerald decided not to run for reelection, Obama won the open U.S. Senate seat in Illinois. Michelle wasn't happy with him becoming a U.S. senator. She decided to remain in Chicago and not move to Washington, D.C. She suddenly felt that she was a single mother with Barack playing politics and constantly being absent. She told him: "You only think about yourself. I never thought I'd have to raise a family alone."

By 2007, Michelle got used to Barack being a career politician, and Barack had to make a tough choice: Should he run for president of the United States or governor of Illinois? On February, 10, 2007, he declared his candidacy for the presidency.

## Winning in the media

Major magazines in the U.S. just loved Michelle Obama. She was selected by *Vanity Fair* for its best dressed list, and *Ebony* voted her and Barack one of the hottest couples in America. In May 26, 2006, *Essence* magazine listed Michelle as one of the 25 world's most inspiring women, and *Maxim* voted her as one of the 100 hottest women in the world.

## Sealing the deal on the campaign trail

As soon as Barack decided to run for president, Michelle was all in. After a rough start on the campaign trail, where Michelle had stated she was proud for the first time of her country after people started supporting her husband, she was subsequently portrayed as an angry Black woman by the press. So, Michelle had to change her image by focusing more on her role as a successful business woman and mother.

Afterwards, she proved to be a great asset during the 2008 campaign. She was authentic and blunt and had a working-class background. She was a working mother who had accomplished much, and voters appreciated that. In her campaign speeches, she humanized Barack, mentioning how he snored and how he left his socks all over the place. She wanted to show the American public that he was just an average American Joe, despite his funny first and last name. She did so well on the campaign trail that soon the Obama campaign called her "the closer" because she was able to convince so many undecided voters to cast a ballot for her husband.

# Serving as mom-in-chief

In 2009, Michelle Obama became the first African American First Lady of the United States. At first, she relied on Laura Bush's White House team for advice, and even Nancy Reagan came by for lunch and told her to have lots of state dinners. Unlike her predecessors, Laura Bush, Hillary Clinton, and Nancy Reagan, who all had been First Ladies at the state level before, Michelle had no experience being a hostess in the White House and running the place. She also didn't do a lot of formal interviews or press conferences like other First Ladies had done but preferred social media and softer outlets, such as local radio and TV stations where she'd face friendly questions.

REMEMBER

The Obamas did entertain a lot, but not the way people expected. Many were hoping for a return of John F. Kennedy's Camelot, where the rich and famous mingled with the president and his wife. Instead, the Obamas invited wounded veterans, successful Black women, friends from college, and community leaders from across the country. As Michelle Obama once said: "This First Lady is interested in community outreach and not social outreach."

Soon, Michelle became an example of how to raise children well. She gave parenting tips to the average American and would always say, "I am a mom first." And the Obamas seemed just like the family next door. Michelle went to soccer games and her daughters' school events and frequented local restaurants with her friends. Her daughters had to make their own beds in the White House and Michelle's mom moved into the White House to make sure the girls had a stable family life.

## Getting kids to move it, move it

As First Lady, Michelle, like her predecessor Laura Bush, became an advocate for children. While Laura Bush dealt with literacy issues, Michelle focused on children's health. She was determined to battle the obesity epidemic in the U.S. For this reason, she invited Washington, D.C., fifth graders to the White House to help with growing an organic vegetable garden. In addition, she started the Let's Move initiative in 2010, to get children off the couch and engaging in physical activity. During her second term, Michelle expanded her Let's Move initiative. She met with school nutritionists and educators to give kids access to healthier meals in school.

REMEMBER

Michelle made the fight against obesity personal. She used her daughters' weight gain as an example of why children need to eat carefully and exercise, and she herself started working out with a personal trainer.

In 2010, she was behind the Healthy, Hunger-Free Kids Act, which made school lunches more nutritious and expanded access to meals for little or no cost to poorer students.

In 2012, Michelle Obama published a book *American Grown,* which introduced families to vegetables and showed the average American how to grow and/or shop for fruits and vegetables. The book also included the story of the White House garden and recipes from White House chefs using items grown in the garden.

To increase publicity among school-aged girls, during Women's History Month, Michelle sent outstanding and accomplished women to schools to tell their story. These included musicians, singers, actresses, military officers, and sports stars.

## Reaching high

As an African American woman, Michelle was able to challenge Black and other minority students who have a higher high school dropout rate compared to white students in ways that other First Ladies could not. Minority students, especially Black females, were more open to her message, which Michelle knew. Thus, she gave numerous speeches in schools throughout the U.S. to motivate students to stay in school. She repeatedly told them not to listen to people telling them what they could or could not do because of their background. She even started a Reach Higher Initiative that included a College Signing Day in high schools. The initiative is still going on today.

## Helping veterans

Michelle's second major project as First Lady was a joint project with Second Lady Jill Biden. The two created a program called Joining Forces to help match employers with returning veterans and their family members who needed jobs.

## Going global

Finally, in 2015, Michelle Obama went global and launched Let Girls Learn, an international campaign for girls' access to education.

In addition, she and Laura Bush got together in Tanzania in 2013 at a forum on women's issues to discuss education, health, and jobs. The two First Ladies got along well, even though they were from different political parties. In 2014, the Obama White House and the Bush Institute sponsored a U.S.-Africa summit in Washington, D.C. Again, the two First Ladies worked together on a symposium on health and education.

# Enjoying retirement

In 2016, near the end of her tenure, Michelle Obama supported and campaigned for Hillary Clinton, after she had declined herself to run for president. This made her the first First Lady to get involved in a presidential campaign not involving her husband. During the campaign, she also became the first First Lady to go negative by attacking Republican candidate Donald Trump for his behavior with women.

In 2018, Michelle published her memoirs *Becoming*, which sold 11.5 million copies by November 2019. Netflix also made a documentary entitled *Becoming* of her book tour promoting the book. The documentary was released on May 6, 2020.

In 2021, Michelle teamed up with Netflix on a new children's show entitled *Waffles+Mochi*, which stars two puppets who have a dream to learn how to cook healthy food from all over the world with the help of Michelle and special celebrity friends.

In addition, Michelle and Barack have signed book and TV deals valued at $65 million.

**IN THEIR WORDS**

When asked about her legacy, Michelle Obama said: "Success isn't about how much money you make; it's about the difference you make in people's lives."

# Chapter **20**

# The Model and the Educator

Melania Trump was one of the most private First Ladies in recent years. She didn't enjoy interacting with the public and the national media. She hated making speeches on her husband's behalf and rarely campaigned for him, unlike most modern First Ladies. When Melania entered the White House, she was at a disadvantage compared to other First Ladies. She had never been involved in American politics nor been the First Lady of an American state. She had no connections to Congress, was a lot younger than President Trump, and was his third wife. She really didn't want to be First Lady and secretly hoped that her husband would lose the election in 2016.

Jill Biden is one of the best-educated First Ladies the U.S. has ever had. She has spent three decades in education teaching at various levels, including the college level. At the same time, she is one of the best-prepared First Ladies ever. She held the office of Second Lady for eight years (2009–2017) and was the wife of a U.S. Senator for more than 30 years. She knows Washington, D.C., and how to play the game of politics. As one magazine stated, "Jill Biden might just be Joe Biden's greatest political asset."

This chapter covers both the most recently retired and the most recently hired First Ladies of the United States.

# Melania Knauss Trump (1970–)

Melanija Knavs, who later used the German spelling of her name, Melania Knauss, to further her modeling career (see Figure 20-1), was born on April 26, 1970, in the small town of Novo Mesto in Slovenia. Slovenia, back then, was a part of the former Communist state of Yugoslavia and didn't become an independent country until 1991. Growing up in a Communist country meant that Melania didn't know much about the United States and wasn't taught English in school. She grew up in a government-owned apartment complex. Her father worked as a traveling car salesman, while her mother worked in the textile industry. Her father was a card-carrying member of the Communist party of Yugoslavia, which was a must at that time if a person wanted to advance economically and socially, and was also a driver in the Yugoslav Army. Many who know him compare him to Donald Trump, with the way he acted and his love for expensive goods, such as foreign cars.

**FIGURE 20-1:**
Melania Knauss
Trump.

Source: Library of Congress, Prints & Photographs Division,
Reproduction number LC-DIG-ppbd-00610 (original digital file)

As soon as Communist Yugoslavia collapsed, Melania's dad embraced the new capitalist system in Slovenia. He opened his own cycle/moped repair shop and started to deal with real estate. He bought the government-owned apartment the family lived in and later built a large house for the family of four.

# Choosing modeling and Donald Trump

Melania's mother made the clothes for Melania and her sister to save money and to make sure that the family was always well dressed. From her mother, Melania gained interest in personal beauty and a sense of fashion. Her mother was always well dressed, she made most of her clothing herself, and she paid attention to the way she looked. It was also her mother who got Melania interested in modeling. She volunteered her as an informal model for a hometown fashion show when she was just a child.

Melania attended a local public school and was an average student. However, she showed a lot of promise in two topics, art and design. Soon, Melania started sewing her own clothes and changed the ones she bought to make them look more distinctive. When Melania was 15, she enrolled in a secondary school for design and photography in the capital of Ljubljana, where she studied industrial design for four years. Afterward, she enrolled at the University of Ljubljana to study design.

By 1992, Melania didn't enjoy her university classes and thought about what to do next. She signed up for a beauty contest and came in second. She then changed her mind, quit her studies, and decided to be a model; the money was better, and it gave her a chance to travel the world. However, her last name proved to be a hindrance, so she Germanized it and changed it to Knauss.

Melania's modeling career didn't take off in Europe, so she moved to the United States in 1996. She lived in Manhattan, sharing a small apartment with other models. She met Donald Trump in 1998 at Manhattan's Kit Kat Club, a famous New York nightclub. Donald asked her for her number, but she said no because he was at the club with another woman. Soon afterward, she changed her mind, and the two started dating. With his support, Melania's modeling career slowly took off. She suddenly had offers from both the United States and Europe and, by 2000, was a sought-after model. Melania and Donald Trump became engaged in 2004.

Melania never was a party girl; she took modeling seriously, and for her, it was a job. She watched her diet, didn't drink too much, and always made sure she got enough sleep. Being a model later helped her when she became First Lady, because she was comfortable in front of cameras and knew how to dress well.

REMEMBER

In 2000, Melania did her famous shoot for the British Gentleman's Quarterly Naked Supermodel Special. She laid naked on a fur rug, wearing only diamond bracelets. The shoot happened on an airplane, and it turned out that plane was owned by Donald Trump, who was present for the shoot. A few weeks later, she was included in the *Sports Illustrated Swimsuit* edition, and she was now considered a supermodel.

Melania married Donald Trump on January 22, 2005. They were married in Palm Beach, Florida, and nearly 500 guests attended. Guests included famous singers, such as Billy Joel, and, ironically, Bill and Hillary Clinton, who were close friends with Donald Trump back then. In 2016, of course, they weren't so friendly when Donald Trump beat Hillary Clinton for the presidency.

## Becoming an American citizen

Melania Trump became an American citizen in 2006. She had received a green card in 2001 and wasn't an American citizen when she married Donald Trump in 2005. She was the first naturalized citizen to become First Lady. (*Note:* Louisa Adams, who is often called the first foreign-born First Lady, was born in London, England, to an American father and had American citizenship by birthright.)

In 2006, Melania gave birth to her only child, son Barron. Her family from Slovenia decided they wanted to be closer to their grandson. Her sister, Ines, already lived in New York, and her parents, Viktor and Amalija, obtained green cards in order to stay in the United States. In August 2018, her parents became American citizens. Melania stayed isolated, being close only to her family. She mostly spoke Slovenian and really didn't have a close group of American friends.

## Taking a backseat to politics

Melania wasn't a political person. She grew up in a country that was Communist until the early 1990s and was never able to freely express her political opinions. Therefore, she rarely talked about politics in public. She didn't become a defender of her husband's policies. In 2016, she said that she was choosing not to go political in public because that was her husband's job.

When asked whether she was interested in and cared about politics, Melania said:

**IN THEIR WORDS**

"I am very political in my private life, and between me and my husband, I know everything that is going on."

At the Republican Convention in August of 2016, Melania embarrassed herself when it was discovered that parts of her speech were nearly identical to Michelle Obama's speech from 2008 given at the Democratic National Convention. She was immediately accused of plagiarism but denied that she had copied Michelle's speech. One of her speech writers took responsibility for the mistake and subsequently quit.

# Being a quiet and private First Lady

Melania had no political experience and no experience as a First Lady. She wasn't familiar with the hosting and other functions she needed to perform in the White House and was the least-prepared First Lady in the history of the United States. As First Lady, she kept most of her activities and life out of the public eye, so it's therefore difficult to judge her tenure as First Lady. She disappeared for weeks in 2018, after having kidney surgery, and then again in 2019. The public was told that she was planning her work for the upcoming year. By mid-2018, she appeared alongside her husband for only the most important formal events in the White House.

While Melania was absent, Donald Trump's daughter Ivanka stepped in and performed many First Lady functions. For example, Ivanka took Melania's place at campaign rallies, fundraising events, and even social occasions in the White House. Ivanka loved the limelight, was good in front of cameras, and enjoyed giving campaign speeches. For this reason, she performed many campaign functions that were usually taken care of by a presidential spouse. For example, Ivanka, and not Melania, introduced Donald Trump at the Republican Convention. As one newspaper printed: "Ivanka Trump: A Real First Lady?"

## Fighting online bullying

In 2018, Melania found her pet issue, called "Be Best," to encourage children's well-being by advocating against substance abuse, especially opiate abuse, and online bullying. Her son, Barron, then 13-years-old, had faced cyberbullying when he was younger, and that is how she became interested in the cause.

## Staying away from the media and the campaign trail

Melania had open contempt for the media, which she perceived to be unfair to her husband, his policies, and herself. She told Sean Hannity on *Fox News* that journalists were "opportunists who are using my name or my family's name to advance themselves." For this reason, Melania rarely gave interviews to media outlets. In one of her most famous interviews, she was asked about her relationship with Donald Trump. Melania said:

**IN THEIR WORDS**

"Do I agree with him all the time? No. I think it is good for a healthy relationship. I am not a yes person. No matter who you are married to, you still need to lead your life. I don't want to change him, and he doesn't want to change me."

During the 2016 and 2020 presidential campaigns, Melania didn't campaign much. She went to only a few important states, kept her speeches very short, and avoided any kind of controversy. She didn't discuss policy issues, instead talking about generalities and telling people how great her husband was.

## Standing her ground

Unlike her predecessors, Melania didn't move with her husband into the White House. She stayed in Manhattan for the first six months of 2017 so that her son could finish school there. Ivanka took her place in the White House during that time. Melania showed up only for select social occasions and celebrations. She finally moved into the White House in June of 2017.

On a few occasions, Melania publicly went against her husband's policies. In June of 2018, she condemned the separation of children from their undocumented parents at the border and then praised NBA star LeBron James, a frequent critic of President Trump, for doing good things to help the disadvantaged in his hometown of Akron, Ohio. Her husband was furious with her.

## Retiring with controversy

After the 2020 election, Melania agreed with her husband that the election was stolen from them and that he legitimately won reelection. She didn't even contact the incoming First Lady Jill Biden to make transition arrangements, as is historically done. She also didn't provide Jill Biden with the tour of the White House as is customary. Melania never felt comfortable in Washington, D.C., and was glad to be out of the White House. She left as quickly as she could. She and her husband didn't even attend President Biden's inauguration, as is customary. A president refusing to attend his successor's inauguration hadn't happened since 1869 when Andrew Johnson refused to attend Ulysses Grant's inauguration.

**TECHNICAL STUFF**

Melania left the White House in January 2021 as the least popular First Lady in the history of the United States. Her approval rating, according to Gallup, was only 42 percent, while her disapproval rating sat at 47 percent. Previous First Ladies, beginning with Pat Nixon in 1974, averaged approval ratings of about 71 percent when they left office. The only other First Lady to have an approval rating below 71 percent was Hillary Clinton in 2001 (see Chapter 18). Her approval stood at 52 percent, with a disapproval rating of 39 percent when she left office.

# Jill Tracy Jacobs Biden (1951–)

Jill Tracy Jacobs (see Figure 20-2) was born on June 3, 1951, in Hammonton, New Jersey, but grew up in the Philadelphia, Pennsylvania, suburbs. She was the oldest of five sisters. Her father, Donald Carl Jacobs, was the head of a savings and loan institution. Her mother, Bonny Jean Jacobs, was a homemaker who had her hands full with five girls in the household. Jill always wanted to have a career and not be a stay-at-home mom like her mother. When she was 15, she started waitressing in Ocean City, New Jersey. In high school, Jill was more interested in having fun than being a great student. However, she did excel in her favorite subject, English.

**FIGURE 20-2:** Jill Tracy Jacobs Biden.

*Source: Library of Congress, Prints & Photographs Division, Reproduction number LC-DIG-ppbd-00606 (original digital file)*

Jill graduated high school in 1969 and enrolled in a local junior college. She wanted to study fashion merchandising but soon got bored with it. Then she met Bill Stevenson, a former football player, and after a brief romance got married in February 1970. He opened one of the most successful college bars in the country near the University of Delaware, and Jill transferred and switched her major to English. Now she was having fun with her college career but not with her marriage. Soon the couple separated. By May of 1975, Jill was going through divorce proceedings and a few month later was finally granted a divorce.

During that time, Jill took a year off college and modeled for an agency in Wilmington, Delaware. Then, in March of 1975, Joe Biden's brother Frank, a college friends of hers, set her up on a blind date with his brother. He was nine years older than she was, but he impressed her with his maturity, his manners, and his formal appearance. She excitedly told her mom: "I finally met a gentleman."

The same year, Jill graduated with a bachelor of arts in English from the University of Delaware. She first became a substitute teacher and then taught high-school English in Wilmington, Delaware. She taught high school for the next 13 years.

**REMEMBER**

When Jill met Joe Biden in 1975, she was a college senior at the University of Delaware, and he was widowed, having lost his wife, Neilia, and their one-year-old daughter in a car accident in 1972. His two sons, Beau and Hunter, had survived the crash.

## Marrying a politician and continuing her education

Joe was intrigued by Jill and fell in love. She provided the stability he needed and the strength to overcome the tragedy he had suffered. He once said: "She gave me back my life; she made me start to think my family might be whole again." Jill finally agreed to marry Joe in 1977 after he had proposed five times. In 1981, they had a daughter, Ashley.

While teaching high school, Jill continued to work on her master's degree in reading from West Chester University. She received the degree in 1981, the same year her daughter was born. Jill stopped working for two years to focus on raising her daughter and then returned to work, teaching emotionally disabled students. She also went back to school. In 1987, she received her second master's degree from Villanova University. This one was in English.

After Joe didn't receive the Democratic nomination for president in 1988, Jill focused on her teaching and taught high-school students at various high schools until 1993. That year, she began to teach English at Delaware Technical and Community College. She taught there until 2008, when her husband was named the vice presidential candidate for the Obama administration.

**FIRST
LADY LORE**

Jill Biden returned to the University of Delaware for a doctorate of education (EdD) degree. She studied under her maiden name, Jill Jacobs, and received her EdD in 2007, at the age of 55.

Jill Biden didn't want her husband to run for president in 2004. She figured that he would have a tough time against the incumbent President George W. Bush. However, after Bush was reelected, she became vocal and pushed him to run in 2008. She did campaign for him during his quest for the Democratic nomination but continued to teach and joined him on the weekends for campaign events. She'd actually take student term papers and grade them on the campaign bus.

Jill became even more active in the campaign after her husband had been named the vice presidential candidate by Barack Obama. She not only campaigned by herself but also staged several campaign events with Michelle Obama.

## Working double-duty

After becoming the Second Lady of the United States, Jill intended to continue teaching at the community college level, but her place of employment had to be closer to Washington, D.C. Several of the local community colleges offered her positions, and she chose Northern Virginia Community College and started teaching English there in January 2009. When asked whether she could perform both functions, as Second Lady and college professor, she said:

IN THEIR WORDS

"I can have my own job, my own life, but also work on issues. I can have it all, really."

By 2011, Jill was promoted to associate professor and taught three English courses per semester. She also advised students during regular office hours and participated in service functions for the college.

REMEMBER

When Jill held office hours and even in the classroom, Secret Service agents were constantly with her. They actually sat in the classroom and in her office. Her reputation was that of a tough but caring teacher who assigned lots of homework.

FIRST LADY LORE

Jill Biden is the first Second Lady to hold a paying job while her husband was the vice president of the United States.

## Serving the community (colleges) and the military

As Second Lady, Jill became an advocate for community colleges, which she referred to as America's best-kept secrets, throughout the United States. In 2009, President Obama put her in charge of an initiative to raise awareness of the value of community colleges. In 2010, she organized the first White House summit on community colleges, which President Obama attended. Then, in 2012, she embarked on a tour of community colleges to highlight alliances between community colleges and the private business sector.

In 2011, Jill and First Lady Michelle Obama founded the national initiative Joining Forces (see Chapter 19) to help veterans and U.S. military families. In 2012, she published a children's book titled *Don't Forget, God Bless Our Troops,* which showed how her granddaughter dealt with her dad, Beau Biden, being deployed in Iraq.

In 2015, Joe's son and Jill's stepson Beau Biden died of cancer. Jill was devastated; she had become his stepmother at an early age and helped raise him. She stated in her 2019 memoirs *Where the Light Enters: Building a Family, Discovering Myself*, "I feel it every day. I think every mother who lost a child must feel this way."

## Leaving D.C. and returning as First Lady

After leaving office as Second Lady in 2017, Jill, for the first time in decades, wasn't involved in politics. Her husband had opted not to run for president in 2016, clearing the way for Hillary Clinton to become the Democratic presidential nominee. Jill continued to teach and focus on her junior college teaching career and literary initiatives she had started. She took a job to chair the board for the Save the Children Foundation and even became a presenter at the 71st Tony Awards. She and Joe bought a vacation home in Delaware and talked about permanent retirement. They both made millions writing their memoirs and hit the speaking circuit, which also proved to be very profitable. By 2019, the two had made almost $15 million.

Jill continued to teach, but then in 2019, she and Joe had to make a big decision. Should Joe run for president a third time? After he decided to give it one more go, Jill enthusiastically supported his choice of running for the Democratic nomination, and on April 25, 2019, Joe Biden announced his campaign for president of the United States.

At the 2020 Democratic National Convention, Joe Biden thanked Jill and called her "so damn tough and loyal." Then for the first time in more than 40 years, Jill took a leave of absence from teaching in the spring and fall of 2020 to campaign for her husband full time. In June of 2020, she published another children's book titled *Joey: The Story of Joe Biden*, describing Joe's childhood battle with stuttering and how he was bullied for it in school. In the summer of 2020, Jill became one of his closest advisors and was heavily involved in choosing Kamala Harris to be the vice presidential candidate.

After she became First Lady in January 2021, Jill said that she wouldn't set aside her teaching career but would continue teaching while serving as First Lady. She is the first spouse to hold both positions of First and Second Lady since Barbara Bush, and she is also the oldest First Lady, at the age of 69, the United States has ever had.

At the time of the writing of this book, Jill Biden has resumed teaching, albeit in online format because of the ongoing COVID-19 crisis. This made her the first First Lady of a sitting president to hold a paying job outside of the White House. In addition, Jill Biden has revived her Joining Forces program and plans to start a new project for autistic children of military families.

# 6

# The Part of Tens

Discover who makes the list of the ten most influential First Ladies in U.S. history.

Check out the ten least-known facts about U.S. First Ladies. Prepare to be amazed — or at least surprised and entertained.

Chapter **21**

# The Ten Most Influential First Ladies

n this chapter, I undertake a truly difficult task — selecting the ten most influential First Ladies out of the 47 First Ladies of the United States. Of course, only 41 First Ladies are really in the running. Why, you may ask?

Four First Ladies died before their husbands assumed office and never had a chance to serve as First Lady, so they have to be excluded. However, because their husbands never remarried, they are considered First Ladies. They are Martha Jefferson, Rachel Jackson, Hannah Van Buren, and Ellen Arthur. In addition, Anna Harrison can't be evaluated because she served as First Lady for only one month before her husband died and never even moved to Washington, D.C. Finally, Dr. Jill Biden, who became First Lady in January 2021, isn't ranked because, at the writing of this book, she's been in her role for only six months. So it's too early to tell what her influence will be.

I base my evaluation on the ten characteristics I discuss in Chapter 2: background, value to country, integrity, leadership, White House steward, own woman, accomplishments, courage, public image, and value to president. For a First Lady to be listed in this top ten list, she has to have shown superior abilities in all categories.

Without any further ado, here are my picks for the ten most influential First Ladies in U.S. history, ranking from one to ten.

# Eleanor Roosevelt

Eleanor Roosevelt deserves the number-one spot on my list. She served as First Lady for 12 years and was one of the most influential figures in American politics during the Great Depression and WWII. Eleanor Roosevelt was one of the first First Ladies to publicly support socioeconomic causes that she believed in and completely changed the role of the First Lady. She was active in advising her husband and was the first First Lady to hold her own press conferences. She wrote articles for newspapers and magazines and even hosted a radio broadcast. She wasn't afraid to express her political opinions, and she dedicated her whole life to helping the economically and socially disadvantaged. She fought for civil rights, racial justice, and gender equality.

After her tenure as First Lady was up, Eleanor didn't retire but stayed active. She sat on the board of the National Association for the Advancement of Colored People (NAACP) and became involved in international affairs, serving as Chair of the United Nations Commission on Human Rights. Without her, there would have been no Universal Declaration of Human Rights in 1948 by the United Nations.

# Abigail Adams

Abigail Adams has the distinction of being the first Second Lady and also the second First Lady. Read that again. She was a prolific letter writer, and so we know much about not only her political views but also life in the late 18th and early 19th centuries in the U.S. She was the first First Lady in what is now called the White House and continued Martha Washington's legacy of being a wonderful hostess.

Unlike Martha Washington, being a hostess wasn't enough for Abigail. Abigail was outspoken and influenced her husband's decision making. She was frequently called Mrs. President because of the influence she had over her husband. She discussed important problems with him and helped him draft official letters. She supported women's right early — many call her the first American feminist — and she also opposed slavery.

Finally, Abigail Adams has the distinction of being one of two First Ladies who was married to a president and also gave birth to a future president. The other one was Barbara Bush.

# Dolley Madison

Dolley Madison is one of the most famous First Ladies in U.S. history. She truly set a new standard for First Ladies. In addition to being very popular, Dolley also possessed negotiating skills and was able to interact with Congress. Congress even gave her her own chair on the floor of Congress, after she was First Lady, to use when she visited Congress, which she did often. She was the first to host an inaugural ball, and through her social charm and extensive social networks, she supported her husband's political career.

Dolley was able to secure more money from Congress for the White House. Therefore, she was able to hire a chef and increase the number of guests invited to White House events. Suddenly, not only could members of Congress or foreign diplomats attend but also well-known artists, writers, and even newsmakers were invited.

In 1814, Dolley single-handedly saved not only a famous portrait of George Washington from the British, who attacked Washington, D.C., and burned down the White House, but also notes from the Constitutional Convention and the White House silver. This act made her a heroine among Americans, and she was celebrated for it the rest of her life. *Note:* The term *First Lady* was actually coined by President Taylor in his eulogy to honor Dolley.

# Hillary Clinton

Hillary Clinton is a controversial choice. However, she was one of the most active and powerful First Ladies in our history and continued to serve her country after leaving office. In terms of her political career and her actions, she created a new path for future First Ladies to follow. At the writing of this book, Hillary Clinton is still one of the best known female politicians in the world. She truly deserves to be on this list.

Hillary built a career as one of the leading attorneys in the United States, before entering politics, and in both 1988 and 1991 was named one of the top 100 attorneys in the United States by the *National Law Review.* As First Lady, Hillary advocated for healthcare reform, child welfare, and women's rights.

After her tenure in the White House, Hillary Clinton went on to become the first First Lady to run for political office. She became a two-term New York U.S. Senator as well as the secretary of state during the Obama administration. In addition, she became the first woman ever to be nominated for president on a major party's ticket in 2016. She ended up narrowly losing the election.

Hillary's greatest contribution wasn't just being an equal with her husband — Sarah Polk and Rosalynn Carter had already accomplished that — but to turn her First Ladyship into the foundation for her own political career. With this, she redefined the role of American presidential spouses in U.S. politics and set a future precedent for First Ladies. Similar to her great idol, Eleanor Roosevelt, she has changed the way we perceive First Ladies forever.

# Betty Ford

Here is another surprise choice. Many people wouldn't think of Betty Ford as one of the top ten most influential First Ladies.

With her honesty and openness about breast cancer and substance abuse, Betty Ford saved thousands of lives. Betty was not only the most openly political First Lady — discussing and supporting abortion and the equal rights amendment, opposing her own husband on these issues — but she connected with millions of Americans through her own battle with breast cancer, which she shared with the American public. She went through and discussed her mastectomy publicly and spoke about cancer awareness. Because of her, people started to actually talk about breast cancer in the U.S. and millions of women decided to have mammograms to prevent the disease. After serving her term as First Lady, she faced a second health battle: substance abuse. Again, she made her fight public and afterward founded the Betty Ford Center in California, which has now expanded to other states, and has treated thousands for addiction-related issues.

# Claudia "Lady Bird" Johnson

Claudia Johnson, more commonly known as "Lady Bird," was a political force in Washington, D.C. She was an invaluable partner to her husband, President Lyndon Johnson, and pursued many initiatives of her own. She is best remembered for her passion for environmental conservation. She was the first American First Lady to work for environmental protection, public conservation, and the beautification of American highways and inner-city areas.

Many consider Lady Bird to be one of the founders of the American environmental movement. With her emphasis on environmental protection, she also established the tradition of First Ladies selecting specific causes or projects to pursue while in office. For her dedication to beautification projects and wildlife preservation, Lady Bird received the Medal of Freedom from President Ford in 1977.

Lady Bird also excelled as White House hostess and was the first First Lady to hire a professional newswoman, Liz Carpenter, as press secretary. Lady Bird ran the White House similar to her own business — a media empire she had created in the 1940s and 1950s, which had turned her into a millionaire. While First Lady, Lady Bird documented all day-to-day activities, which not only became the foundations for her own memoirs but also constitute some of the best documentation we have today of the Johnson administration and its activities.

# Sarah Polk

The selection of Sarah Polk for this list may surprise some. Sarah was well educated for her time and considered a progressive among the women of her era. She had no children but was fully politically engaged. She even told her future husband that she would marry him only if he entered politics. Soon she became a political partner to her husband, President James Polk.

As First Lady, Sarah used her skills to craft speeches for her husband and even wrote and answered letters for him. The two shared an office, and Sarah wasn't afraid to express her political opinions publicly, which was unheard of at the time. Like her husband, Sarah believed in Manifest Destiny, the view that the U.S. had the God-given right to expand, and that is what the Polk administration did.

Sarah learned the skill of being a White House hostess from none other than Dolley Madison and soon became famous for entertaining. She was nonpartisan and well respected throughout the capital. In fact, she was so well liked that during the Civil War, her estate in Tennessee, Polk Place, was considered sacred ground. It was considered neutral territory, and Sarah entertained both Northern and Southern military leaders there during the war.

# Rosalynn Carter

Rosalynn Carter followed in the footsteps of her idol Eleanor Roosevelt. She was politically and socially active and tried to become intimately involved in her husband's campaigns and later in his White House politics. She did become his right-hand woman and considered herself and her husband full partners in politics. She was a clear equal to him, she sat in Cabinet meetings, and she became one of his closest advisors. She even traveled as his official envoy to Latin America in 1977. As First Lady, Rosalynn was an ardent supporter of the Equal Rights Amendment and became an advocate for mental health issues.

After leaving office, Rosalynn stayed active. She became a vocal advocate of human rights throughout the world and has traveled extensively, monitoring elections in many countries. Rosalynn continues her work with Habitat for Humanity, where she helps to build low-income housing and advocates on behalf of the mentally ill. She also cofounded Every Child by Two, a program that provides for early childhood immunization. In 1999, President Clinton awarded Jimmy and Rosalynn Carter the Presidential Medal of Freedom for their humanitarian service. Rosalynn Carter today is considered the most successful former First Lady and is one of the most respected individuals not just in the United States but in the world.

# Harriet Lane

Now here is another controversial choice. Ironically, Harriet Lane wasn't even married to a president. However, when her uncle, President James Buchanan, became president, he asked her to serve as his First Lady. He was a lifelong bachelor and needed someone to run the White House for him. He made a great choice. Harriet Lane turned out to be a great First Lady, admired not only in the U.S. but also in Europe.

Harriet Lane was orphaned at a young age and raised by her uncle James Buchanan. He took her along when he became Ambassador to England, and that is where she developed her social and diplomatic skills. Queen Victoria took a liking to her, and she soon became a court favorite and was allowed to participate in diplomatic activities at her court. This came in handy when she as First Lady hosted the Prince of Wales, future King Edward, which ended English-American hostilities in 1860.

When she was 27, her uncle asked if she wanted to be his First Lady, and she became a wonderful White House hostess. She was well liked and well respected, she knew how to throw a party, and she was soon called the First Lady of the land.

As soon as she became First Lady, Harriet became involved in several social reform activities. She advocated for prison reform, public education, and healthcare for Native Americans. Native Americans appreciated her help and referred to her as the "Great White Mother."

Finally, Harriet donated her collection of art, which became the foundation for what is today the National Collection of Fine Arts at the Smithsonian.

# Michelle Obama

In 2009, Michelle Obama became the first African American First Lady in U.S. history. Unlike some of her predecessors, Michelle didn't focus much publicly on policy but emphasized her role as mother and focused on family-related issues such as childhood obesity and empowering women and girls in the United States and globally. She had previously worked as a lawyer and hospital administration executive in Chicago and had always been involved in community affairs.

As First Lady, Michelle focused on the Let's Move program, to reduce childhood obesity in the United States, and lobbied for the Healthy, Hunger-Free Kids Act, which allowed the U.S. Department of Agriculture to set new nutritional standards for all food in schools. In addition, she started an organic garden in the White House with the help of local fifth graders and later published a book *American Grown,* which chronicles the story of the White House Garden and includes recipes from White House chefs using items grown in the garden.

Together with Second Lady Jill Biden, Michelle started a program called Joining Forces to help military families by matching employers with returning veterans and their family members. Finally, she and former First Lady Laura Bush got together to promote women's issues in Africa, culminating in a U.S.-Africa summit in 2014 sponsored by the Obama White House and the Bush Institute.

Out of the White House, Michelle Obama has remained active, releasing a bestselling memoir and signing a multimillion-dollar television deal with Netflix.

# Chapter **22**

# The Ten Least-Known Facts about U.S. First Ladies

In this chapter, I decided to have some fun. While writing this book I encountered many interesting and fun stories about some of the First Ladies. Some stories are well known; others aren't. So I decided to combine the ten most unique stories, at least in my opinion, into the last chapter of the book. Feel free to disagree, but have fun reading about the ten least-known facts about U.S. First Ladies. The stories are listed chronologically by First Ladies and aren't ranked one through ten.

## Dolley Madison: Dining and Dashing

In 1812, the United States went to war with Great Britain. In 1814, the British landed a large army in the U.S. to win the war quickly. According to the British Commander Admiral Sir George Cockburn, the objective was to conquer the capital of Washington, D.C., and to capture the First Lady, Dolley Madison. The admiral wanted to take her prisoner, ship her back to England, and parade her through the streets of London as a war prize.

When the British troops approached Washington, D.C., Dolley hastily began to evacuate the White House. She saved several national treasures, including a famous portrait of George Washington. Before leaving the White House, Dolley set the dining room table and put a tasty dinner on the table for the British admiral. When he arrived with his troops, Dolley was gone, but the British did eat dinner and then burned down the White House.

# Julia Grant: Using Foresight

Julia Grant believed that she had psychic abilities, especially the gift of foresight, which today is known as premonitions or having an inner voice. On April 14, 1865, a strange man knocked on her door and gave her an invitation from Mary Todd Lincoln to meet her and President Abraham Lincoln at Ford's Theater for a play called "Our American Cousin." Julia was troubled right away. The man appeared creepy, and something seemed off. Furthermore, she and Mary Todd Lincoln didn't like each other. So her inner voice told her not to go. She hastily arranged for her and her husband to leave town by train to see their children. The same night, President Lincoln was assassinated, and we know today that General Ulysses Grant, Julia's husband, was the other target.

# Caroline Harrison: Leaving the Light On

Caroline Harrison, like many First Ladies, tried to renovate the White House and bring it up to the standards of the time. So she bought new curtains and furniture and also installed the first private bathrooms. To combat the rat problem the White House had, she even released several ferrets to kill the rats.

Caroline also modernized the White House, installing the first switchboard in the building so it could have more than one phone line and having electricity installed. She soon regretted this, because both she and her husband were afraid of electricity and refused to touch the light switches. They thought they would be electrocuted and die. So the White House staff had to turn the lights on and off for them, even in their bedroom. On some occasions, the staff forgot to turn the lights off, and the Harrisons just laid there all night with the lights on.

# Edith Roosevelt: Playing I Spy

Edith Roosevelt was a very strict woman who considered herself to have the highest moral standards. She especially despised alcoholics and adulterers. To combat immoral behavior in the capital, Edith held weekly meetings with the women of influence — wives of Congressmen and Cabinet members. Everybody attending her meetings had to spy on other members of society and report to her. Soon, everybody with a lax moral code was watched by Edith's spies and then reported on. Edith had created her own little spy agency. To punish immoral people, she made sure that they were off the White House invitation list until they improved their moral standards.

# Edith Wilson: Wielding a Famous Relative

Edith Wilson was a direct descendant of the famous Native American Pocahontas. She was very proud of that fact and let everybody know about it. During WWI, the Navy asked her to pick names for American warships. She picked Native American names for the ships to honor her ancestors.

The story goes that Edith, who accompanied her husband to Europe after WWI, had ended up benefitting greatly from her famous ancestor. While in France to work on the Treaty of Versailles, the French aristocracy looked down upon Edith. She wasn't blue-blooded and therefore didn't receive an invitation to one of the biggest parties of the year. However, as soon as the hostess of the party heard that Edith was a descendant of Pocahontas, she was invited, and then the French treated Edith like royalty.

# Lou Hoover: Dodging Bullets

Besides being the first woman to receive a college degree in geology from Stanford University, Louise (Lou) Hoover was a world traveler who enjoyed adventures. She was an outdoors person and was excited to be in China with her husband exploring the feasibility of Chinese mines. However, she had picked a bad year to be in China. The Boxer Rebellion, an uprising against foreign domination, had just started in 1900. She and her husband, Herbert, lived in the Chinese city of Tientsin, and she refused to leave. Instead, carrying a rifle, she transported medical supplies by bike to a local hospital. She was shot at on many occasions, and one day, a bullet even blew out her bicycle tire. Her obituary actually appeared in a Chinese newspaper. Lou was thrilled to read her obituary, because she got a full three columns, which was usually reserved for important people. She actually said: "I was never so proud in my life."

As a side note, becoming fluent in Chinese did come in handy when she became First Lady. Whenever she and her husband, Herbert Hoover, didn't want other people to know what they were saying, they just conversed in Chinese.

# Mamie Eisenhower: Working from Bed

Mamie Eisenhower loved the color pink and being in bed. Her bedroom was all pink, including the bed. She ate breakfast in bed and also did most of her work there — writing letters, dictating correspondence, and planning formal dinners. She even held staff meetings while in bed. One of her favorite sayings was, "Every woman over 50 should stay in bed until noon."

Not surprisingly, Mamie also listened to her favorite soap opera, *As the World Turns*, in bed. Nobody was allowed to disturb her, and meetings that overlapped with the soap opera had to be rescheduled.

To be fair, Mamie suffered from Meniere's disease, a disorder of the inner ear, and had balance issues. She also had rheumatic fever as a child and was told by her doctors to spend three days a week in bed. So she did.

# Jacqueline Kennedy: Upsetting the Public

In 1962, Jaqueline Kennedy went on vacation in Italy with her two children. She was having fun on the beach wearing a fairly skimpy bathing suit (for 1960s tastes, at least). She was stalked by the paparazzi and was photographed in her bathing suit. Her pictures were all over the newspapers in Europe and the United States. She had become the first First Lady to be photographed in a bathing suit. Conservative groups in the U.S. were incensed that a First Lady would do such a thing. They were afraid that she was corrupting their children, and when Jackie retuned to the U.S., demonstrators greeted her at the airport.

# Lady Bird Johnson: Not Letting Anything Stop Her

In 1948, Claudia "Lady Bird" Johnson was campaigning on her husband's behalf who was running for a U.S. Senate seat. On the way to San Antonio for a campaign appearance, she got into a car accident, flipping her car twice. She got out of the car and hitched a ride with a stranger. Upon arriving at the campaign event, she asked for new clothing to change into and then proceeded with her address. After it was all over, she went to the nearest hospital and finally had X-rays taken.

# Barbara Bush: Taking Chances

Barbara Bush needed glasses badly. However, she often refused to wear them, believing they didn't look that great on her. On one occasion, a state dinner for the Australian Prime Minister, she opted not to wear glasses. During dinner, she decided to go for the lobster in front of her. As she was about to eat, the Australian Prime Minister, who was sitting next to her, turned to her and whispered, "Barbara you are about to eat the adornment." See, the lobster shells on the table were actually not food but a part of the decorations. Afterward, Barbara got contact lenses so this wouldn't happen again.

# Index

Booth, John Wilkes, 113
Boston Tea Party, 39
Boxer rebellion, 187, 307–308
breast cancer, 239, 300
British Gentleman's Quarterly Naked Supermodel Special, 287
Britton, Nan, 178
Bryan, William Jennings, 170
Buchanan, James, 101, 102–103, 105
bullying, Melania Trump's fight against, 289
Burma, oppression in, 276
Burr, Aaron, 47
Bush, Barbara Pierce
  accomplishments criterion, 23
  admiration for Jackie Kennedy, 219
  early life, 253
  family as priority for, 254
  as First Lady, 255–257
  later life, 257–258
  least-known facts about, 309
  marriage, 253
  overview, 241
  political involvement, 8, 255–256
  popularity, 257
  road to presidency, 254–255
  as Second Lady, 255
  similarity to Laura Bush, 271
  value to country criterion, 23
Bush, George H. W., 253–255, 257, 258, 263, 274
Bush, George W., 258, 272, 273–274, 275, 276
Bush, Laura Welch
  accomplishments criterion, 23
  activity after White House, 276–277
  campaigning by, 274, 276
  career, 273
  early life, 272

  as First Lady, 274–276
  as First Lady of Texas, 274
  marriage and early married life, 273–274
  and Michelle Obama, 277, 282
  political involvement, 275–276
  popularity, 271
  similarity to Barbara Bush, 271
Bush, Robin, 254

# C

Camelot, 218, 221
Camp David Accords, 245
campaigning by First Ladies
  Eleanor Roosevelt, 200
  Florence Harding, 179
  Jackie Kennedy, 218
  Lady Bird Johnson, 227, 228
  Laura Bush, 274, 276
  Lucretia Garfield, 136
  Melania Trump, 289–290
  Michelle Obama, 280
  overview, 14–15
  Pat Nixon, 234
  Rosalynn Carter, 243, 244
Carter, Eleanor Rosalynn Smith (Rosalynn)
  early life, 242
  as First Lady, 1, 11, 12, 244–246
  as influential, 301–302
  later life, 246
  marriage and early married life, 242–243
  political involvement, 8, 241, 243, 244–246
  run for presidency, 244
Carter, Jimmy, 242–244, 245, 246, 249
Cassini, Oleg, 219
celebrity status of Jackie Kennedy, 219
ceremonial powers, 11

Cheat Sheet, explained, 3
Checkers Speech (Nixon), 233
cherry trees in Washington D.C., 167
Children's Defense Fund (CDF), 261, 262
China, Boxer rebellion in, 187, 307–308
china collection, White House, 150, 250
civil rights, 202–203, 228
Civil War
  Benjamin and Caroline Harrison in, 149
  Chester and Ellen Arthur in, 141
  Harriet Lane in, 104
  James Garfield in, 135–136
  John and Julia Tyler in, 81–82
  Mary Todd Lincoln in, 111, 112, 113
  Rutherford and Lucy Hayes in, 130
  Sarah Polk in, 91
  Ulysses and Julia Grant during, 126
Clay, Henry, 52, 62, 86, 108
Cleveland, Frances Folsom
  early life, 142–143
  as First Lady, 144–146
  later life, 147–148
  marriage, 143–144
  overview, 139
  popularity of, 145, 146
  remarriage, 147
Cleveland, Grover, 142–147, 151
Cleveland, Rose Elizabeth, 143
Clinton, Bill
  advice for Hillary in 2016 campaign, 269
  Congressional Gold Medal for Fords, 240
  and Donald Trump, 288
  as governor of Arkansas, 262–263

Hayes, Lucy Ware Webb
   abstinence from alcohol, 133
   bumpy road to White
      House, 131
   compassionate nature of,
      133–134
   early life, 129–130
   as First Lady, 131–134
   involvement in civic causes,
      130–131, 132
   marriage, 130
   overview, 119
Hayes, Rutherford, 129, 130–
   131, 133, 154
head of government position, 11
head of state roles, 11
Head Start Program, 228–229
Health Security Act
   (Hillarycare), 264
Healthy, Hunger-Free Kids
   Act, 282
Hemings, Sally, 44
Herndon, William Lewis, 140, 141
Herron, John, 163
Hickok, Lorena, 204
Highway Beautification Act, 229
Hinckley, John, 251
Hoover, Herbert, 187, 188,
   189, 191
Hoover, J. Edgar, 203
Hoover, Louise (Lou) Henry
   accomplishments of, 10,
      187, 188
   charitable nature of, 189
   in China, 187, 307–308
   early life, 186–187
   as First Lady, 189–191
   later life and death, 191
   least-known facts about,
      307–308
   marriage, 187
   overview, 175–176
   political involvement, 188–189
   world travels and wealth of
      family, 188

hostess role
   Abigail Adams, 40
   Angelica Van Buren, 73
   Bess Truman, 211
   Edith Roosevelt, 160
   Edith Wilson, 173
   Eliza Johnson, 123
   evolution of, 12–13
   filled by substitutes, 71–72
   Frances Cleveland, 145, 146
   Grace Coolidge, 184
   Harriet Lane, 102, 103–104
   Jane Pierce, 101
   Julia Grant, 127
   Julia Tyler, 80–81
   Lady Bird Johnson, 228
   Louise Hoover, 190, 191
   Lucretia Garfield, 136
   Mamie Eisenhower, 214
   Martha Johnson Patterson, 123
   Martha Washington, 32–34
   Mary Elizabeth Bliss, 95
   Mary McElroy, 141–142
   Mary Todd Lincoln, 110–111
   Michelle Obama, 281
   Nancy Reagan, 250
   Priscilla Tyler, 78
   in rankings, 18
   Rose Elizabeth Cleveland, 143
   Sarah Polk, 85, 87, 88
   unseen powers related to, 11
   White House Steward
      criterion, 22
Howe, Louis, 198

**I**

icons, explained, 3
image campaigns, 75
impeachment
   of Andrew Johnson, 123–124
   hearings for Bill Clinton, 266
   as possibility for Richard
      Nixon, 262

In Their Words icon, explained, 3
institutionalization of First Lady
   role, 12, 157, 245
integrity criterion, in
   rankings, 24
Intolerable Acts, 39
Iran-Contra Affair, 250, 252

**J**

Jackson, Andrew, 13, 62, 65–67,
   84, 86
Jackson, Rachel Donelson
   early life, 63–64
   early married life, 65, 66
   exclusion from list of
      influential First Ladies, 297
   illness and death, 54, 67
   inability to perform First Lady
      functions, 13
   marriages, 64–65
   opinions on husband's
      presidential ambitions, 66
Jay Treaty, 59
Jefferson, Martha (daughter),
   45–46
Jefferson, Martha Wayles
   Skelton (wife)
   early life, 43
   exclusion from list of
      influential First Ladies, 297
   marriages, 43–44
   sickness and death of, 45, 46
Jefferson, Thomas, 33, 41,
   43–45, 47, 56
JFK. *See* Kennedy, John F.
Johnson, Andrew, 120–121, 122,
   123–124
Johnson, Claudia Alta Taylor
   (Lady Bird)
   campaigning by, 227, 228
   ceremonial powers of, 11
   early life, 224–225
   familiarity with politics, 226
   as First Lady, 227–229
   as influential, 300–301

# R

ranking First Ladies
  evaluation criteria for, 22–24
  overview, 18, 19–20
  rankings in order, 20–22
Reach Higher Initiative, 282
Reagan, Nancy Davis
  acting career, 247–248
  as advisor to Ronald, 251
  ceremonial powers of, 11
  early life, 246–247
  as First Lady, 249–252
  as First Lady of California,
    248–249
  health problems of, 252
  as informal chief of staff, 252
  later life, 252–253
  leadership criterion, 23
  marriage and early married
    life, 248
  political involvement, 241,
    250–251
  ranking, 18
  relationship with Barbara
    Bush, 255
Reagan, Ronald
  assassination attempt
    against, 251
  and George H. W. Bush, 255
  as governor of California,
    248–249
  health problems of, 250,
    251, 253
  Iran-Contra Affair, 252
  later life, 253
  marriage and move into
    politics, 248
  Nancy's protection of, 250, 251
Regan, Donald, 252
Remember icon, explained, 3
Revolutionary War, 29–30, 39
Robards, Lewis, 64, 65
Robinson, Charles, 101

Robinson, Craig, 277, 279
Robinson, Fraser, 277
Robinson, Marian, 277
Rockefeller, Margaretta
  (Happy), 239
Roosevelt, Alice Hathaway
  Lee, 159
Roosevelt, Anna, 196
Roosevelt, Anna Eleanor
  (Eleanor)
  accomplishments of, 195
  as activist First Lady, 201–204
  and Bess Truman, 210
  early life, 196–197
  as First Lady of New York, 200
  Franklin's early political
    endeavors, 198
  later life and death, 205
  legacy of Edith and Teddy
    Roosevelt, 162
  marriage and early married
    life, 197
  as most influential First
    Lady, 298
  overview, 195
  political involvement, 7, 8, 18,
    195, 198–205
  ranking, 22, 23
  work at United Nations,
    205, 206
  writing career, 203
Roosevelt, Edith Kermit Carow
  early life, 158
  as First Lady, 12, 159–161
  and Helen Taft, 164
  later life, 161–162
  least-known facts about, 307
  marriage, 159
  overview, 157
Roosevelt, Elliott, 196
Roosevelt, Franklin Delano (FDR)
  affair with Lucy Mercer,
    199, 205
  death, 205

  early political endeavors, 198
  Edith Roosevelt's campaign
    against, 162
  as governor of New York, 200
  and Harry Truman, 210
  legacy of Edith and Teddy
    Roosevelt, 162
  marriage to Eleanor, 197
  as president, 201–202
Roosevelt, Quentin, 162
Roosevelt, Sara, 197, 199
Roosevelt, Theodore (Teddy),
    154, 158–159, 160, 161, 164
Rough Riders, 154
Russia, John Quincy and Louisa
  Adams in, 60

# S

Sadat, Anwar, 245
Sartoris, Algernon, 127
Sartoris, Nellie Grant, 127
Saxton, James, 151, 152
Secret Service protection,
    203, 212
Sedition Act, 41
September 11, 2001 terrorist
  attacks, 275
Shawnee tribe, 75
Siena College Research Institute
  Survey on First Ladies
  evaluation criteria for, 22–24
  overview, 18, 19–20
  rankings in order, 20–22
Skelton, Bathurst, 43
slavery
  Abigail Adams' viewpoint
    on, 39
  abolition movement, 85,
    111, 130
  Andrew Johnson's freeing of
    slaves, 122
  Andrew Johnson's support
    of, 121

slavery *(continued)*

Julia Tyler's defense of, 81

Mary Todd Lincoln's view on, 111

Pierce's differences in opinion on, 101

Sarah Polk's support of, 87, 90

split in Democratic Party over in 1852, 100

Thomas Jefferson's slave ownership, 44

Ulysses and Julia Grant's views on, 125–126

Washington's viewpoints on, 35

Zachary Taylor's support for, 95

Slum Clearance Bill, 171

Smith, Al, 200

social events organized by First Ladies. *See also* hostess role

Souvestre, Marie, 197

Spanish-American War, 154, 164

Spoken from the Heart (Bush), 276

Stanton, Edwin, 124

Stevenson, Bill, 291

Stuart, John, 110

substance abuse

Betty Ford's fight against, 238, 240, 300

war against, 250–251

substitute First Ladies

Angelica Van Buren, 71, 73

Emily Donelson, 67

Harriet Lane, 102

Ivanka Trump, 289, 290

Jane Irvin Harrison, 76

Martha Jefferson, 45–46

Martha Johnson Patterson, 123

Mary Abigail Fillmore, 97, 98

Mary Elizabeth Bliss, 95

Mary Harrison McKee, 151

Mary McElroy, 141–142

overview, 13, 71

Priscilla Tyler, 71, 78

Rose Elizabeth Cleveland, 143

suffrage movement, 14, 146. *See also* voting rights for women

Summersby, Kay, 214

# T

Taft, Helen (Nellie) Herron

ambitions for husband, 164, 165

contributions to U.S. history, 8

early life, 162–163

as First Lady, 166–167

as free thinker, 163–164

health problems of, 166

later life, 167–168

love of politics, 8, 9

marriage, 163

memoir written by, 10, 167

overview, 157

in the Philippines, 164

Taft, William Howard, 163, 164, 165, 166, 167

Taylor, Margaret (Peggy) Smith

early life, 93–94

as First Lady, 13, 93, 95–96

later life, 96

marriage and early married life, 94

Taylor, Zachary, 32, 52, 94, 95

Tea Act, 39

Teapot Dome Scandal, 181

Technical Stuff icon, explained, 3

temperance movement, 130, 133

Tenure of Office Act in 1867, 124

Texas, annexation of, 81, 85, 86, 89

Texas Rangers, 274

Tilden, Samuel, 131

Todd, John, 46

Todd, Payne, 51

Treaty of Guadeloupe Hidalgo, 89

Truman, Elizabeth (Bess) Virginia Wallace

early life, 208

as First Lady, 210–211

friendship with Mamie Eisenhower, 215

later life, 211–212

marriage and early married life, 209–210

overview, 207

Truman, Harry, 147, 205, 209–210, 211

Trump, Donald, 283, 287–288, 289, 290

Trump, Ivanka, 289, 290

Trump, Melania Knauss

approval rating, 290

becoming American citizen, 288

early life, 286–287

as First Lady, 289–290

marriage, 288

media scrutiny of, 19

modeling career, 287

overview, 285

retiring with controversy, 290

taking backseat to politics, 288

Tsar Alexander of Russia, 61

Tuskegee airmen, 203

Twain, Mark, 128

Tyler, John, 76, 77–78, 80–81

Tyler, Julia Gardiner

defense of slavery by, 81

early life, 79

as First Lady, 80–81

marriage, 78, 80

support for Confederacy, 81–82

Tyler, Letitia Christian
  early life, 76
  as First Lady, 13, 78
  help from Dolley Madison, 52
  marriage, 76
  ranking, 22
  road to presidency, 77–78
Tyler, Priscilla Cooper, 71, 78

# U

United Nations (U.N.), 205
Universal Declaration on Human
  Rights, 205

# V

value to country criterion, in
  rankings, 23
value to president criterion, in
  rankings, 22
Van Buren, Angelica, 71, 73
Van Buren, Hannah Hoes,
  72–73, 297
Van Buren, Martin
  friendship with Andrew
    Jackson, 67
  James Polk as alternative to, 86
  marriage, 72, 73
  Sarah Polk's banning from
    White House, 88
  substitute First Ladies for, 13,
    51–52, 73
veterans, support for, 180,
  282, 293
Victoria (Queen of England), 103
Voorhis, Jerry, 232
voting rights for women, 14,
  146, 174, 179, 189

# W

Wagner-Rogers Bill, 185
Walker, Alice, 257
Wallace, David, 208

Wallace, Henry, 210
War of 1812, 49–50, 65, 75,
  305–306
Warren, William G., 237
Washington, George, 29–35, 42
Washington, Martha Dandridge
  Custis
  active role in Revolutionary
    War, 29
  ceremonial powers of, 11
  contributions to U.S. history, 8
  early life, 28
  executive mansions used
    by, 42
  as First Lady, 30–33
  friendship with Abigail
    Adams, 33
  infighting between friends
    of, 33
  later life, 33–35
  marriage, 29
  as national hero, 29–30
  overview, 27
  traditions started by, 32–33
  undefined role of, 12
Watergate scandal, 19,
  235–236
Where the Light Enters
  (Biden), 294
whistle stop campaign by Lady
  Bird Johnson, 228
White House
  Abigail Fillmore's changes to,
    97–98
  Caroline Harrison's
    improvements to, 149–
    150, 306
  china collection, 150, 250
  destruction by British in
    1812, 50
  Dolley Madison's changes
    to, 49
  Dolley Madison's evacuation
    of, 49–50
  Easter Egg hunt on lawn, 132

  Edith Roosevelt's updating
    of, 161
  Florence Harding's changes
    to, 180
  history of, 42
  Jackie Kennedy's restoration
    of, 219
  Johnsons' frugalness when
    restoring, 123
  Louisa Adams' opinion of, 61
  Lucy Hayes' improvements
    to, 133
  Mary Todd Lincoln's spending
    on, 111, 112
  Nancy Reagan's spending
    on, 250
  openness for visits, 12
  Pat Nixon's restoration of, 235
  Sarah Polk's administration
    of, 87
  Trumans' remodeling of, 211
  use of term in book, 2
  White House steward role, 22
A White House Diary
  (Johnson), 229
Whitewater scandal, 19, 265
widowed First Ladies, pensions
  for, 76, 82, 114
Wilson, Edith Bolling Galt
  after Woodrow's stroke, 14,
    173–174
  early life, 171
  as First Lady, 173–174
  later life, 174
  least-known facts about, 307
  marriages, 171–173
  memoir written by, 10
Wilson, Ellen Louise Axson
  artistic talents of, 169–170
  early life, 168–169
  as First Lady, 170–171
  involvement in policy making,
    157, 170, 171
  marriage, 169
  overview, 157

# Z

# About the Author

**Marcus A. Stadelmann** is a professor of political science and chair of the Department of Political Science and History at the University of Texas at Tyler. Dr. Stadelmann received his PhD from the University of California at Riverside in 1990 and has subsequently taught at universities in California, Utah, and Texas.

He presently teaches classes on American government, international relations, and comparative politics. In addition, he has given many public and academic presentations on American presidential elections and international topics such as the collapse of the Soviet Union, German unification, the rise of populism in Europe, and the politics of Russia and Ukraine.

Dr. Stadelmann's other publications include *The Dependent Ally—German Foreign Policy from 1949 to 1990, The Quest for Power—An Introduction to World Politics in the 21st Century, U.S. Presidents For Dummies,* and *Political Science For Dummies.* In addition, Dr. Stadelmann has contributed chapters to many books and has published numerous academic articles.

# Dedication

This book is dedicated to the people who had the most impact on my life: my parents, Wolfgang and Heidi; and my two daughters, Katarina and Holly.

# Author's Acknowledgments

Special thanks go to my parents and my two daughters, Katarina and Holly. They kept me on track for the last months, supported me in this endeavor, and patiently waited until my work was done. Without their support, this work would not have been possible.

I would also like to express my gratitude to my editor, Linda Brandon, who did an excellent job working with me on the book. Without her input, this book would not have become what it is today.

## Publisher's Acknowledgments

**Acquisitions Editor:** Lindsay Lefevere
**Development Editor:** Linda Brandon
**Copy Editor:** Jennette ElNaggar

**Technical Editor:** Diana Carlin
**Production Editor:** Mohammed Zafar Ali
**Cover Image:** ©dszc/Getty Images